Marketing Strategy for Small- to Medium-Sized Manufacturers

Marketing Strategy for Small- to Medium-Sized Manufacturers

A Practical Guide for Generating Growth, Profit, and Sales

Charles E. France

business**expert**
Press

First published in 2013 by
Business Expert Press, LLC
222 East 46th Street, New York, NY 10017
www.businessexpertpress.com

ISBN-13: 978-1-60649-614-5 (paperback)

ISBN-13: 978-1-60649-615-2 (e-book)

Business Expert Press Marketing Strategy collection

Collection ISSN: 2150-9654 (print)
Collection ISSN: 2150-9662 (electronic)

Cover and interior design by Exeter Premedia Services Private Ltd., Chennai, India

First edition: 2013

10 9 8 7 6 5 4 3 2 1

Printed in the United States of America.

Abstract

Small and medium manufacturers' attempts to grow their business often produce less-than-desired results due to self-inflicted obstacles and pitfalls that defeat their well-intended efforts. Many do not follow generally accepted basic business practices such as knowing product costs and margins, obtaining strategically useful information about customers, conducting market research to identify prospective customers, and understanding competitors' advantages and disadvantages needed to build effective growth strategies. Their approach to pursuing growth strategies—a.k.a shotgun marketing—is akin to ready, shoot, aim—and often the business' working capital, cash flow, financial ratios, and overall profitability are insufficient to afford the costs of needed sales, marketing, and promotional strategies typically called for to find and develop new customers, markets, and products.

Based on 21 case studies and 126 reviews of manufacturers' sales and marketing practices, the book explains the common pitfalls these companies experienced and offers common sense, practicable, and affordable step-by-step "how to's" for cost and profitability analyses on products and customers, finding prospective new customers, conducting marketing research, and deciphering and using competitor intelligence. It also provides guidelines for determining the best combination of sales coverage for inside/outside sales and independent reps and for estimating the cost to implement sales, marketing, promotional, and growth strategies.

It is a handy self-help resource that the approximate three hundred thousand small-to-medium manufacturers will need as the economy rebounds and creates opportunities for profitable growth—not just sales volume.

Keywords

B2B sales, B2B marketing, B2B strategy, B2B customer, product, and market development, B2B small business, B2B strategic planning, B2B sales planning, B2B marketing research, B2B new product development, B2B growth planning, B2B marketing and sales, manufacturing marketing and sales, manufacturing marketing strategy, manufacturing growth strategy

Contents

List of Tables

List of Figures

List of Graphs

Acknowledgments

David Cranmer
Manager Industrial Marketing Systems
National Institute of Standards and Technology's Hollings
Manufacturing Extension Partnership (MEP)
(*late 90s to early 2000s*)

Senior Research Engineer
National Institute of Standards and Technology's Hollings
Manufacturing Extension Partnership (MEP) *(current)*

Many thanks to Dave for spearheading the MEP's Industrial Marketing initiative in the late 90s and early 2000s that led to the Industrial Marketing Assessment—referred to in the book as the "questionnaire"—making possible the research and findings about manufacturers' sales and marketing business practices and procedures upon which most of the book is based. His leadership of the Assessment's four-person development team, his camaraderie, and sense of humor resulted in lifetime friendships.

Michael P. Collins
President, MPC Management, Inc.
Portland, OR
mpcmgt.com

Mike generously provided the MEP and the development team access to the material in his first book, "The Manufacturer's Guide to Business Marketing: How Small and Mid-Size Companies Can Increase Profits with Limited Resources." His first hand experience as line manager with bottom line responsibility and as a consultant to manufacturers proved invaluable to the development of the questionnaire. He and I have enjoyed close collaboration over the past 16 years on various consulting engagements, in the writing of his second book, "Saving American Manufacturing," and in the writing of this book.

Thanks, Mike, for your unwavering generosity and friendship.

Peter LaPlaca, Ph. D

Founding Diretor of CONN/STEP Connecticut State Technology
Extension Program *(late 90s to 2000s)*

Editor, Industrial Marketing Management and Emeritus Professor,
University of Connecticut
24 Quarry Drive, Suite 201
Vernon, CT 06066-4917   USA
860-875-8017 *(Current)*

Peter's hands-on experience with manufacturers and in-depth education
in sales and marketing brought a beneficial counter-balance to Collins'
and my private-sector consulting backgrounds, which contributed
immensely to the holistic quality of the questionnaire, making it unique.
His Italian sense of humor and fellowship provided levity to the late-night
development sessions and deadlines. And special thanks, Peter, for your
advice and recommendations during the early writing of this book.

Ann Brown

Marketing Specialist
Mid-America Manufacturing Technology Center (MAMTC),
Long Island, KS

In memory of Ann, whose work with and insights into small manufacturers
emphasized that manufactures are not all the same—that size does matter
and solutions and recommendations must take into account company
size and resource limitations—that one size does not fit all, that solutions
and recommendations appropriate to larger companies cannot always
be simply down-sized for smaller companies, and that solutions and
recommendations must be tailored to the company and its circumstances.

The Southeastern Trade Adjustment Assistance Center (SETAAC) is a
40-year federal program operating at Georgia Tech under a grant spon-
sored by the U.S. Department of Commerce, which provides technical
assistance to improve a manufacturer's competitiveness adversely affected
by import competition.

During our careers at Georgia Tech Bob, Paul, Marla, Ann, and
I worked in SETAAC and assisted hundreds of manufacturing companies

with their finances and accounting, production, operations, administration, and sales and marketing functions. This experience provided much of the background for findings and conclusions in the book.

Robert W. Springfield

Director, Southeastern Trade Adjustment Assistance Center (SETAAC)
Georgia Institute of Technology *(1979–1986)*

Senior Research Engineer
Georgia Institute of Technology *(Retired, 2006)*

Thanks to Bob for his 37 years as friend and co-worker, who always provides candid advice and insightful feedback. His comments and suggestions improved the organization of the book and helped refine many of the explanations, examples, and illustrations.

Paul N. Lewis

Director, Southeastern Trade Adjustment Assistance Center (SETAAC)
Georgia Institute of Technology *(1994–2003)*

Chief Operations and Finance Officer
Enterprise Innovation Institute Georgia Institute of Technology *(Current)*

Paul for his encouragement and support to emphasize the importance of sales and marketing to manufacturing companies and that their competitive problems cannot be solved solely from inside the factory.

Marla Gorges

Director, Southeastern Trade Adjustment Assistance Center (SETAAC)
Georgia Institute of Technology *(2003–2011)*

Associate Director
Health and Information Services
Enterprise Innovation Institute
Georgia Institute of Technology *(Current)*

Marla for her charming humor and willingness to review the book despite her work and family commitments. Her comments and feedback, based on her experience working with manufacturing companies as Director of SETAAC, supported the book's general findings and conclusion about manufacturers' lack of cost and margin data, customer information, marketing research and competitor intelligence.

Ann O'Neill

Program Manager, TRACS

Georgia Institute of Technology

Enterprise Innovation Institute

Georgia Institute of Technology

Ann for her excellent marketing research and competitor investigations during our many client engagements and for her review and constructive comments about the marketing research and competitor material in the book.

————————

Tom Madison

General Manager, Pipe Group

Skyline Steel, Inc.

Ben Wells

President

Delta Metals, Inc.

Thanks to Tom and Ben for their generous cooperation during reviews of their companies' operations, taking the time to review the book, and for their encouraging comments about its central message that in order to be successful and profitable companies must have good information about their costs and margins, customers, markets, and competitors.

Their companies are excellent examples of being positioned for growth due to having adhered to good business practices.

Charles H. Brandon, Ph. D. *(Retired)*

Professor of Accounting at the Crummer Graduate School of Business

Rollins College

Visiting Professor of Accounting at the Goizueta School of Business

Emory University

Another longtime friend of over fifty years, many thanks to Charles for his technical advice and clarifications on the financial and cost accounting examples and illustrations in the book.

Foreword

Many owners and senior managers understand and articulate that their businesses need to grow, but often cannot specify "how" they intend to make that happen. They say they need to find additional customers and markets and occasionally say they want or need to find new products; but infrequently specify what or how they intend to make those things happen.

Much has been written about "what" manufacturers need to do to find and enter new markets, diversify, add customers, innovate, and develop new products. But most of this—taught in business schools both at undergraduate and at graduate levels—pertains to large consumer products companies and a few large industrial companies; there is little material directed to the small company. If you do not believe this, then look at the typical case studies presented in university curriculum and articles in national publications. The solutions described therein are too sophisticated and costly for small businesses and it is assumed that sufficient knowledge of costs, margins, market potential, and competition are readily available, which is not the case for most small companies as the data in this book show. A vast majority of manufacturing companies in this country have less than 100 employees, and my own experience is that much of the sales, marketing, and strategy material I learned in college and have read in national publications are not applicable to them.

While it is argued that consumer marketing and sales principles are universal and can be applied to any business—at a conceptual and intellectual level this might be so—my experience tells me that business-to-business (B2B) market analysis, planning, strategy development, and execution is markedly different for business-to-consumer (B2C) and particularly for small-to-medium manufacturers (SMMs).

In this book, by presenting a systematic and methodical "how to" approach, I endeavor to help SMMs simplify strategy development and the challenges of growing their businesses. It focuses on only three things: customers, products, and markets. By identifying the "right" mix of customers and products to sell into the "right" markets, a company will shift its focus from sales volume to operating for profit.

The concept is simple, and when a company focuses on its customers, products, and markets, it will find the complexities of "how to" decisions greatly minimized. Many SMMs, however, are not positioned to do this due to a lack of good "strategic" information about their costs, profit margins, customers' needs and wants, competitors, and markets.

This book presents the methods and procedures for overcoming this lack of strategic information so that owners and managers can make reasonably informed decisions about growing their businesses and sustaining that growth.

Two demographics have significant implications for the design and delivery of programs and assistance targeted to SMMs.

First, over 90 percent of these companies have less than 100 employees (see Table 1).

These employees typically wear many hats and do not have the time and specialization to conduct in-depth analyses of costs, margins, competitors, and markets needed to develop effective growth strategies.

Table 1. *U.S. Manufacturing Establishments by Employment Size, 2003–2010*

U.S. manufacturing establishments by employment size, 2003 to 2010								
Employ-ment size	2003	2004	2005	2006	2007	2008	2009	2010	Cum. % of total
1–4	121,315	121,338	118,782	117,391	119,182	116,660	115,521	115,374	38%
5–9	59,595	58,709	57,899	57,171	57,779	57,220	54,287	51,794	56%
10–19	53,594	53,064	52,001	51,627	51,422	50,596	47,604	46,526	71%
20–49	52,406	51,854	50,773	50,800	50,094	49,645	45,281	42,985	86%
50–99	25,146	24,944	24,797	24,819	24,359	24,102	21,727	20,469	92%
100–249	19,548	19,227	19,361	19,381	18,943	18,694	16,467	15,428	98%
250–499	6,574	6,349	6,340	6,375	6,172	5,957	5,162	4,764	99%
500–999	2,531	2,486	2,426	2,412	2,384	2,340	2,024	1,847	100%
1,000 or more	1,140	1,112	1,081	1,086	1,020	1,002	861	795	100%
Total	341,849	339,083	333,460	331,062	331,355	326,216	308,934	299,982	

Source: U.S. Census Bureau, 2010 County Business Patterns.

Public and private service providers with expertise in cost accounting, financial and data analysis, and market research could help SMMs obtain this information.

Second, most SMMs are family-owned and -operated and often do not have the financial and human resources needed to be successful in finding and diversifying into new markets, adding customers, innovating, and developing new products. Growth of this nature requires a business to increase investment in working capital and capital equipment and to potentially take on risk that can compete with the family's budget, priorities, and life style that the business's cash flow supports. Therefore, strategies to expand the business that might jeopardize the family's well-being could encounter stiff opposition.

These situations—lack of "strategic" information about costs and margins, customers, competitors, and markets, thinly spread employees wearing many hats who do not have the time to focus on data analysis and strategy development and execution, limited financial resources, and competing family demands and priorities—call for growth strategies that must be tailored to the company's ability to pay for and implement those strategies and not compete with family priorities.

Most published materials on marketing deal with consumer businesses and presume that consumer marketing principles and techniques apply almost universally to all businesses, whether consumer or industrial. While commonalities exist between consumer and industrial/B2B marketing, the specifics and nuances associated with SMMs' B2B growth and marketing strategies require a much different approach.

B2B companies' products and services are used or consumed in other businesses' products, production, operations, and selling activities where there is an economic justification for the sellers' products and services; consumer products are mass marketed to individuals, families, and households, and bought on emotional factors. B2B sales channels require different skills and expertise to sell to purchasing agents, engineers, plant managers, owners, or executive committees; consumer products move through sales distribution channels for point-of-sale and coupon offerings in retail space or Internet. B2B sales frequently derive from considerable bidding, quoting, and negotiating, thus considerably extending the selling cycle; consumer products are scanned and packaged at retailers' stamped or bar-coded price. B2B unit prices tend to be much higher and can involve leasing and long-term financing and contracts; consumer products are purchased via cash, check, credit, or debit card.

The book combines my personal experience of assisting SMMs and is also based on the findings and insights gained from hundreds of reviews of manufacturing companies' sales and marketing business practices conducted from the late 1990s and early 2000s. These reviews took the form of a questionnaire that my three colleagues and I developed under a contract with the U.S. Department of Commerce, National Institute for Standards and Technology, NIST-Manufacturing Extension Program, in the mid-1990s. During the 7 years, between March 1997 and March 2004, I personally conducted 126 reviews of companies in 23 states and Canada. Throughout the chapters I have combined the findings and insights gained from the reviews with hands-on experience involving the efforts of 21 companies to find opportunities to grow—some successful and some not—and present the lessons learned. The names used for the 21 companies are fictitious for confidentiality and any resemblance or similarity to existing or past companies or exact match of existing companies' names is unintentional and purely coincidental.

Over the course of developing and administering the questionnaire and subsequently assisting firms, the critical importance of the interdependence of accounting, operations and manufacturing, customer service and support, marketing research and competitor intelligence, and sales and marketing management practices became too obvious. I call this "connecting the dots." Effective strategy development requires input from all these components.

The following diagram illustrates all the areas involved in B2B industrial marketing that must be addressed to be able to successfully develop and execute sales, marketing, and growth strategies for B2B SMMs. It represents the holistic nature of strategy development—that all facets of the business must be taken into account when developing strategy—that all the "dots" must be connected.

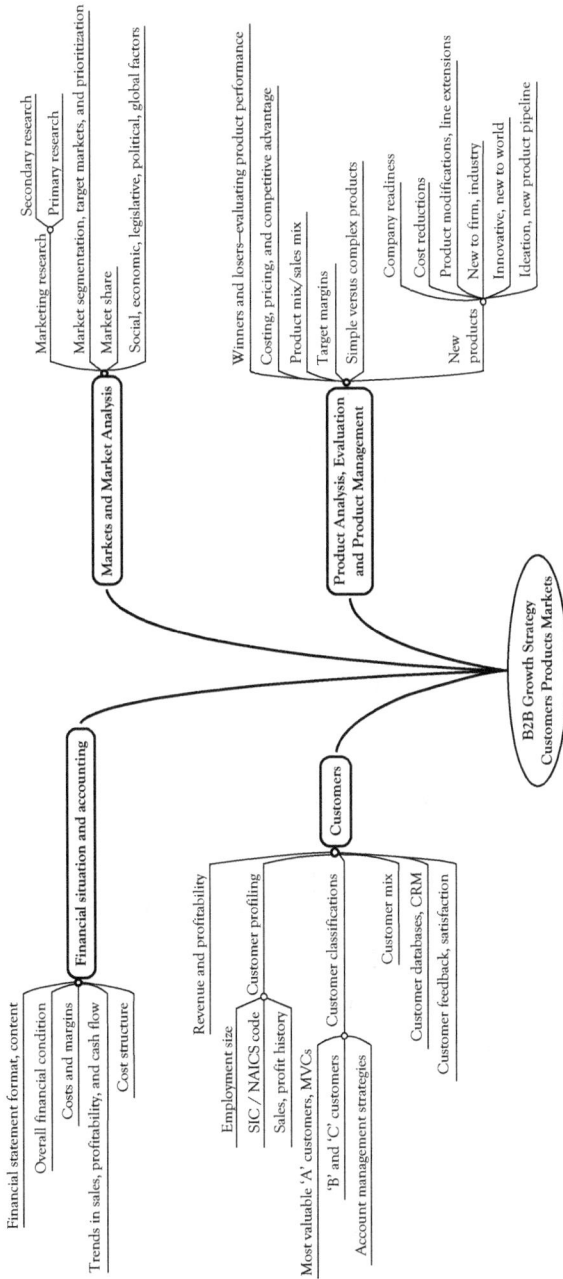

A mind-map diagram titled "B2B Growth Strategy, Customers Products Markets" with the following branches:

Markets and Market Analysis
- Marketing research
  - Secondary research
  - Primary research
- Market segmentation, target markets, and prioritization
- Market share
- Social, economic, legislative, political, global factors

Product Analysis, Evaluation and Product Management
- Winners and losers—evaluating product performance
- Costing, pricing, and competitive advantage
- Product mix/sales mix
- Target margins
- Simple versus complex products
- Company readiness
- Cost reductions
- New products
  - Product modifications, line extensions
  - New to firm, industry
  - Innovative, new to world
  - Ideation, new product pipeline

Financial situation and accounting
- Financial statement format, content
- Overall financial condition
- Costs and margins
- Trends in sales, profitability, and cash flow
- Cost structure

Customers
- Revenue and profitability
- Customer profiling
  - Employment size
  - SIC / NAICS code
  - Sales, profit history
- Customer classifications
  - Most valuable 'A' customers, MVCs
  - 'B' and 'C' customers
  - Account management strategies
  - Customer mix
  - Customer databases, CRM
  - Customer feedback, satisfaction

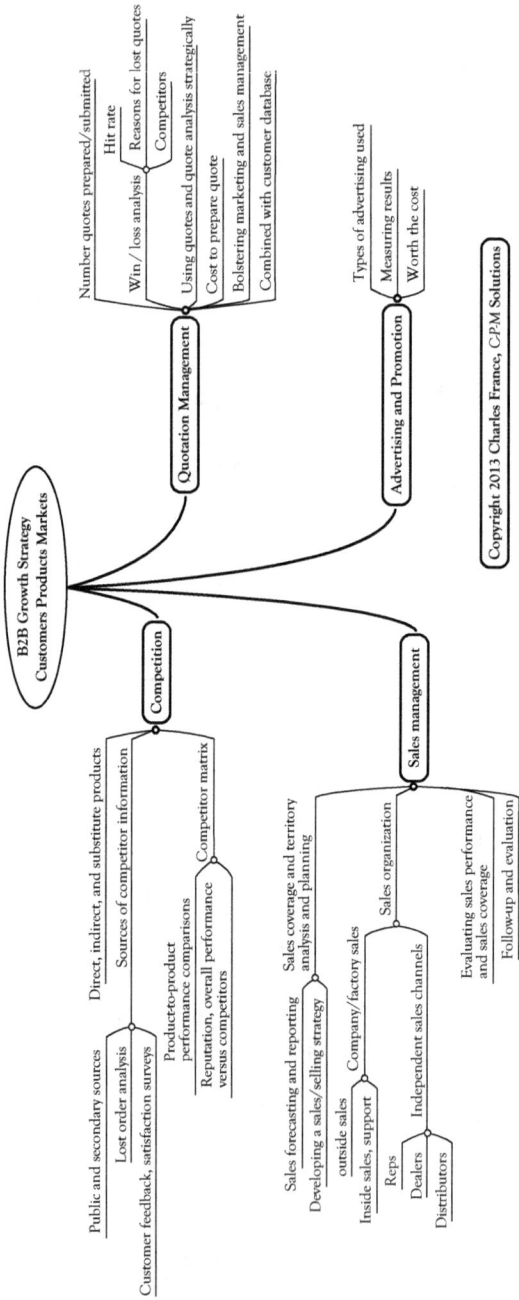

B2B Growth Strategy
Customers Products Markets

Quotation Management
- Number quotes prepared/submitted
- Hit rate
- Win / loss analysis — Reasons for lost quotes
  - Competitors
- Using quotes and quote analysis strategically
- Cost to prepare quote
- Bolstering marketing and sales management
- Combined with customer database

Advertising and Promotion
- Types of advertising used
- Measuring results
- Worth the cost

Competition
- Direct, indirect, and substitute products
- Sources of competitor information
- Public and secondary sources
- Lost order analysis
- Customer feedback, satisfaction surveys
- Product-to-product performance comparisons
- Reputation, overall performance versus competitors
- Competitor matrix

Sales management
- Sales coverage and territory analysis and planning
- Sales forecasting and reporting
- Developing a sales/selling strategy
- Sales organization
  - outside sales
  - Company/factory sales
  - Inside sales, support
  - Reps
  - Dealers — Independent sales channels
  - Distributors
- Evaluating sales performance and sales coverage
- Follow-up and evaluation

Copyright 2013 Charles France, CPM Solutions

Background and Acknowledgments

As mentioned in the Foreword, much of the material in the book derives from the findings of the questionnaire used to review companies' sales and marketing practices. It was collaboratively developed by four people and myself who were involved with the Manufacturing Extension Partnership (MEP, www.nist.gov/mep), a federal program under National Institute of Standards and Technology (NIST) headquartered in Gaithersburg, Maryland, comprising a nationwide network of more than 70 not-for-profit centers whose purpose is to assist small- and medium-sized manufacturers in implementing operational and strategic practices to strengthen their businesses.

1. Mike Collins, a marketing and strategy consultant with many years of hands-on and profit experience in industrial products companies (www.mpcmgt.com),
2. Ann Brown of the Kansas MEP, Mid-America Manufacturing Technology Center (MAMTC)
3. Peter LaPlaca of the Connecticut MEP, and
4. David Cranmer, the MEP contract manager overseeing the questionnaire's development.

MEP selected the four of us to design and develop a questionnaire to be used nationally throughout the MEP network to help manufacturers identify constraints to developing sales and marketing strategies. Our backgrounds, a combination of academics, graduate level education, and real-world experience, proved invaluable in developing an instrument unique to government and industry; our collective fifty plus years' experience encompassed over a thousand manufacturers in multiple industries.

We decided at the start not to create another "one size fits all" questionnaire that typically results in generalizations about a company's situation; but rather that findings and conclusions would be specific to the company and provide insights into how it could improve its chances for successfully developing sales, marketing, and growth strategies.

We divided manufacturing into two groups: (a) companies that produce and sell products and (b) job shops and machine companies that sell capacity rather than products. Product companies operate much differently than job shops and machine companies, having dissimilar cost structures and expenses, as evidenced in their income statements, and employing different skill sets and organizational designs. We further divided manufacturers by their employment size—small, medium, and large—to account for differences in resources and proficiencies needed to develop and execute growth strategies. Smaller firms tend to have fewer resources than larger ones and generally do not have employees dedicated to accounting and cost control, customer service and tech support, and sales and marketing management. Rather, in smaller firms, many employees wear multiple hats. Table 2 illustrates the two types of companies combined with the three employment sizes resulting in six versions of the questionnaire.

The employment ranges in the table are not cast in concrete because there always are exceptions to rules and guidelines. Nevertheless, the hundreds of reviews conducted nationally since the late 1990s show that employment size is a useful criterion for anticipating financial, organizational, and strategic issues and problems that affect a company's ability to develop and execute sales and marketing strategies.

The scope of the questionnaire did not include publicly owned companies because it was designed primarily for the small-to-medium sized manufacturer (SMM).

As Table 3 shows, the questionnaire covered many areas that at first might seem only marginally relevant to the development of sales, marketing, and growth strategies. Following basic information about the company, Parts 2 and 3 address information typically generated for operational purposes and day-to-day management, such as accounting, costing, and estimating, production, and quality and customer data. Parts 4 and 5 deal

Table 2. Six Versions of the Questionnaire

	Small-to-medium size manufacturers (SMMs)			
	Small Up to 25 empls.	Medium26 to 75 empls.	Large 76 to 750+ empls.	Publicly-owned
Product Producers	1	3	5	n\a
Job/Machine Shop	2	4	6	n\a

Table 3. Five Areas of the Questionnaire

		Five areas of the questionnaire		
Part one	**Part two**	**Part three**	**Part four**	**Part five**
Basic information	**Measuring the availability of basic information**	**Using information about customers**	**Information about competitors and markets**	**Market planning, strategies, and sales channel management**
• Sales, profitability, and cash flow trends • General problems	• Accounting systems • Forecasting and reporting • Estimating and costing • Production scheduling and control • Quality control	• Customer concentration, profitability, and MVCs. • Quotation management and analysis • Customer satisfaction and service	• Competitor intelligence • Market research and analysis	• Market planning and documentation • Product management and NPD • Pricing • Advertising and promotion • Channel management

with the more germane strategic issues, such as market and competitor information, sales and marketing management, channel, and product management.

The questionnaire was holistic, covering all facets of a manufacturing business that could affect its ability to competitively produce and sell products and services. The hundreds of reviews conducted since its 1997 launch have validated its efficacy in identifying problems that predictably hinder or defeat SMMs' efforts to develop and implement marketing and sales strategies. Further, the use of employment size and the dichotomy of the Product–Job Shop versions avoid the "one size fits all" syndrome and confirm the questionnaire's uniqueness: No other publicly funded effort has produced as effective an instrument to assess a manufacturer's readiness to tackle challenges of growing its business.

Table 4 summarizes 126 companies who were surveyed by type of company, sales, and number of employees.

The questionnaire covered a very broad range of companies, accounting for:

- Over 7,800 employees, ranging from as few as 7 up to 685, averaging 63. This is very representative since most manufacturing companies have fewer than 100 employees, averaging 35, according to the U.S. Census Bureau, 2011 Annual Survey of Manufactures.
- Over $900 million in sales derived from summing all 126 companies' sales for one fiscal year, averaging $7.5 million per company, and selling to over 31,000 industrial and consumer products customers, via factory sales, reps, dealers, and distributor sales channels.
- Eighty-four different classifications of businesses based on Standard Industrial Classification (SIC) codes http://www. osha.gov/pls/imis/sicsearch.html and NAICS (North American Industrial Classification System) http://www.census. gov/eos/www/naics, two systems used by Federal statistical agencies in classifying business establishments for the purpose of collecting, analyzing, and publishing statistical data related to the U.S. economy. The 84 classifications encompass

Table 4. *Number and Type of Companies Surveyed*

		Job shop				Product				
		Breakdown of types of firms, sales, and employment								
Type										
		Job shop				Product				Total
Size		1	2	3	Total	1	2	3	Total	Total
Number		12	27	16	55	14	36	21	71	126
Sales $1,000s										
Total		$15,325	$71,790	$276,700	$363,815	$15,430	$159,670	$370,100	$545,200	$909,015
Minimum		504	500	2,000		100	120	3,900		
Maximum		3,500	6,500	73,500		2,500	34,000	45,000		
Average[1]		$1,393	$2,761	$17,294	$6,864	$1,102	$4,696	$17,624	$7,901	$7,451

(*Continued*)

Type	Job shop				Product				Total
Size	1	2	3	Total	1	2	3	Total	Total
Employees									
Minimum	7	9	50		3	3	30		
Maximum	26	61	425		19	82	685		
Average	12	33	145	61	9	35	148	64	63
Total	148	902	2,320	3,370	130	1,271	3,113	4,514	7,884
Customers									
Minimum	8	3	25		10	10	5		
Maximum	82	1,500	3,500		600	1,400	1,200		
Average	40	216	435	246	215	394	250	313	282
Total	403	5,608	6,524	12,535	2,580	11,432	4,752	18,764	31,299

¹ not all companies reported sales; 118 reported

a wide range of products and industries, including food, printing, plastics, agriculture, automotive, chemicals and basic materials, electronics, and general machining.

• 23 states and Canada.

In addition to the considerable variety of businesses in terms of their employment sizes, sales, and industry designations, Table 5 shows they also sold into a combination of industrial and consumer markets, as determined by descriptions of their products and by their definitions of their market segments.

Table 5. Companies by Market Served

Companies by market/customer											
	Job shop				Product				Type			
Market	1	2	3	Total	1	2	3	Total	1	2	3	Total
Industrial	9	22	15	46	8	24	20	52	17	46	35	98
Both	3	4	1	8	2	4	0	6	5	8	1	14
Consumer	0	1	0	1	4	8	1	13	4	9	1	14
Total	12	27	16	55	14	36	21	71	26	63	37	126

Many thanks to Mike Collins whose hands-on experience, both as a V.P. Sales and Marketing for industrial companies and as a national consultant, provided more insight into the inner workings of SMMs than anyone else I have encountered.

Dave Cranmer, the NIST/MEP administrator who oversaw the development of the questionnaire and working team member, provided key insights into the questionnaire's scope and design.

Ann Brown, with her 30 years in working with small manufacturers in rural Kansas, and Peter LaPlaca, with his PhD in marketing at the University of Connecticut and experience with northeast manufactures, brought divergent experiences that enriched the questionnaire's design and effectiveness.

My appreciation and gratitude to all of them for a once-in-a-lifetime experience.

CHAPTER 1

Necessary and Sufficient Conditions for Increasing Sales and Profit

Most small to medium-sized manufacturers (SMMs) generally can produce or obtain information and data they feel are necessary to make decisions about how to grow their businesses. However, as the questionnaire data reveal and as the following case studies will show the information and data that many SMMs have are not sufficient for choosing the right combination of customers, products, and markets that will produce the most profit.

Many SMMs know who their most valuable customers are but do not know the true profitability accruing to the business from selling to them, because SMMs mainly focus only on sales volume—and having too much business from too few customers is not uncommon. SMMs need to know not only the profitability of trading with customers, but also where and how to find new and profitable customers to expand their customer bases. Too few customers are a strategic time bomb and marginally profitable customers are a drag on profit and cash flow.

Similarly, there are winners and losers in product lines. Profitable growth depends on selling products that are profitable and culling out less profitable and aging ones. Product profitability, however, is typically unknown or inaccurate owing to lack of capturing and reporting of actual direct costs—primarily direct labor—at the individual product level. This lack of good data on cost and margin by product makes difficult the task of deciding whether the existing products can provide the desired growth or whether the firm needs new products. It also leads to pricing problems, as the data will show, and causes some SMMs to compete on price alone, which works against profitable growth.

While most SMMs know their markets, they do not know the number of establishments and prospective new customers therein because most have never conducted marketing research. This presents a formidable limiting factor to a growth strategy that calls for adding new customers or products and entering new markets.

SMMs generally know their direct competitors but cannot make "apples-to-apples" comparisons on competitive factors such as price and terms, quality, performance, shipping, warranty, parts replacement, technical service, sales coverage, or customer satisfaction. As with not having conducted marketing research, lack of competitor intelligence is another impediment to growth. Unless an SMM knows the changes it must make to its products and services to better compete, it is relegated to a "me too" competitive position where only the factor on which it can compete is price: the company will have increased sales but at lesser profit.

While having information and data on costs, margins, customers, markets, and competitors is a *necessary* condition to growing profitably, the *sufficient* condition requires that that information and data identify winners and losers among the firm's customers and products, identify new markets—including the number of establishments and prospects—and provide good comparative information about competitors' products, services, pricing, customer service, tech support, sales force and sales coverage, warranty, and so forth.

The following list of questions and SMMs' responses illustrates this lack of information.

Sample questions

When was the last time the firm conducted marketing research?

Is the total number of establishments in the company's target markets known?

Does the firm know the number of prospective customers in its market segments?

Describe the firm's top three market segments.

- 78 of the 126 firms surveyed had never conducted formal marketing research.

- 107 provided a market definition, but only 71 of the definitions were descriptive enough to be able to determine the number and location of prospective customers.
- 68 of the 126 firms did not know the number of businesses or prospective new customers in their defined market segments.
  - Clearly, many SMMs do not have sufficient information or knowledge about their markets to effectively direct their sales efforts to find new customers or markets.

Do the firm's products/services have a competitive advantage?
Can an "apples-to-apples" comparison be made of the firm's products and services with those of direct competitors?
Are there problems defending prices?

- 51 of 71 firms who answered competitor intelligence questions reported they did not routinely collect data on competitors.
- 90 of all 126 named at least one direct competitor but only 61 reported they could make an "apples-to apples" comparison of competing products, services, and prices.
- 85 of 126 reported at least some or sure competitive advantage; yet, 79 reported problems establishing and maintaining prices and 59 said they had to discount price to meet competitive pricing.
- 79 of 126 reported problems maintaining and defending prices; about 30% of the respondents offered more than 25% discounted prices to get orders.
- Three frequent reasons given for pricing problems included (a) prices too high, (b) unsure of actual costs, (c) no competitive advantage—and therefore had to meet competitors' pricing.
  - While most firms know who their direct competitors are they don't have the information to make changes to products and services, pricing, sales coverage, customer service and support, selling and promotional strategies to improve their competitive situation. This lack of good competitive data also results in pricing problems.

> Companies believing that they possess a competitive
> advantage should not have to discount price.

Does the firm prepare reports that show actual costs to produce and sell a
product/service?

- 42 of 126 firms reported knowing actual material and labor
  costs; 34 reported not knowing any of the actual costs.
  - SMMs' lack of accurate cost information is a fundamental
    problem that can adversely affect their efforts to increase
    sales profitably. As the previous material show, pricing
    based on questionable or unknown costs can lead to
    competing primarily on price, which lowers margin and
    profitability, and often signals a lack of competitiveness. In
    the broader sense, not knowing the inherent profitability of
    products compromises product management and will make
    it difficult to identify winners to support profitable growth
    strategy.

Does the company prepare a sales forecast and sales report?

- 73 of 126 firms reported preparing a sales forecast and sales
  report, but only 30 forecasted and reported to the product
  level, and only 19 compared forecasted sales to actual sales to
  the product level. Most firms forecasted only at the company
  level.
  - As with having to know costs, sales forecasting should be a
    basic business practice. That only 23% forecast and report
    sales to the product level further illustrates some of the
    problems that SMMs encounter when trying to expand
    their businesses—problems that can adversely affect both
    product management and sales management.

What percentage of sales derives from your largest customer?

- 31 of 107 firms that answered the question had more than
  30% of sales attributed to their single largest volume customer.

- 60 of 126 did not know the profit margin generated by 80% of their customers.
  - Too much business in too few customers represents the most common critical strategic weakness facing SMMs—particularly smaller ones who have but a few customers and whose margins might be low, resulting in weak cash flow to the business. Knowing the percentage of business deriving from key customers as well as the profit and cash flow they produce is, therefore, important not only for operating for profit but, in some cases, also for survival. While the solution to having too much business with too few customers is to add more customers, the data show that most SMMs simply do not have sufficient information about markets to readily do so.

Are there problems/issues with the performances of the company's sales force, reps, and distributors and with sales coverage?

- Approximately 25% of firms reported dissatisfaction with sales performance (inside, outside, reps) and nearly 30% said sales coverage overall (inside, outside, reps) was satisfactory.
  - Three factors contribute to firms' dissatisfaction with sales performance. As previously noted, first, many firms forecast sales only at the company level; without a detailed sales forecast, evaluating actual sales performance to forecast is difficult. Second, most firms did not have a formal evaluation system by which to evaluate inside, outside, and rep performance. Third, performance evaluation occurred mostly on a semi-annual or annual basis; performance evaluation and feedback should occur more frequently to be effective.

Typical Sales and Marketing Problems

Table 6 summarizes the responses to an open-ended question in the questionnaire investigating the main sales and marketing problems facing the company. The responses, grouped into nine categories, corroborate findings that many SMMs simply lack usable information about their markets and competitors and that sales force performance is problematic.

Table 6. Top Problems Cited

Top areas of problems, issues cited	No. of times Mentioned
Marketing research and analysis and market knowledge.	35
Sales force capabilities, performance, and sales coverage.	28
Competitor intelligence, differentiation, and competitive advantage.	18
Prospect and lead identification.	16
Product management and new product development.	14
Advertising and promotion.	8
Costing and pricing.	6
Customer mix and customer diversification.	5
Quotations and hit rate.	5

Assume you are the sales manager of ABC, Inc. and have just been directed to add five new customers with potential annual orders of $100,000 each and your sales force perceives its markets like the descriptions shown in the following table, *and* you have never researched markets, *and* you and your sales force do not know the number of prospective customers. This is a good example of the reasons most manufacturers experience problems and constraints to growth.

Table 7 further illustrates the difficulty that SMMs have with finding new customers and markets—"turning on their sales spigots." The actual responses to the item, "Describe the firm's top 3 market segments," are

Table 7. Actual Market Segment Descriptions

Actual market segment descriptions	
Auto industry	Restaurants/hotels
Telecommunications	Fireplace, hearth, BBQ type companies
Die-casting	Mid-size electrical equipment manufacturers
Consumer products	Mid-size consumer appliance manufacturers
OEMS	New and used equipment, repair &
Spiral wound (composite cans, dry mix, soap)	rebuilding, parts and accessories
	Jobbers, distributors, wholesalers
Fertilizer dealers	Roll and web business 45% (85% of this is
Growers	conversion)
Contract Health Care	Consumer products – primarily 1–2 key customers
	Military/aerospace 9% (primarily 1–2 key customers)

too vague to be used to determine the number and location of prospective new customers, and some are industries—not markets, for example, auto industry, telecommunications, and manufacturing. These descriptions cannot begin to provide sufficient detail by which to effectively and efficiently direct sales efforts to prospective customers and markets. In addition, many of them refer to an industry–not a market. I define "industry" as a group of sellers and producers and a "market" as a group of buyers.

The Industry–Market Hierarchy and the "Macro Market Fallacy"

I use the following hierarchy shown in Figure 1 to put into perspective the relationship of industries with markets to help SMMs redefine their markets and market segments so that they can determine the number and location of prospective new customers and eventually identify their target markets— those which management prioritizes and directs the sales force to. This

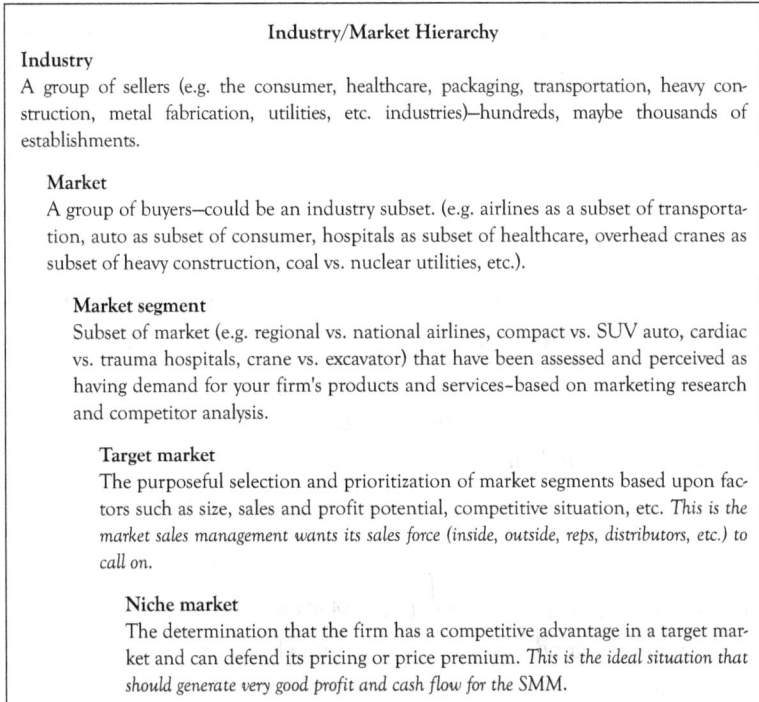

Industry/Market Hierarchy

Industry
A group of sellers (e.g. the consumer, healthcare, packaging, transportation, heavy construction, metal fabrication, utilities, etc. industries)–hundreds, maybe thousands of establishments.

  Market
  A group of buyers–could be an industry subset. (e.g. airlines as a subset of transportation, auto as subset of consumer, hospitals as subset of healthcare, overhead cranes as subset of heavy construction, coal vs. nuclear utilities, etc.).

    Market segment
    Subset of market (e.g. regional vs. national airlines, compact vs. SUV auto, cardiac vs. trauma hospitals, crane vs. excavator) that have been assessed and perceived as having demand for your firm's products and services–based on marketing research and competitor analysis.

      Target market
      The purposeful selection and prioritization of market segments based upon factors such as size, sales and profit potential, competitive situation, etc. *This is the market sales management wants its sales force (inside, outside, reps, distributors, etc.) to call on.*

        Niche market
        The determination that the firm has a competitive advantage in a target market and can defend its pricing or price premium. *This is the ideal situation that should generate very good profit and cash flow for the SMM.*

Figure 1. Industry/market hierarchy.

avoids the typical approach that SMMs use to find new business—"shotgun marketing"—where the priority is any sale or new customer as long as it increases the top line. As the remainder of the book shows, not all sales, products, or customers are equally profitable—some are much more profitable than others—and the objective of this book is to find and focus on the best combination of customers, products, and markets to maximize profit.

The descriptions of market segment shown in Table 7 illustrate the "macro market fallacy," which goes something like this:

"If I can only get 1% to 2% of the multi-million-dollar growers market I'll be rich."

But since the multi-million dollar *growers* market is never defined in terms of number and location of prospects—only in the aggregate—a company will not know where to begin to get a piece of it. The company will not be able to break it down into segments (subset of a market), prospects, and target customers (the target market). It will not be able to quantify sales and profit potential or prioritize sales and marketing resources and initiatives. The questionnaire findings indicate that most SMMs operate at the industry/market levels because few investigate markets and competition sufficiently to be able to segment and prioritize opportunities—a.k.a. shotgun marketing.

Operating in the Dark

After working with hundreds of companies over the years and reflecting on the insights gained from the questionnaire, I have concluded that a formidable impediment to manufacturers' ability to grow—to be able to turn on their sales spigot—is lack of good, strategic data and information by which to design focused and targeted growth strategies, as shown in Figure 2.

Summary

One of the biggest impediments that SMMs have to growing their businesses is lack of good insight into and knowledge about their markets. Most do not have clear definitions of the markets they serve or want to target. They think in terms of industries rather than market segments or

Four areas of insufficient information	
Area	Strategic implication
1. Costs and margins	To calculate the inherent profitability of products, services, and customers, to calculate break-even sales level and to determine the most profitable combination of products and services.
2. Information about customers	To determine the best combination of customers, products, and markets.
3. Markets, market segments, and target markets	
4. Competitor information	To change products, pricing, quality, sales channels, and advertising and promotion strategies to gain competitive advantage.

Figure 2. Four areas of insufficient information.

target markets, which results in their pursuing the macro market fallacy and in shotgun marketing.

Because complete information about costs and margins is often absent and therefore unavailable for pricing, SMMs find that they must offer discount prices or meet competitors' prices to sell, even when they believe they possess competitive advantage. Some of this can be attributed to their accounting and financial reporting systems, which frequently do not provide profit analysis on products and customers. Some pricing problems, however, are due to being unaware of competitor's pricing, which results in SMMs simply pricing what they think the market will bear. Good cost and margin data therefore are essential not only for pricing but also for being able to identify winners and losers in both the product line and the customer base.

Customer profitability analysis is just as critical—if not more so—for profitable growth as is product profitability analysis. A company faces a potential strategic time bomb where it has one or a few customers accounting for the majority of sales, profit, and cash flow. If any of those customers reduce purchases or deflect to competitors then that company's survival could be at risk. This is particularly true for smaller companies where typically they have few customers. Having information about customers, particularly the percentage of sales each customer represents as well as the profit and cash flow it produces, should be one of the first steps in developing a growth strategy. Along with determining which products will support future growth, an SMM also needs to know which customers will support growth.

A company's financial situation and trends in sales, profitability, and cash flow affect its ability and readiness to develop and execute growth strategies. SMMs desiring to grow should be on a good financial and cash flow footing and know their break-even sales and overall profitability before embarking on a growth plan. In-depth information about costs and margins, customers, markets, market segments, and competitors represent the building blocks and the necessary and sufficient conditions for growth.

CHAPTER 2

Getting Down to Basics

Some of my experiences and observations of companies pursuing growth strategies involved a two-day offsite meeting where management reviewed historical sales and some financial data and discussed the pros and cons of various opportunities. These meetings usually ended with an agreement to increase sales by 10% and with general statements about targets and goals, usually documented by sticky notes on the walls. I don't recall any that specified the number of new accounts to open or existing ones to prioritize, new market potential described in number of prospective new customers or realistic sales potential, products to cull or new ones to develop, and, most importantly, where a solid company financial analysis was presented to shed light on its ability to pay for the expected growth. A company financial analysis and assessment of its ability to fund growth should be a necessary and sufficient condition in conjunction with having information on costs and margins, customers, markets, and competition.

Growth plans should be tailored not only to a company's ability to pay for them but also to their ability to execute. Smaller SMMs might not have the financial and human resources and skills as do larger companies to take on various growth strategies. For example, smaller companies might be better off just trying to grow by adding a few more customers whereas a larger company could consider aggressive new product development or acquisitions. The former is a much less expensive and less risky strategy than the latter and can be accomplished with basic marketing research and lead generation whereas the latter requires extensive engineering, marketing research, competitor intelligence, and financial and cost accounting.

Four Types of Manufacturers

Years ago, Mike Collins introduced the following chart to explain why strategies developed for big companies cannot be simply dropped on to or "down sized" for smaller companies and why strategies for small companies must be markedly different and simpler. Figure 3 illustrates four types of manufacturers, based on employment size as a proxy of their overall ability to execute growth strategies.

Note: The use of employment size is a rule-of-thumb—not a scientific or statistical metric—and is not cast in concrete. It is simply a way to anticipate the problems and issues confronting an SMM that could limit its alternatives to grow or that could defeat their execution.

Collins' four types of manufacturers			
Type 1	Type 2	Type 3	Type 4
Empl. up to 25	Empl. 26 to 75	Empl. 76 to 250	Empl. over 250
Survival Mode	Fledgling Business	Professionally Managed	Giant Public
Few assets	Growing assets	Assets as collateral	Huge assets
Cash flow awful	Cash flow erratic and problematic	Working capital management	Formally managed cash flow
Quartly financial statements, basic or manual accounting system	Some monthly/ quarterly statements, more detailed accounting system	Detailed, formatted statements, dedicated accounting software and MIS systems	Audited statements, sophisticated MIS, MRP, etc.
Any sales, no goals, just survive	Informal, verbal sales volume goals	Written sales and profit goals, forecasts, and budgets	Strategic plan, profit, bottom line focus
Sole proprietorship, sub 'S' corporation	Sole proprietorship, sub 'S' and some 'C' corporations	Sole proprietorship, 'C' corporations	Publicly owned
No marketing/sales function, inside sales	Inside sales, reps, agents, distributors	Inside sales, company outside sales and/or reps, informal channels	Sophisticated sales marketing organization and channels

Figure 3. Four types of manufacturers.

Types 1 and 2 businesses (employment up to about 75) operate with relatively less sophistication and with informal business systems and procedures, employ mostly family members who wear many hats, are primarily focused on sales volume, and often experience chronic cash flow problems. Sales and marketing goals and objectives are verbal, subject to frequent change, and are focused on getting the next sale—not on longer-term growth planning. They tend to have a few customers that account for most of the business and are routinely reacting to the crisis du jour. Sales and marketing functions are carried out mostly by inside positions and reps; dedicated outside company sales positions are too expensive. These firms typically pursue shotgun marketing that results in low repeat business, quality and customer service problems, low margins, and high selling costs.

Type 3 businesses are larger (employment between 76 and 250 and up) and operate with relatively more formalized systems for planning, budgeting, and forecasting; use assets as collateral; conduct long-term planning with follow-up and evaluation; employ specialists for account-ing, finance, production, and sales/marketing; and have a sales organiza-tion composed of inside and outside employees, reps, and possibly dealers and distributors. Type 3 firms also are not immune to shotgun marketing. Type 4 companies are publicly traded businesses who, because their problems and issues are much different from SMM's, are not addressed in this book.

Customers, Products, and Markets (C-P-M™)—the Essential Components of Growth Strategy

After many years of working with SMMs and learning about Collins' four types of manufacturers, I realized that Types 1–3 needed some-thing tailored to their situations and distilled all this experience and material down to C-P-M™—customer, products, and markets—because at the end of the day, SMMs must focus on these three items to grow. I consider C-P-M™ the DNA of growth strategy development. More specifically, manufacturers desiring to grow should determine the com-bination of C-P-M™ that will generate the most profit and cash flow. It is that simple.

Note: *C-P-M*™ is not to be confused with CPM, the critical path method or critical path analysis, developed in the 1950s by the DuPont Corporation that uses a mathematically based algorithm for scheduling a set of project activities.

The thrust of the work I have done with companies is to help them acquire these data and then use the same to develop strategy. As you will see, the material in this book is mostly about gaining insights derived from *C-P-M*™ analyses in order to make effective strategic decisions. It should help owners and managers answer the *C-P-M*™ question, "Given our current customers, products, and markets what should we do with the business?"

Strategy Is 90% Planning and Analysis and 10% Execution; Paralysis by Analysis

The B2B industrial marketing I practice involves gaining insight and knowledge about a company's cost of doing business (cost and margins of product and services costs, cost to generate a new customer, and sales and marketing costs), about current and prospective customers, target markets, and competition. It focuses on market analysis and planning before implementation. I believe, and have experienced, that strategy is 90% planning and analysis and 10% execution.

A couple of years ago, a professional facilitator told me that all this data and analysis amounted to paralysis by analysis. He took at face value whatever data a company presented and proceeded to help it develop strategy—admittedly never challenging the accuracy, relevance, completeness, or strategic value of the data the company presented. He helped prioritize issues based on anecdotal and qualitative data and then facilitated the development of solutions to address the issues—leading up to a grand plan.

Granted, good strategy development is time consuming and focusing on and prioritizing the right problems, issues, and data is important. However, strategy development can progress very effectively— and efficiently—simply by focusing on *C-P-M*™ because it will lead to critical and strategically important issues quickly and in the process strategic options and practicalities will become evident.

The following material presents three steps to finding out if the business is financially ready to pursue growth and lays the groundwork for conducting *C-P-M*™ analyses.

Step One: Assess the Company's Financial Situation

A company's financial situation affects its ability to develop and execute growth strategies. Many Type 1 and 2 SMMs' format and content of financial statements generally are not suitable for use in determining the best *C-P-M*™. Some expenses pertaining to the family, co-mingled with business expenses, often obscure the actual costs of the business, and the business' production, general, and administrative expenses also are co-mingled. All this must be sorted out to be able to assess the financial situation of the business and its ability to fund growth.

Knowing a company's financial situation is vitally important and should be the first step before setting it on a growth trajectory. SMMs whose working capital, cash, and credit are weak are questionable candidates for growth because, financially, they might not afford the costs to grow. These companies should first focus on becoming more operationally efficient to improve profitability and working capital, and conduct marketing research and market planning to ready the business to grow.

Five basic financial ratios to assess your business' financial readiness to grow

SMMs can quickly determine if their financial situation can support growth by compiling a few numbers from from their balance sheet balance sheet and income statement and calculating the following five ratios, which most bankers and creditors use to assess a business' creditworthiness.

1. Current ratio
2. Quick ratio
3. Sales-to-working capital ratio
4. Accounts receivable ratios
5. Debt-to-equity ratio

1. *Current ratio*—The amount of cash, accounts receivable, and inventory (the sum of these is called "current assets") compared with trade accounts payable, line of credit, and current maturity of long-term debt (the sum of these is called "current liabilities"). Current assets should exceed current liabilities and the ratio of current assets to current liabilities should be greater than 2.0, generally between 2.0 and 3.0.

$$\text{Current ratio} = \frac{\text{current assets}}{\text{current liabilities}}$$

2. *Quick ratio (also the acid test)*—This is the *current ratio* without inventory since inventory cannot always be readily converted to cash and is a more stringent assessment of a firm's ability to convert assets to cash. Similar to the current ratio, the amount should exceed current liabilities and the ratio should be greater than 1.0.

$$\text{Quick ratio} = \frac{\text{cash + accounts receivable–inventory}}{\text{current liabilities}}$$

- *Creditors routinely use these two ratios in their determination of a company's creditworthiness and ability to repay debt and interest. Similarly, SMM owners and managers can use them to see if the firm can support additional investment in materials, labor (manufacturing and sales), and overhead to execute sales, marketing, and growth strategies.*

3. *Sales-to-working capital ratio*—Working capital is the difference between current assets and current liabilities, and should be positive. It represents the amount of current assets in excess of current liabilities. Negative working capital requires credit or additional equity to meet the demands for cash to pay trade suppliers, creditors, and short-term debt obligations.

$$\text{Working capital} = \text{current assets} \div \text{current liabilities}$$

The sales-to-working capital ratio associates annual sales revenue with working capital.

$$\text{Sales-to-working capital ratio} = \frac{\text{annual sales revenue}}{\text{working capital}}$$

The following illustration shows the sales-to-working capital ratio calculation using $1,000,000 for annual sales.

$$\text{Sales-to-working capital ratio} = \frac{\$1,000,000}{180,500} = 5.5$$

While this example shows a sales-to-working capital ratio of 5.5, there is no recommended range for the working capital ratio because it varies by industry, inventory, and cash and financial management practices of the company, and whether the company sells into seasonal markets. For example, companies that manufacture and sell low-cost products and turn inventory quickly might experience a higher ratio (higher sales to working capital) than a high-fixed-cost company with higher-priced products that turns inventory slower.

	Current situation	Forecast
Sales	$1,000,000	$1,100,000
Working capital	180,500	198,600

SMMs can use this ratio to assess quickly the additional working capital needed to grow their business that might involve increased sales coverage, new product development, and advertising and promotional initiatives. Using the previous example, the firm's working capital ratio is 5.5 to 1.0—sales are five and a half times greater than working capital—and it expects to increase sales by 10 percent. The firm will need an additional $18,100 (up to $198,600; $100,000 increase in sales divided by 5.5) in working capital to support this growth strategy.

- *This is a key preliminary indicator of a firm's ability to afford its growth plan—if it does not have $18,100 or access to credit, it might have to reconsider its intent to increase sales.*

The working capital ratio can also alert management to potential credit squeezes when increases in sales outpace working capital. For example, if orders unexpectedly rose to $2,000,000, the firm could need up to about $360,000 in working capital ($2,000,000 ÷ 5.5). The 5.5 factor is used because it represents the firm's historical sales-to-working capital ratio.

4. *Accounts receivable ratios*—Since accounts receivable hold a lot of cash, businesses want to collect them quickly to avoid delinquencies and uncollectable accounts. Two components of A/R, the turnover ratio and the collection period, shed light on the firm's credit and collection policies and on the speed by which it converts sales to cash.

   The A/R turnover ratio shows the number of times A/R is paid by customers. The higher the number, the faster the business collects its receivables and converts credit to cash.

$$\text{Accounts receivable collection period} = \frac{365}{\text{accounts receivable turnover}}$$

This number shows the number of days it takes to collect all accounts receivable, but unlike the turnover ratio, the smaller the number the better.

Example: Annual sales = $2,000,000
          A/R (average) balance = $250,000

$$\text{Accounts receivable turnover} = \frac{\$2,000,000}{\$250,000} = 8 \text{ times per year}$$

Accounts receivable
collection period = $\frac{365}{8}$ = 45 days to collect

   While most businesses want to collect within 30 days, it's my experience many B2B relationships average somewhat longer particularly when the economy is slow—up to 60 days or more.

   In addition to calculating the collection period on all accounts, businesses can do this on individual accounts and group them into time periods, such as 30 days or less, 31 to 45 days, 46 to 90 days, 91 to 120 days, thus identifying slow-paying accounts and potentially uncollectible. Accounts exceeding 90 days generally require special collection efforts or might have to be written off.

- *This ratio should be particularly significant to smaller SMMs whose business is concentrated in one or two major customers—if they are "slow pay" the SMM's survival could be in jeopardy.*

5. *Debt-to-equity ratio*—Also called *debt-to-net worth*, this ratio shows the proportion of equity the owners and investors have in the business and the amount of funding provided by creditors and suppliers. Lenders rely heavily on this ratio to decide on a company's credit worthiness and ability to service debt. The higher the ratio, the more risk perceived by a creditor. A lower ratio indicates a more stable financial situation and a more likely approval of credit. Before the recession, bankers and creditors wanted a ratio between 1.5 and 3.0, but now might have to consider a somewhat higher since the recession may have weakened some balance sheets.

   The current and quick ratios deal with obligations foreseeable during the next 12 months (current or short term), whereas the debt-to-equity ratio includes all debt, both short and long term, and includes credit issued by trade suppliers and lines of credit. The term "equity," for this purpose, is synonymous with retained earnings or net worth.

$$\text{Debt-to-equity ratio} = \frac{\text{total liabilities}}{\text{net worth}}$$

- SMMs with high debt-to-equity ratios or negative net worth (total liabilities exceeding total assets) are in a precarious situation that calls for caution. When net worth is negative, the firm is insolvent and needs to consider a turnaround strategy—not a growth strategy—or at worst bankruptcy or liquidation. Unfortunately, without funds or credit it may not even be able to afford the development and implementation of a turnaround plan, let alone a growth strategy.

SMMs that effectively manage these five ratios will be well positioned to develop and take on strategies that call for increasing market share and expanding into new markets, developing new products and services, expanding sales personnel and sales coverage, and committing resources to advertising and promotion. Figure 4 summarizes the commonly acceptable ranges of the financial ratios.

A company can use the formulas to calculate company ratios and compare them with the generally accepted ranges, as shown in the following example. If the current ratios and quick ratios are near or less than their minimums, the debt-to-equity ratio is near or greater than 3.0, and accounts receivable days outstanding is more than 60, it may not be financially sound enough to pursue aggressive growth strategies. However, as with most rules of thumb, there are always exceptions and SMMs should consult with their accountant or CPA before taking any actions as a result of the calculations.

	Financial Ratios		
Ratio	Generally Accepted Ratios		Company Ratios
Current	=> 2.0 to 3.0		
Quick	=> 1.0 to 2.0		
Sales-to-working capital	Varies with industry, company, policies regarding credit, collections, inventory, and seasonality. Use historically derived ratio.		
Accounts receivable days outstanding	30 to 45 days		
Debt-to-equity	1.5 to 3.0		

Figure 4. Sample financial ratios.

The obvious solution for shoring up weak financial ratios is to increase sales and generate more profit, but there is no magic key by which to turn on the sales spigot, according to questionnaire findings. SMMs whose financial ratios fall outside of the acceptable ranges, however, are not without options.

SMMs improve their financial situation in three ways:

1. By reducing costs and operating more efficiently.
2. By increasing sales volume.
3. By selling more inherently profitable products and services.

Cost reductions and efficiency improvements increase profitability, but their impact is limited to the extent that the company can reduce excessive costs and inefficiencies. Companies whose ratios are weak might pursue cost reduction and efficiency improvement before taking on growth strategies.

Selling more products and services certainly boost sales, but if products' margins are low they will not generate commensurate profit to improve the ratios. Still, selling more products and services to existing customers is a viable, relatively lower cost, less risky, and a short-term strategy. Finding new customers, however, as questionnaire results show, is difficult since most firms do not know where to find new customers. In the short term, SMMs with weak ratios could consider cost reduction and efficiency improvement and increasing sales to existing customers with existing products.

Longer-term selling of more profitable products and services requires a robust strategic overview to determine if existing products and services can be made more profitable, and if not, finding or developing profitable new products and markets. This is the thrust of the book—to explain how SMMs can develop sound and practicable strategies to operate for higher profit as well as for sales volume.

Step Two: Calculate the Company's Profitability before Developing Sales, Marketing, and Growth Strategies

The financial ratio analyses presented in the previous discussion involved mostly balance sheet items to see if the company's cash and credit situation can support growing the company. Income statement analysis, on the contrary, sheds light on the profitability of products and services. It leads to the overriding strategic question, "Can the business' products and services generate the desired amount of profit for future growth?" This analysis should be the second step toward setting the ground work for developing a growth strategy.

After reviewing the balance sheet to make a preliminary assessment of the business' financial situation, an SMM should look at its income statement for trends in sales and profit. Many Type 1 and Type 2 income statements, however, do not report expenses in a format that allows an insightful and meaningful breakdown of costs and margins.

Reformatting the Income Statement

Before the typical Types 1 and 2 SMMs begin to consider how and what to do to grow, they usually need to reformat their income statements because often the expenses for manufacturing, office and administration, and sales and marketing are co-mingled, making it difficult to conduct any cost and profit analysis. Reformatting makes it easy to look at costs according to their function—for example, costs associated with production and manufacturing cost of goods sold (CGS), office and administrative, and sales and marketing (SG&A)—and to gauge whether they are in line with typical manufacturing operations. CGS typically ranges within 25–35% of sales, SG&A within about 8–15% of sales, and sales and marketing about 5% of sales. These ranges will vary with the size of the firm and with the types of products and services produced. Although income statement cost and margin analysis often results in cost reduction to improve profitability, it also can lead to the investigation of strategic questions such as:

- "What is the level of sales needed to be profitable?"
- "What is the profitability of the business and its products and services?"
- "What combination of customers, products, and market will produce the most profit?"

There are two problems with the typical format shown in Figure 5. First, **Cost of Goods Sold** includes Materials only whereas it should also include manufacturing labor and manufacturing overhead. Consequently, this format overstates Gross Profit at 75% of sales; a manufacturing company usually experiences Gross Profit at about 25–35% of sales. Second, **Expenses** co-mingles manufacturing, general, administrative, selling, and advertising expenses, making any cost or financial analyses difficult—and therefore distorts profitability ratios.

The reformatted statement rearranges the expenses, puts them into the generally accepted accounting format, and results in more accurate percentages of sales for ratio analysis. The expenses, although typical of most SMMs' income statements, will change depending on how a company actually reports and describes its expenses.

In the reformatted example, Mfg. Direct Labor and Mfg. OH moved up to Cost of Goods Sold, showing a Gross Profit of $549, 000 at 22% of sales. (Production inefficiencies, low material utilization, weak pricing, or low sales volume could account for the Gross Profit percentage below

Typical Format		
	($1,000's)	
Sales	$2,488	100%
Cost of Goods Sold		
Materials	623	25%
Cost of Goods Sold	$623	25%
Gross Profit	$1,865	75%
Expenses		
Advertising	$15	1%
Commissions	102	4%
Insurance	14	1%
Interest	17	1%
Mfg. Direct Labor	442	18%
Mfg. OH	874	35%
Miscellaneous	24	1%
Office/sales salary	49	2%
Officer salary	45	2%
Outside services	4	0%
Rent	30	1%
Travel expenses	5	0%
Utilities	7	0%
Total Expenses	$1,628	65%
Pre-tax Profit	237	10%

Reformatted		
	($1,000's)	
Sales	$2,488	100%
Cost of Goods Sold		
Materials	623	25%
Mfg. Direct Labor	442	18%
Mfg. OH	874	35%
Cost of Goods Sold	$1,939	78%
Gross Profit	$549	22%
General and Administrative		
Officer salary	$45	2%
Office salaries	24	1%
Rent	30	1%
Miscellaneous	24	1%
Interest	17	1%
Insurance	14	1%
Utilities	7	0%
Outside services	4	0%
Total Expenses	$165	7%
Operating Profit	$384	15%
Sales/Marketing Expenses		
Commission	$102	4%
Selling salaries	25	1%
Advertising/trade shows	15	1%
Sales Travel	5	0%
Total	$147	6%
Pre-tax Profit	$237	10%

Figure 5. Typical and reformatted income statements.

the typical range.) However, general and administrative expenses (G&A) at 7% of sales is better than normal (usually about 10–12% depending on the industry), and the 10% Pre-tax Profit is pretty good. Sales and marketing expenses vary, similar to G&A, by circumstance, so the 6% could be high or low. Thus, the reformatted statement provides much more insight into the business' expenses that now can be evaluated accurately on a percentage of sales basis.

This example shows a business that is operating at a profit. But when a business is not operating at a profit and wants to grow, it needs to do more than just reformat its income statement—its needs to determine if the loss is due to insufficient sales volume, due to unprofitable products and services, or both.

"Contribution Margin" and "Break-even sales"—Two Very Useful Financial Tools

When a firm is operating at a loss, a growth strategy must—at a minimum—focus on the level of sales that will bring the firm up to profitability. It is called the "break-even" point—where sales equal total expenses. Finding break-even sales (BE) requires calculating the *contribution margin*, another measure of profitability.

Contribution margin (CM) = unit selling price minus the variable costs for direct material and direct labor. This is the dollar amount of profit remaining from the selling price after paying for the variable (direct) costs for materials, labor, and commissions (if paid) for the product or service. Dividing CM by the selling price results in a percentage that shows the profitability of the product. The greater the percent, the greater the profitability. *Note.* Contribution margin as a measure of profit differs from gross profit, which takes into account manufacturing overhead. Gross profit = sales—direct material, direct labor, and manufacturing overhead. Contribution margin = sales—direct material—direct labor—sales commissions. A more detailed explanation follows.

Products A and B both sell for $100, but A's total cost at $48 (direct material, direct labor, and commissions—not overhead) is greater than

	A	B
Contribution Margin–A		
Selling Price	$100	$100
Direct Material	$25	$15
Direct Labor	20	5
Commissions	3	3
Total Variable Cost	$48	$23
Contribution Margin $	$52	$77
Contribution Margin %	52%	77%

Figure 6. Sample contribution margin–A.

B's at $23, which produces a lower CM $ ($52 versus $77) and CM % than B. Therefore, B is more profitable than A, and will generate $25 more profit ($77 – $25), or contribution margin, per unit. Given a choice, an SMM would want to sell more B than A because B generates more profit at the same sales volume. (*Note*: This does not consider operational issues pertaining to production capacity or limitations, machine speeds, or constraints, which can have a bearing on the amount of a given product that can be made. Also, it does not consider market demand or competitive pressures that could affect the company's ability to sell as much of B as it would like.)

Since most SMMs sell more than one product, the CM% for a combination of products will be the weighted average of the total volume sold, as shown by the 69% CM% at the bottom right of Figure 7. Note that if the proportion of sales between the two products differed, for example, more of A than of B, the total CM % would decrease since A is less profitable.

Contribution Margin-B			
	A	B	Total
Selling Price	$100	$100	
Direct Material	$25	$15	
Direct Labor	20	5	
Commissions	3	3	
Total Variable Cost	$48	$23	
Contribution Margin $	$52	$77	
Volume	100	200	
Total Revenue	$10,000	$20,000	$30,000
Contribution Margin $	$5,200	$15,400	$20,600
Contribution Margin %	52%	77%	69%

Figure 7. Sample contribution margin-B.

Job shops and machine companies can use CM on a per-job or per-order basis to see the profitability between the different types of jobs, orders, and processes. One company, BuzzCo Machining, Inc., listed its 1,215 work orders for a year in descending order of contribution margin, ranging from 81% to –40%, averaging 60% for the company overall. The owner attributed the higher margins to repairs he did on aircraft landing gears for which he had FAA Air Station Certification. This obviously represented a competitive advantage for him since most job shops will not invest in this market because of the stringent quality, machining, and delivery requirements needed for certification—barriers to entry into the FAA market segment. The higher margin orders represented an opportunity to increase profits should he focus on further penetrating FAA-type business.

The break-even sales calculation—the sales volume at which the firm makes neither a profit nor loss—requires the use of CM% and fixed costs, which include factory and office rent, utilities, depreciation, insurance and taxes, and factory, office, and sales salaries (but not factory hourly wages). These costs are *fixed* in the sense that they do not vary with sales or production. Rent, for example, remains the same whether a hundred units are produced and sold or a thousand are produced and sold. Direct material and direct labor costs, on the contrary, do vary with sales and production, and are called *variable* costs. An SMM cannot make a profit until its sales exceeds its total fixed costs and all variable costs associated with producing and selling products. Figure 8 illustrates breakdown of sales, variable costs, fixed costs, and break-even sales volume for a single product, Product A.

Figure 8 uses Product A's variable costs as illustrated in Figure 7 and adds $1,000 in fixed costs to illustrate the BE calculation. Sales at 10 units × SP $100 generates $1,000 total revenue. Product A's contribution margin, at $520 for 10 units, does not cover fixed costs, resulting in a $480 loss. At 19 units × SP $100, the $988 contribution margin almost covers fixed costs. Break-even sales, therefore, is just above 19 units. The company's sales volume will need to be 20 units before it will make a profit.

The break-even (BE) formula is

$$BE = \frac{\text{fixed costs}}{\text{CM\%}} \quad BE = \$1,923 = \frac{\$1,000}{52\%}$$

The formula for BE is fixed cost $1,000 divided by CM % (52%). Contribution margin is the amount of revenue remaining after paying for direct material, direct labor, and commissions, if applicable. It represents the "inherent" profit of the product. These costs—variable costs—are directly associated with raw material, "hands-on" labor to

Break-even Sales				
	A	Sales Volume		
Selling Price	$100	$1,000	$1,900	$2,000
Variable Costs				
Direct Material	$25	$250	$475	$500
Direct Labor	20	200	380	400
Commissions	3	30	57	60
Total Variable Cost	$48	$480	$912	$960
Contribution Margin $	$52	$520	$988	$1,040
Contribution Margin %	52%			
Fixed costs	$1,000	$1,000	$1,000	$1,000
Profit/(Loss)		($480)	($12)	$40
Break-even Sales	$1,923			

Figure 8. Break-even sales.

convert material into a saleable product, and commission to sell the product—they vary directly with production and sales. Fixed costs include all other costs: manufacturing (including depreciation), office salaries, rent, administration, and sales and marketing and advertising expenses. A higher CM % will reduce BE and generate profit faster. Figure 9 shows two products—Product A from the previous example— and Product B with a higher contribution margin at 77% than A's contribution margin at 52%. B's higher CM% at the same fixed cost of $1,000 results in a lower breakeven of $1,299 compared with $1,923 for Product A. Higher fixed costs will increase BE and take longer to reach profitability. Higher CM% at the same fixed cost will lower BE and shorten the time to reach BE. Therefore, the ideal situation is high CM% and low fixed costs. A sales volume of higher-profit products and services will generate more profit than the same unit sales volume of lower-profit products and services.

The strategic implication for profitable growth is that selling higher-margin products (higher CM%) will accelerate a company's profits and profitability. Hence, operating for profit means determining the combination of customers, products, and markets that will produce the most profit.

Contribution Margin–C		
	A	B
Selling Price	$100	$100
Variable Costs		
Direct Material	$25	$15
Direct Labor	20	5
Commissions	3	3
Total Variable Cost	$48	$23
Contribution Margin $	$52	$77
Contribution Margin %	52%	77%
Fixed costs	$1,000	$1,000
Breakeven	$1,923	$1,299

Figure 9. Sample contribution margin–C.

When a firm is operating below BE, it is important to know the difference between current sales and BE sales so that the amount of growth—and resources—needed to put the firm in the black can be established. The two income statements in Figure 10 compare a loss situation and a break-even situation for the same company.

The Loss example in Figure 10 shows the company's year-end income statement with a pre-tax loss of –$128,000 at sales of $1.8 million, thus operating below breakeven. Assume, for example, that management has determined that financial ratios are okay and wants to make the business profitable within 18 months as part of a longer-term growth strategy, and needs to prioritize sales, marketing resources, and working capital. Its next step requires determining the sales volume that will produce a profit, which is shown in Figure 11. It shows that additional sales of $242,000—a 13% increase to $2,042,000—will put the firm at break-even. The income statement on the right side of Figure 10 confirms the firm will reach break-even sales at $2,042,000.

The break down of fixed and variable costs in Figure 11 illustrates total variable and fixed costs to make the BE calculation. Total variable costs of $844,000 subtracted from sales results in the $956,000 contribution margin, and CM$ divided by sales equals CM%, 53%. Total fixed costs, $1,084,000, divided by CM% equals BE sales, $2,042,000.

This calculation reveals two things that will help management prioritize sales and marketing resources and working capital. First, its 53%

Loss				Breakeven			
($1,000s)				($1,000s)			
Sales		$1,800	100%	Sales		$2,042	100%
Cost of Goods Sold				Cost of Goods Sold			
Materials		451	25%	Materials		511	25%
Mfg. Direct Labor		320	18%	Mfg. Direct Labor		363	18%
Mfg. OH		874	49%	Mfg. OH		874	43%
Cost of Goods Sold		$1,644	91%	Cost of Goods Sold		$1,748	86%
	Gross Profit	$156	9%		Gross Profit	$294	14%
General and Administrative				General and Administrative			
Officer salary		$45	3%	Officer salary		$45	2%
Office salaries		24	1%	Office salaries		24	1%
Rent		30	2%	Rent		30	1%
Miscellaneous		24	1%	Miscellaneous		24	1%
Interest		17	1%	Interest		17	1%
Insurance		14	1%	Insurance		14	1%
Utilities		7	0%	Utilities		7	0%
Outside services		4	0%	Outside services		4	0%
Total Expenses		$165	9%	Total Expenses		$165	7%
	Operating Profit	-$9	0%		Operating Profit	$129	5%
Sales/Marketing Expenses				Sales/Marketing Expenses			
Commission		$74	4%	Commission		$84	4%
Selling salaries		25	1%	Selling salaries		25	1%
Advertising/ trade shows		15	1%	Advertising/ trade shows		15	1%
Sales Travel		5	0%	Sales Travel		5	0%
	Total	$119	5%		Total	$129	5%
Pre-tax Profit		-$128	-5%	Pre-tax Profit		$0	0%

Figure 10. Comparing loss and breakeven.

CM indicates that the firm's products are relatively profitable (generally, contribution margin higher than 30% is good). Second, although the 9% gross profit is much lower than expected for a manufacturing business, management recognizes that the firm simply has not been generating enough sales volume to cover overhead—profitability will increase just by increasing volume and that the high 53% CM will help reach profitability sooner. After reviewing the product line and customer mix, and discussing with the sales force, the need to bring on a couple more accounts, management believes it can close the $242,000 sales gap in 18 months, which will require averaging an additional $13,000 in sales per month. It now has a factual-based sales forecast to increase sales—it's now a matter of researching markets and deciding from where the additional sales will come.

However, Types 1 and 2 and most Type 3 SMMs that do not conduct marketing research, who do not know how and where to find prospective new customers, who do not have good competitive information, and who most likely do not know actual costs and margins, are at a formidable disadvantage in the game of growth strategy development, particularly if their contribution margins are low. The only way they will be able to generate profit is by selling volume—yet, as the questionnaire data show, they don't produce or have the information to find new customers. In Figure 11, the firm had good cost and margin data, a high CM, but needs more sales volume to reach profitability.

If your company is not profitable, or you are interested in calculating its profitability, or you want or need to determine the level of sales that will bring it up to profitability, you can use the following formats.

The first is a blank income statement, Figure 12. Enter sales dollars and dollars for Cost of Goods Sold and subtract CGS from Sales to get Gross Profit. Enter General and Administrative Expenses and subtract from Gross Profit to get Operating Profit. Enter Sales and Marketing Expenses and subtract from Operating Profit to get Pre-tax Profit. Divide each of these numbers by Sales to get their percentages of sales. Lastly, enter the corresponding margin numbers for your company's industry (SIC or NAICS codes), which you can find via the Internet or at most public libraries. This will enable you to compare your business with others in the same SIC/NAICS group.

Percentages that fall on the favorable side of the generally accepted percentages should not require any follow-up. However, low margins for Gross Profit, Operating Profit, or Pre-tax Profit should trigger some inquiry into the causes, particularly if the firm is operating above break-even, which you can determine using the next format, Figure 13.

Enter the company's annual sales, costs for direct material and direct labor, commissions if they are paid, and sum at Total variable costs. Divide those dollars by Sales and enter under Company % of Sales. Subtract Total variable costs from Sales to get Contribution Margin $, divide this by Sales, and enter Contribution Margin % under Company % of Sales.

Break-even Sales Calculation				
	($1,000's)		Fixed	Variable
Sales	$1,800	100%		
Materials	451	25%		$451
Mfg. Direct Labor	320	18%		320
Mfg. OH	874	49%	$874	
Cost of Goods Sold	$1,644	91%		
Gross Profit	$156	9%		
General and Administrative				
Officer salary	$45	3%	45	
Office salaries	24	1%	24	
Rent	30	2%	30	
Miscellaneous	24	1%	24	
Interest	17	1%	17	
Insurance	14	1%	14	
Utilities	7	0%	7	
Outside services	4	0%	4	
Total	$165	9%		
Operating Profit	($9)	-1%		
Sales/Marketing Expenses				
Commission	$74	4%		74
Selling salaries	25	1%	25	
Advertising/trade shows	15	1%	15	
Sales travel	5	0%	5	—
Total	$119	7%		
Pre-tax Profit	-$128	-7%		
Total Costs			$1,084	$844
% of Sales				47%
Contribution Margin $				$956
Contribution Margin %				53%
Break-even Sales				$2,042

Figure 11. Break-even sales calculation.

Enter the amount for Overhead and divide by CM % to get BE sales. Example calculations are shown under Example.

To determine the months to get to BE, divide annual sales by 12 to get average monthly sales, and divide this into BE sales. In this example, the firm will reach BE sales in 4.4 months, assuming pricing and volume remain constant.

Income statement margin analysis

	Company numbers here		Generally
	Dollars	% of Sales	Accepted %
Sales		100%	100%
Cost of Goods Sold			65–75%
Gross Profit			25–35%
General and Administrative Expenses			8–15%
Operating Profit			17–20%
Sales and Marketing Expenses			5–10%
Pre-tax Profit			5–10%

Figure 12. Blank income statement format.

Break-even calculation

Annual	Company		Example	
	Dollars	% of Sales	Dollars	% of Sales
Sales		100%	$1,000,000	100%
Direct material			350,000	35%
Direct labor			200,000	20%
Commissions			40,000	4%
Total variable costs			$590,000	59%
Contribution margin $ (sales - variable costs)			$410,000	41%
Contribution margin % (sales + variable costs)			41%	
Overhead, fixed costs			$150,000	15%
Break-even sales (Overhead ÷ cm%)			$365,854 ($150,000 ÷ 41%)	
Break-even sales			$365,854	
Average monthly sales			$83,333	
Months to breakeven			4.4	

Figure 13. Blank break-even format.

At 4.4 months of average sales, sales volume will be $365,854 and with a 41% CM the firm will have generated contribution margin sufficient to cover annual fixed costs, resulting in no profit. Again, assuming constant pricing and sales volume, the company will accrue pretax profit at $3,417 per month ($83,333 monthly sales × 41% CM) for the rest of the year.

Average monthly sales	$83,333
Months to BE	4.4
Sales	$365,854
Contribution margin %	41%
Contribution margin $	$150,000
Fixed costs	$150,000
Profit	$0

Estimating Working Capital to Fund Growth

To estimate the amount of working capital needed to fund the sales increase, divide 1 by the firm's working capital ratio (1 ÷ working capital ratio) and multiply the result by the sales gap. In the following example, Figure 14, if the firm's annual sales are $1,000,000, the sales gap to BE is $125,000, and working capital is $180,500, the working capital ratio is 5.5. Additional required working capital is $22,562.

Working capital calculation		
	Example	Company
Curent annual sales	$1,000,000	
Working capital	180,500	
Sales-to-working capital ratio	5.5	
Sales gap to BE	125,000	
Additional working capital needed to reach BE		
(1 ÷ 5.5) × $125,000 =	$22,562	

Figure 14. Working capital calculation.

SMMs can use these sample calculations and example formats to assess their company's financial situation before pursuing growth, to avoid inadvertently depleting cash, worsening credit and debt situations, and jeopardizing chances for successful and profitable growth.

Step Three: Assess Preliminary Strategic Options Based on Financial Trends

Here are examples of preliminary strategic implications stemming from the assessment of a company's financial situation that should influence its development and execution of sales, marketing, and growth strategies. It entails looking at five situations that involve trends in sales, profitability, and cash flow.

Cash flow involves the movement of cash in and out of the business and corresponds to the firm's working capital—accounts receivable and payable, inventory, credit line, and debt repayment. It basically is the amount of available cash in the business. Slow-paying customers and slow-turning inventory hold up cash flow. Similarly, payments to suppliers and creditors deplete cash.

The first situation, Figure 15, illustrates the most desirable situation where sales, profitability, and cash flow all are increasing or good, allowing for many growth options, such as increasing sales of existing products to existing customers, finding and entering new markets, and developing new products, all of which require working capital and possibly capital investment, particularly new product development. If the balance sheet is strong enough (not too leveraged, good equity and cash), the company could even consider more aggressive strategies, such as acquisition or merger.

The second situation, Figure 16, the worst situation, involves decreasing sales, profitability, and cash flow. This is the classic turnaround situation.

	Increasing or good	Decreasing or weak
Sales	×	
Profitability	×	
Cash Flow	×	

Figure 15. Most desirable situation.

	Increasing or good	Decreasing or weak
Sales		×
Profitability		×
Cash Flow		×

Figure 16. Worst situation.

Critical questions: Are sales down due to general economic activity, poor sales planning and execution, or competitor strength? Is profitability affected by inefficient operations, inherently low-profit products and sales mix (the proportion of each product's sales of total sales), or operating below break-even? Is cash flow affected by slow-paying customers, low profitability, or debt reduction and investment? Aggressive growth should not be considered in this situation because the amount of working capital to pay for materials, labor, and other operating costs, and sales and promotional efforts associated with growth could outpace the firm's cash and credit and push the firm further into debt. Rather, the firm should seek to stabilize cash and profitability through cost reduction and better working capital management.

The next three examples involve variations of trends in sales, profitability, and cash flow.

In Figure 17, sales and cash flow are okay, but not profitability. This could be due to a couple of things. First, the firm could be operating below breakeven, which by definition means there is no profit. However, if the firm is operating above breakeven the search for causes of low profitability could involve checking for operational inefficiency, too much overhead, low-profit products, and inefficient and ineffective selling strategies. Each one of these possibilities should be addressed before pursuing growth because it will most likely still result in inadequate profits. Growth can be pursued but it should be accompanied by strategies

	Increasing or good	Decreasing or weak
Sales	×	
Profitability		×
Cash Flow	×	

Figure 17. Profitability not okay.

to lower costs and increase product profitability (increasing production efficiency and competitive analysis). This is likely practicable because cash flow is okay—the firm has the money to do it.

The fourth situation, Figure 18, shows sales as okay, but profitability and cash flow are not. The company can consider moderate, careful growth, but management must find out why profitability is low (operating below BE, due to low-profit products, inefficiencies or high overhead) and keep an eye on cash.

	Increasing or good	Decreasing or weak
Sales	×	
Profitability		×
Cash Flow		×

Figure 18. Profitability and cash flow not okay.

The fifth situation, Figure 19, shows the firm's sales and profitability as okay but cash flow is a problem. Sales could be outpacing working capital (the firm's sales-to-working capital ratio is too high). In financial parlance, this is "overtrading," typical of many firms who experience a rapid increase in sales. This is a borderline situation depending on how problematic profit and cash flow are. Another possibility is that the firm could be paying down debt, which puts growth and debt retirement on a collision course due to their mutual need for cash. This situation calls for strong credit and bank relationships to support growth and a strong balance sheet—good ratios. Management should investigate why cash flow is problematic. Again, this is a working capital situation involving all or some receivables, payables, capital investment, and debt service.

	Increasing or good	Decreasing or weak
Sales	×	
Profitability	×	
Cash Flow		×

Figure 19. Cash flow not okay.

Table 8. Preliminary Strategic Implications of Financial Situation

		Preliminary strategic implications of financial situation	
		Cash flow and working capital	
		OK	Not OK
Below BE	Products and services are profitable–good CM	OK to proceed with growth strategies. Prepare a sales, marketing, promotional and working capital budget to make sure the firm can "afford" to grow.	Caution–working capital issues (e.g. debt service, A/R turns, etc.). Stabilize cash flow before proceeding.
	Products and services are not profitable–low CM	Caution – find out why products and services are unprofitable (e.g. high production and selling costs, competitive disadvantage, etc.) before developing and implementing growth strategies.	Red flag. The company is not ready to grow; fundamental problems. Focus on cost reduction, working capital. Stabilize before proceeding.
At or above BE	Products and services are profitable–good CM	Green flag, best situation—OK to proceed with growth strategies. Depending on cash flow and working capital strength, the firm can consider customer/market expansion, product development and innovation, merger/acquisition.	Caution–working capital issues (e.g. debt service, A/R turns, etc.). Stabilize cash flow before proceeding.
	Products and services are not profitable–low CM	Yellow flag. Find out why products and services are unprofitable (e.g. high production and selling costs, competitive DISadvantage, etc.). OK cash flow buys time to fix profitability situation.	Yellow flag. The company's growth should be put on hold. Focus on cost reduction, working capital, and competitive situation. Stabilize before proceeding.

Table 8 presents preliminary strategic implications using break-even sales, cash flow, and working capital—a slightly different perspective from the trends just shown in sales, profitability, and cash flow.

The examples presented in Step 3 are not cast in stone but rather presented as guidelines, with the underlying message that growth strategies should align with a company's financial situation and ability to pay for the growth. They should not distress the company by inadvertently depleting cash or credit. This particularly applies to companies that are struggling financially.

Note: The previous examples for breakeven use one or two products, such as A and B, for simplicity. Companies with many products and product lines can still use breakeven but require a different income statement format and possibly the help of an accountant or CPA. More examples of break-even and multiproduct profitability analysis are in Chapter 6—Product Analysis and Evaluation and Product.

Summary

This chapter dealt with preparing a company for growth by first reviewing its financial situation, ability to fund growth, and assessing preliminary strategic options given its financial situation and trends in sales, profitability, cash flow, and working capital—with the underlying message that a company should have a good financial footing before pursuing growth.

There are three simple and quick steps to assessing a company's ability and financial readiness to pursue growth strategies:

1. Assessing working capital, cash, and debt and credit using five ratios: current, quick, accounts receivable days outstanding, sales-to-working capital, and debt-to-equity.
   * *Weak financial situations should moderate companies' impulses to pursue growth that could inadvertently harm the business by depleting working capital and straining credit and debt.*

2. Determining the company's profitability, which involves gross profit, operating profit, pretax profit, contribution margin, and BE sales volume.

- *Promoting and selling inherently low-profit products and services require higher sales volume to generate profit, but most SMMs do not know how or where to find new customers.*

3. Matching preliminary strategic actions to the company's financial situation.

- *Weak financial situations (red and yellow flags) call for conservative, less cash-intensive and working capital-intensive strategies, and might justify delaying growth until working capital, debt, profitability, and the identification of market potential are strengthened.*

Preparation and some basic analysis at the start of a growth-planning project will avoid paralysis by analysis and ensure that management has accurate and current data for choosing the best combination of *C-P-M*™ to achieve the desired level of growth and profit.

The first high-level core strategic questions to answer early in the planning process are as follows:

"What is the company's financial situation with respect to working capital, cash flow, and debt, and what are its trends in sales, profitability, and cash flow?"

"If the company is not profitable, what is its break-even sales level, and can its overall profitability generate sufficient profit if growth does occur?"

"What are the preliminary courses of action and strategic alternatives indicated by the two previous questions?"

The remainder of this book presents similar methods for determining the profitability of customers, products, and markets and how to determine their strategic value to the future growth of a company.

CHAPTER 3

Customer Analysis to Improve the Top and Bottom

Questionnaire data show that many SMMs are missing an opportunity to use information about their customers to improve profitability and cash flow, to avoid having too much business in a single or few customers, and to find new customers and markets. Graph 1 shows the number of companies listing information about customers, with dollar sales and zip code the top items listed. Of 122 companies reporting, 74 listed dollar sales by customer and 71 listed zip codes. Only 31—25%—maintain profit information by customer. Knowing the profit that a customer generates is critical where one or a few customers account for most of the firm's business. Graph 2 shows the breakdown of job shops (J) and product companies (P) where their largest customer accounts for at least 30% of sales. In total, 42% of the companies had at least 30% of their sales coming from their largest customer. Small job shops—Type J1—and smaller companies in general—Type 1—reported a much higher percent of business in one customer: 75% (6 of 8 J1 firms) and 52% (11 of 21 Type 1 firms). Having too much business in one customer is a strategic time bomb particularly where that customer's profit to the business is low or unknown. Small job shops and small companies in general (Types 1 with less than 25–30 employees) are particularly susceptible to reduced cash flow and low profitability or worse if a big-volume customer reduces purchases, defects to competition, or goes out of business. Whether an SMM believes in having 30% or more of its business in a single customer is good or bad, the reasons against increasing that percentage should be obvious. It is not strategically sound to be so dependent on one or a few customers. The solution, obviously, is to find more customers to dilute the risk, but as previous data show, most SMMs do not have the information to find

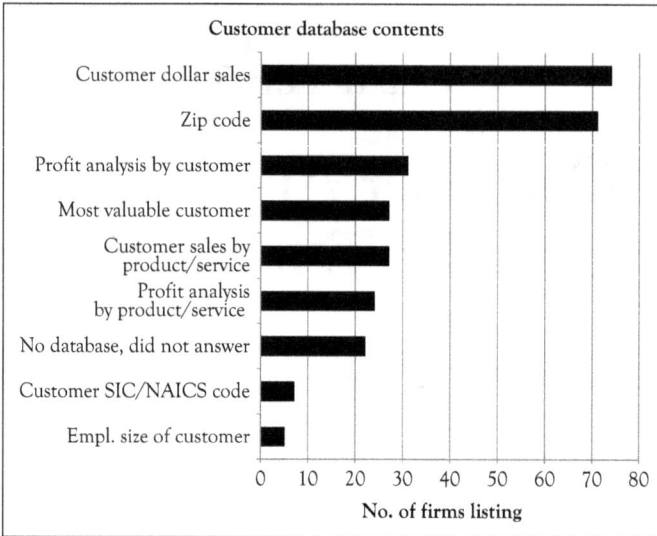

Graph 1. *Customer information.*

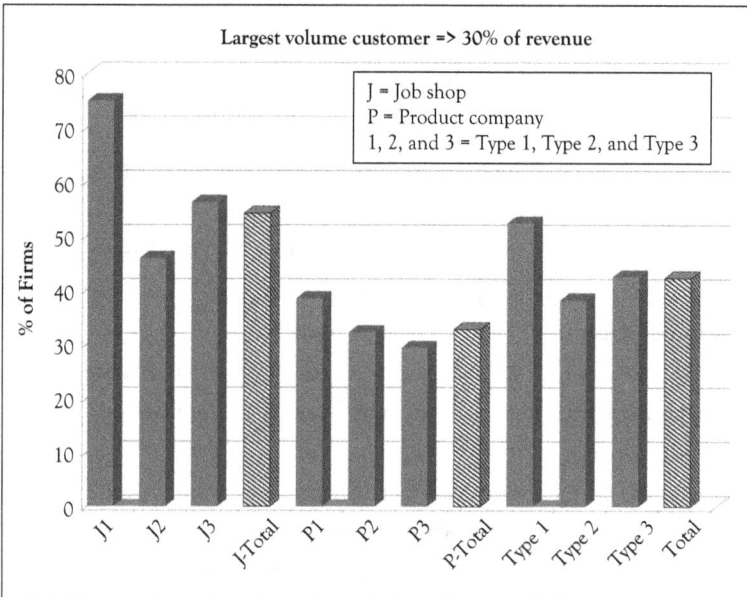

Graph 2. *Largest volume customer.*

them or do not know where to go to get them. Two pieces of information that could help SMMs find new customers are existing customers' SIC/NAICS codes and their employment sizes, shown in Graph 1 as the least items listed, but most companies don't have or maintain that data on their customers.

Finding New Customers by Using Data on Existing Customers

Standard Industrial Classification (SIC) and North American Industrial Classification System (NAICS) are federal designations for classifying all goods and services produced in the economy, both public and private. Every business must list its SIC/NAICS code for income tax reporting (some have more than one code where multiple products and services are involved) and therefore can be identified by searching commercially available marketing databases that list millions of companies specifically for marketing and prospecting purposes. An SMM that wants to find more customers can simply search one of these databases for SIC or NAICS codes matching that of its best customer to find the number and location of prospective new customers. The SMM can then contact the prospect to see if it is interested in learning more about its products and services. That is the simplest and most direct method for finding more customers.

The second piece of information, the customer's employment size, is used as a proxy to quickly assess if a prospect is worth pursuing. For example, conventional wisdom says larger companies are ideal target customers for smaller suppliers, but the small supplier might not have the organization, resources, systems, procedures, and capacity to effectively meet the demands for price, quality, delivery, and customer and technical support that many larger firms require. Smaller companies also have difficulty gaining entry into larger companies because they tend to have more sophisticated voice-mail and receptionist screeners that make it difficult to get through to the right person when prospecting for new customers. This burdens the small firm with extra sales, marketing, and promotional costs to win the larger customer and is a major obstacle for Type 1 and Type 2 firms that do not have the time and expertise to overcome these hurdles. Since the commercially available databases profile companies by SIC, NAICS, employment size range (and many other factors), a company seeking new customers can easily identify prospects that are a better fit for their situation using SIC, NAICS, and employment size in their search criteria.

The first step to finding new customers based on data about existing customers is to develop a *MVC profile* (most valuable customer) that defines what a valuable customer is. For example, most businesses regard their most valuable customer as the one generating the most revenue. Sales volume alone, however, should not be conclusive. Figure 20 lists questions SMMs could use to identify and define their most valuable customers and expand the concept of "valuable" beyond sales volume:

- The profitability and cash flow accruing to the business by selling to the customer
- Future profit potential
- Leverage to other new customers
- Strategy fit
- Long-term viability of the customer
- Consumption of indirect services and overhead.

These areas are not all inclusive and other criteria can be established on the basis of the circumstances of the individual SMM. Margin data such as gross margin and contribution margin per customer could be used to assess the value of a customer to the business.

Additional factors, such as receivables payment history, use of customer service and tech support, frequency of quality problems and ease of resolution, and consumption of other services and overhead, are also appropriate if they can be identified and "attached" to a specific customer. A large-volume customer whose consumption of services exceeds the

---

Sample MVC questions

Are they profitable (e.g. good margins)?
Is there potential for significant additional future revenues?
Do they truly value what the firm does well?
Are they a springboard to other similar prospective customers (e.g. referrals)?
Is there a fit with them that gives the firm a competitive advantage?
Can the firm serve them better than competitors?
Is the customer financially healthy?
Does the customer pay invoices on time?
Do costs to maintain the customer reduce profitability, such as returns, discounts, warranty, paperwork, field and technical support, credit terms, high selling costs, repetitive quotes that are not awarded, etc.?

Figure 20. MVC sample questions.

margin and cash flow it generates could actually be less valuable (profitable) to the business. The owner of Metro Plastics, Inc., a 30-employee plastics products company, conducted a margin and overhead analysis on its largest-volume customer and wound up firing him because he was consuming more resources than the margin he generated and would have been a drag on growth. This is an exception, but it makes the point that all customers are not equal, which is 180 degrees different from the perception that sales volume alone is the best indicator of a customer's value to a company.

Accounts-receivable-days-outstanding is another example where a large-volume customer pays invoices between 90 and 120 days. Although the customer's sales are attractive, the SMM must use credit and pay interest to "float" the cash the customer is holding. The situation worsens if a margin analysis on that customer shows lower than expected profit, and exemplifies the "Achilles heel" of having too much business tied up in a single large-volume customer or in too few customers.

Table 9 shows sales and margin for BuzzCo Machining, Inc., a Type 2 company, and illustrates the concept of using sales as a criterion for determining MVC and 80/20 analysis (80% of customers accounting for 20% of sales) to see if the firm's customers are concentrated—too much business in too few customers. Customer A, at $287,226 in descending order of sales, is the high-volume customer, accounts for 12% of sales, which is satisfactorily below the 30% threshold for one customer. Fifteen customers, down to O, make up 58% of the customers and account for 80% sales. Another way to look at this is that 5 customers down to E make up 19% (5 ÷ 26) of customers and account for 43% of sales. Therefore, the firm's sales are not concentrated in too few customers; sales are favorably distributed among its 26 customers.

Table 10 sorts BuzzCo's margin percent in descending order, putting the most profitable customers at the top—H, G, M, and so on. Note customer A, the highest-volume customer with a 64% margin, dropped to sixteenth. BuzzCo assigned direct material costs to individual work orders, had invested in systems to track direct labor hours per work order, and was able to aggregate direct costs to the customer; getting to contribution margin was easy.

Table 9. BuzzCo Customer Sales

Customer	Sales			Contribution margin	
	Total	% of Total	Cum %	Profit	Margin
A	287,266	12%	12%	184,819	64%
B	239,975	10%	21%	162,713	68%
C	194,857	8%	29%	50,473	26%
D	177,232	7%	37%	114,214	64%
E	158,232	6%	43%	65,659	41%
F	139,487	6%	49%	101,335	73%
G	118,889	5%	54%	95,746	81%
H	105,905	4%	58%	88,080	83%
I	101,966	4%	62%	72,618	71%
J	99,487	4%	66%	66,694	67%
K	93,325	4%	70%	39,538	42%
L	79,755	3%	73%	48,186	60%
M	78,422	3%	76%	61,190	78%
N	77,321	3%	79%	54,747	71%
O	72,926	3%	82%	52,112	71%
P	69,330	3%	85%	32,158	46%
Q	53,260	2%	87%	24,295	46%
R	48,589	2%	89%	34,011	70%
S	43,075	2%	91%	12,429	29%
T	37,916	2%	93%	27,511	73%
U	35,109	1%	94%	24,167	69%
V	31,887	1%	95%	(12,603)	–40%
W	31,358	1%	97%	19,313	62%
X	27,725	1%	98%	15,135	55%
Y	26,986	1%	99%	18,304	68%
Z	25,765	1%	100%	19,735	77%
Totals	$2,456,045	100%		$1,472,580	60%

Which customer now is the MVC—A, H, G, M, and so forth? Customer A contributes $184,819 in CM$, but only 64% in CM percent, whereas H contributes $88,080 in CM$ but its CM% is much higher. There are no clear-cut criteria to say which is a better candidate for MVC, since the MVC question should be addressed in broader

Table 10. BuzzCo Customer Margin

Customer	Sales			Contribution margin	
	Total	% of Total	Cum %	Profit	Margin
H	105,905	4%	58%	88,080	83%
G	118,889	5%	54%	95,746	81%
M	78,422	3%	76%	61,190	78%
Z	25,765	1%	100%	19,735	77%
F	139,487	6%	49%	101,335	73%
T	37,916	2%	93%	27,511	73%
O	72,926	3%	82%	52,112	71%
I	101,966	4%	62%	72,618	71%
N	77,321	3%	79%	54,747	71%
R	48,589	2%	89%	34,011	70%
U	35,109	1%	94%	24,167	69%
Y	26,986	1%	99%	18,304	68%
B	239,975	10%	21%	162,713	68%
J	99,487	4%	66%	66,694	67%
D	177,232	7%	37%	114,214	64%
A	287,266	12%	12%	184,819	64%
W	31,358	1%	97%	19,313	62%
L	79,755	3%	73%	48,186	60%
X	27,725	1%	98%	15,135	55%
P	69,330	3%	85%	32,158	46%
Q	53,260	2%	87%	24,295	46%
K	93,325	4%	70%	39,538	42%
E	158,232	6%	43%	65,659	41%
S	43,075	2%	91%	12,429	29%
C	194,857	8%	29%	50,473	26%
V	31,887	1%	95%	(12,603)	–40%
Totals	$2,456,045	100%		$1,472,580	60%

terms, as the list of MVC questions suggest. It is not uncommon for a company to have more than one MVC and more than one MVC profile.

The BuzzCo example (in Georgia, as with other states, businesses often adopt the name of school mascots, for example, the Georgia Tech

Yellow Jackets mascot is named Buzz) involved just 26 customers and calculating contribution margin was easy. Even though companies can have hundreds of customers, the number of customers should not be a problem since spreadsheets make analysis of large numbers of customers' sales and margins easy.

Table 11 illustrates customer sales and margin information for a product company, Kudzu Manufacturing Co., Inc. (Kudzu is a climbing, coiling, and trailing vine introduced from Japan into the United States in 1876 at the Philadelphia Centennial Exposition, where it was promoted as a forage crop and an ornamental plant. Unfortunately, it has since taken over most of the southeastern countryside, fences, yards, and telephone poles due to near-perfect hot, humid, and moist growing conditions, no natural predators, and resistance to herbicides. It has become part of southern lore, often referred to derisively.)

Table 11 also sorts Kudzu's customer sales in descending order. The largest-volume customer, D, accounts for 30% of sales, and along with customer F, combines for over half the firm's business, obviously problematic having two customers controlling that much business.

Kudzu's overall profitability, shown as gross profit rather than contribution margin, is good at 33% of sales, and individual customer gross profit margin ranges between 40% and 56%, depending on the products they buy.

Kudzu must consider customer D and possibly F as MVCs because they generate most of the business. With so few customers, however, the loss or decrease of any customer's business could hurt the firm. Accounts receivable and cash flow are critical to Kudzu because of the few customers; more so than with BuzzCo's 26 customers. Customer concentration is not so much a problem as is the few customers unless Kudzu's owners and managers are content with this number of customers and with the firm's sales, profit, and cash flow.

The BuzzCo and Kudzu examples illustrate how an SMM can analyze its customer base to identify preliminary issues that could affect its ability to successfully pursue growth. Some customers generate sufficient sales and cash flow that can be used to fund growth (the MVCs, for example) while others consume relatively too much indirect cost and support resources and retard cash flow via slow pay. Too much business in too few customers could eventually harm the business' long-term potential.

Table 11. *Kudzu Customer Sales and Profit*

Kudzu customer and product sales and profit

Customer	Product	Sales		Cum. %	Gross Profit		Margin
D	A	$150,000			$55,500		37%
	B	$102,750			$68,400		67%
	C	$47,250			$16,065		34%
	Subtotal	$300,000	30%	30%	$139,965	42%	47%
F	A	$125,000			$46,250		37%
	B	$117,500			$78,525		67%
	C	$7,500			$2,550		34%
	Subtotal	$250,000	25%	55%	$127,325	39%	51%
B	A	$75,000			$27,450		37%
	B	$52,000			$34,840		67%
	C	$23,000			$7,820		34%
	Subtotal	$150,000	15%	70%	$70,110	21%	47%
A	A	$50,000			$18,300		37%
	B	$15,000			$10,050		67%
	C	$40,000			$13,600		34%
	Subtotal	$105,000	11%	81%	$41,950	13%	40%
E	A	$100,000	10%	91%	$37,000	11%	37%
C	B	$65,000			$43,450		67%
	C	$30,000			$10,200		34%
	Subtotal	$95,000	10%	100%	$53,650	16%	56%
Company Total		$1,000,000	100%		$330,035	100%	33%

While sales volume is a common determinant of a customer's value to a business, profit is just as meaningful because it is the root of cash flow. High-sales-volume, low-profit customers not only might seem to absorb a lot of overhead, but also might not generate commensurate cash flow. Because BuzzCo was able to use contribution margin, it found the relative profitability of its 26 customers ranged from–40% to 83% and will easily be able to sort out desirable from less desirable customers. Kudzu, by contrast, using gross profit margin, which adds allocated overhead costs to a product's direct costs, might not be able to easily determine a product's or customer's inherent profitability because of the overhead allocation.

Getting accurate margin can be often difficult, depending on the type of accounting system and the frequency and format of financial statements, as discussed in Chapter 2. Some accounting systems simply do not capture costs and margins that allow routine reporting of margin by customer or product. And, in most cases, accounting data show gross profit rather than contribution margin. In addition, accounting systems typically assign a predetermined "standard" cost and markup to a product, such as 35%, that results in all products showing a 35% gross profit, regardless of the actual selling price and cost to sell, produce, and ship. Consequently, a margin analysis would show all products (and aggregated up to customers that buy them) with a 35% profit, thus diminishing the usefulness of margin analysis. In Kudzu's case, each of the three products showed the same gross margin no matter which customer bought them (A at 37%, B at 67%, and C at 34%). However, in many cases, gross profit, operating profit, or even net profit, are the only available margins.

These last examples illustrate that not all customers are equal. SMMs should seek to understand why margin varies so much, in BuzzCo's case from –40% to 83 percent.

Customer sales and margin information illustrated in the BuzzCo and Kudzu examples should stimulate critical questions, such as "Are variations in margin due to the way we do business with an individual customer, the type of customer, their particular service and quality requirements, the size of the customer, the product mix , production situations, or other factors?"

The search for answers to these questions is the first step to operating for profit as well as sales volume—to evolving from shotgun marketing to target marketing. The key is to determine the reasons for margin variation, for example, due to sales mix (higher- versus lower-margin products), issues in production (scheduling, materials availability, quality, delivery, repairs, and maintenance), office procedures, customer and technical service and support, selling costs associated with certain customers, and so forth. These examples, involving both operational and strategic aspects of the business, suggest considerable analysis. But remember, the development of effective strategy requires insight. Operating for profit as well as sales volume requires operational efficiency (expediency in taking, producing, and shipping orders, lowering costs, and lean manufacturing) and strategic effectiveness (targeting the right customers and markets, good customer service and technical support, and attaining competitive advantage).

Tables 12 and 13 using BuzzCo's sales and margin data from Tables 9 and 10 show six steps needed to identify your company's MVCs and to determine if the company is exposed to customer concentration.

1. List customers in descending order of sales for the last fiscal year.
2. Calculate the percentage of sales for each, and then cumulate the sales, as illustrated using BuzzCo's customers from A to Z.
3. Any customer accounting for more than 30% of sales is a red flag because there could be too much business coming from this customer, and if it is a slow-pay customer the firm's cash flow could be hurt.
4. Determine the number of customers that make up 80% of sales. Find in the **Cum %** column the customer that equates to 80% or more. In BuzzCo's case, it is the fifteenth customer (customer O) of the 26 total customers. Divide 15 by 26, resulting in 58 percent. Therefore, 58% of BuzzCo's customers account for 80% of sales. If less than 20% of your customers account for 80% or more of your company's sales, there is customer concentration—too few customers accounting for too much sales. The obvious conclusion is that you need to increase sales with other customers or find more customers to dilute the risk that these large-volume customers pose.

Table 12. Sales in Descending Order (from Table 9)

Customer	Sales		
	Total	% of Total	Cum %
A	287,266	12%	12%
B	239,975	10%	21%
C	194,857	8%	29%
D	177,232	7%	37%
E	158,232	6%	43%
F	139,487	6%	49%
Z	25,765	1%	100%
Total	$2,456,045	100%	

Table 13. Margin in Descending Order (from Table 10)

Customer	Sales			Contribution margin	
	Total	% of Total	Cum %	Dollars	Margin
H	105,905	4%	58%	88,080	83%
G	118,889	5%	54%	95,746	81%
M	78,422	3%	76%	61,190	78%
Z	25,765	1%	100%	19,735	77%
F	139,487	6%	49%	101,335	73%
T	37,916	2%	93%	27,511	73%
O	72,926	3%	82%	52,112	71%
I	101,966	4%	62%	72,618	71%
N	77,321	3%	79%	54,747	71%

5. Calculate the profit margin generated by your customers. BuzzCo used contribution margin, but gross profit margin or operating profit margin will suffice if they are the only numbers available. Divide profit dollars by sales dollars for each customer, resulting in margin percent, and sort in descending order of margin, Table 13.

   Customer H has the highest margin percent at 83%, but not in dollars. Customer F has a higher dollar margin at $101,335 but its percent margin is 73%. Sorting customers by margin percent shows one perspective while sorting by margin dollars might show another;

the highest percent margin customer might not have the highest dollar margin. Ideally, the highest sales dollar volume customer, such as A would have both the best margin percent and margin dollars, but that is rarely the case. Using margin percent and margin dollars as criteria for determining MVCs are good preliminary metrics, but are not always conclusive. A combination of high sales volume dollars coupled with margin percent and margin dollars is best.

6. Determine MVCs using sales and margin. Customers A and B are good MVC candidates, accounting for the two highest sales volumes and profit dollars, although their margin percentages are not the highest, at 64% and 68%, respectively. Nevertheless, contribution margins in this range are very good, further supporting A and B as MVCs. (Gross profit margins above 30% are good.) Having preliminarily identified A and B as MVC candidates, apply the MVC questions to see if they meet the other qualifications pertaining to long-term growth potential, strategic fit, and payments.

Compiling sales and margin data by customer is the first step in arranging information about customers by which to assess their long-term strategic value. Other factors, such as those indicated in the MVC questions, produce very useful criteria for identifying, locating, and qualifying prospective new customers. The process for developing such criteria is *"customer profiling."*

Using Customer Profiles to Sharpen Market Descriptions and Find New Customers

The sales manager of hypothetical ABC, Inc., introduced in Chapter 1, charged with adding five new customers, could not have pointed his sales team to potential new customers because of vague market descriptions. Customer profiling removes the guesswork of determining the "who" and "where" of finding prospective customers, reduces sales costs, and streamlines the sales and marketing function. It is fundamental to evolving from a shotgun marketer to a target marketer, sharpens the definition of the type of customer to pursue, and makes selling both more efficient and effective—thus operating for profit as well as sales volume.

SIC and NAICS codes and employment size used in conjunction with sales, profit margin, and the answers to the MVC questions form the basis for profiling. The following examples illustrate the use of profiling with SIC and NAICS codes and employment size to find new customers and to avoid the pitfalls of vague, poorly defined markets.

Dan's Machine Shop, a Type 1 company in metro Atlanta, found over 30 prospects, with estimated sales potential of $500,000, (based on plant purchases of prospects called) interested in learning more about his machining capabilities.

Swiss Solutions Co., Inc., a Type 1 seven-employee start-up company, making specialized rubber rollers for carpet and textile high-speed production, found several prospective customers in the packaging industry within one hundred miles of its location. The owner, also the sole salesman, had been attempting unsuccessfully to increase sales through networking with local banking and economic development groups. Profiling allowed him to optimize his selling efforts to get in front of prospects in a different industry that also uses high-speed conveyors.

Coastal Industrial Equipment, Inc., a Type 2 company that produces pipe-cutting equipment for consumer and industrial markets, found over 200 prospects its 6 national reps did not know about.

Conveyor Specialty, Inc., a Type 3 producer of highly engineered and computerized palletizing equipment, identified over 50 factories to which it was not selling. This led the sales VP to increase his sales coverage by augmenting existing company sales force with factory reps with exclusive sales territories, targeted sales call plans, and qualified sales leads.

Profiling sometimes allows a company to reassess assumptions of its markets and to redirect its sales and marketing efforts. Madsen Pipe, Inc., a Type 3 producer of large steel pipe used in highway, bridge, and foundation construction had been selling to a couple dozen small dealers and brokers who, in turn, sold to prime contractors. Profiling resulted in learning that identifying more of these small middlemen would be difficult and too expensive. The company's subsequent decision to go direct to the prime contractors resulted in changing the sales channel—not the market.

SIC and NAICS codes, as a means by which to find new customers and prospects, do not work in all cases. Forashe International, a dry-chemical company that specializes in rigid foams and adhesives, developed a formulation that eliminated styrene emissions in the fiber-reinforced plastics (FRP) industry, on which EPA imposed stringent regulations. The new formula represented a disruptive new technology that would eliminate existing chemicals used in FRP. An SIC/NAICS search to identify companies with products that might use polyester resin and gel coat resulted in thousands of establishments in various industries—housing, marine, consumer, industrial—too many for the company to evaluate. The firm needed a way to narrow down the search.

After pursing trade association membership lists, industry publications, and other secondary data sources to identify prospective products and companies, it discovered an EPA report listing fiberglass products that emitted styrene and the amounts. This information led to the identification of prospective companies and enabled the firm to not only develop a market entry plan but also develop a detailed revenue and expense forecast based on the amounts of styrene emitted at each prospective plant.

Table 14 shows the addition of customer employment size and SIC/NAICS codes to BuzzCo's customer sales and margin data. Tables 15 and 16 summarize Table 14.

Table 15 shows BuzzCo's major SIC groups in descending margin percent, giving BuzzCo a preliminary indication of the industries containing the types of companies that could match the profiles of its existing profitable customers. The company seems to be making good margins in all major groups except the bottom two: 2900 Petroleum and coal products and 2200 Textile mill products. At a high-level strategic and marketing perspective, BuzzCo would want to reduce efforts to generate more business in these two industries. To pursue more business in its other SIC groups, the company can now identify the number and location of prospects by searching marketing databases in those SIC groups. For example, within 2300 Apparel and other textile products, BuzzCo could specify 2392 Other Household Textile Product Mills as shown in Table 14. The equivalent NAICS code is 314129.

Customer employment size, the other criterion for targeting prospective new customers, shows BuzzCo making smaller margins with customers employing 101 to 500 people, Table 16. While this finding might not be materially significant at this point in the review (since only three low margin customers—C, E, and V—are involved with G an exception

Table 14. BuzzCo's SIC/NAICS and Employment Size

Customer	Sales			Contribution margin		Emp. Size	SIC Code	NAICS	Description
	Total	% of Total %	Cum %	Profit	Margin				
A	287,266	12%	12%	184,819	64%	1,249	3714	336211	Motor Vehicle Body Manufacturing
B	239,975	10%	21%	162,713	68%	1,461	3714	336211	Motor Vehicle Body Manufacturing
C	194,857	8%	29%	50,473	26%	169	2952	324122	N/A
D	177,232	7%	37%	114,214	64%	1,233	3069	313320	Fabric Coating Mills
E	158,232	6%	43%	65,659	41%	138	3724	336412	Aircraft Engine and Engine Parts Manufacturing
F	139,487	6%	49%	101,335	73%	1,213	3089	326121	Unlaminated Plastics Profile Shape Manufacturing
G	118,889	5%	54%	95,746	81%	103	3728	332912	Fluid Power Valve and Hose Fitting Manufacturing
H	105,905	4%	58%	88,080	83%	1,842	3621	335312	Motor and Generator Manufacturing
I	101,966	4%	62%	72,618	71%	89	N/A	N/A	N/A
J	99,487	4%	66%	66,694	67%	87	3081	326113	Unlaminated Plastics Film and Sheet (except Packaging) Manufacturing
K	93,325	4%	70%	39,538	42%	974	3089	326121	Unlaminated Plastics Profile Shape Manufacturing
L	79,755	3%	73%	48,186	60%	69	3559	332410	Power Boiler and Heat Exchanger Manufacturing

M	78,422	3%	76%	61,190	78%	68	N/A	N/A	N/A
N	77,321	3%	79%	54,747	71%	1,009	3675	334414	Electronic Capacitor Manufacturing
O	72,926	3%	82%	52,112	71%	824	2111	312221	N/A
P	69,330	3%	85%	32,158	46%	60	3644	332212	Hand and Edge Tool Manufacturing
Q	53,260	2%	87%	24,295	46%	46	N/A	N/A	N/A
R	48,589	2%	89%	34,011	70%	42	3519	333618	Other Engine Equipment Manufacturing
S	43,075	2%	91%	12,429	29%	37	3089	326121	Unlaminated Plastics Profile Shape Manufacturing
T	37,916	2%	93%	27,511	73%	989	2392	314129	Other Household Textile Product Mills
U	35,109	1%	94%	24,167	69%	31	3639	333298	All Other Industrial Machinery Manufacturing
V	31,887	1%	95%	(12,603)	-40%	277	2299	313111	N/A
W	31,358	1%	97%	19,313	62%	2,727	2679	322211	N/A
X	27,725	1%	98%	15,135	55%	3,616	3728	332912	Fluid Power Valve and Hose Fitting Manufacturing
Y	26,986	1%	99%	18,304	68%	23	3494	332919	Other Metal Valve and Pipe Fitting Manufacturing
Z	25,765	1%	100%	19,735	77%	3,361	3728	332912	Fluid Power Valve and Hose Fitting Manufacturing
Total	$2,456,045	100%		$1,472,580	60%				

Table 15. *BuzzCo's Major SIC Groups*

SIC major group	Description	Sales	Contribution margin $	Contribution margin %
2300	Apparel and other textile products	37,916	27,511	73%
2100	Tobacco manufactures	72,926	52,112	71%
3600	Electrical and electronic equipment	287,665	199,153	69%
3400	Fabricated metal products	26,986	18,304	68%
3700	Transportation equipment	1,091,500	701,909	64%
3500	Industrial machinery and equipment	128,344	82,197	64%
2600	Paper and allied products	31,358	19,313	62%
3000	Rubber and miscellaneous plastics products	552,606	334,211	60%
2900	Petroleum and coal products	194,857	50,473	26%
2200	Textile mill products	31,887	(12,603)	–40%
	Grand Total	$2,456,045	$1,472,580	60%

Table 16. BuzzCo's Customers by Employment Size

		Contribution margin	
Empl. size	Sales	$	%
Up to 100	635,979	394,052	62%
101 to 500	503,864	199,276	40%
501 to 1,000	204,167	119,162	58%
1,001 to 2,000	1,027,186	705,908	69%
Over 2,000	84,848	54,183	64%
Total	$2,456,045	$1,472,580	60%

with an 81% margin, Table 14), it might cause inquiry as to why, along with investigating reasons for the low margins in 2900 and 2200 SIC codes, Table 15. Using SIC/NAICS and employment size as search criteria often results in hundreds—if not thousands—of matches, which, at this early stage, are "suspects" and not "prospects" because they have not been qualified. Such a large number of "suspects" must be culled down to a more manageable size for follow-up to determine if the suspects are bona fide prospects. This process is discussed in more detail in Chapter 8—Marketing Research and Competitor Information.

Using Kudzu's sales, margin, SIC/NAICS codes, and employment size data are shown in Table 17, as an example. Unless satisfied with its current sales volume and few customers, it needs to increase sales not only with its existing six customers, but also add new ones to avoid customer concentration. Unlike BuzzCo, Kudzu's need to identify winners and losers in the customer base is less important because there are so few; all are important. It cannot afford to lose any of them and therefore can consider all its customers' six SICS/NAICS industries should it decide to expand the customer base. In addition, its customers' sizes are all within a couple hundred employees, which might be strategically suitable since Kudzu itself is small. In contrast to BuzzCo with several SIC/NAICS industries and a wider range of employment size from which to choose, Kudzu's pursuit of new customers is simpler.

Customer profiling, which involves establishing criteria by which to define the customer, as well as the type of prospective business or customer to target and pursue, helps SMMs answer the question, "Where is

Table 17. Kudzu's Customer Profile

Cust.	Sales	%	Cum. %	Margin	SIC	NAICS	Description	Emp. size
							Kudzu's basic end-user customer profile	
D	$300,000	30%	30%	47%	2821	325211	Plastics, Materials & Nonvulcanizable Elastomers	25
F	250,000	25%	55%	51%	3411	332431	Metal Cans	175
B	150,000	15%	70%	47%	3728	332912 336411 336413 541710	Aircraft Parts & Equipment, NEC	150
A	105,000	11%	81%	40%	3625	335314	Relays & Industrial Controls	50
E	100,000	10%	91%	47%	3679	334310 334418 334419	Electronic Components, NEC	250
C	95,000	10%	100%	56%	3443	332313 332410 332420 333415	Fabricated Plate Work	25
Total	$1,000,000							

the potential to grow profitably?" It begins with identifying the winners and losers in the firm's customer base, gaining insight into why there are winners and losers, and directing the sales force to find prospective new customers that match the profile of winners. It is consistent with the sales and marketing axiom that the best way to increase sales is to sell more to existing customers. In this case, the SMM is essentially replicating its MVC customers—seeking to add new customers based on existing customers' profiles.

Profiling helps firms understand the value derived from doing business with a single customer or groups of customers. It leads to better-defined and clearer market descriptions and results in more efficient and effective sales and marketing. The goal of profiling, then, is to identify the variables, such as SIC and NAICS codes, employment size, profit margin, operational, administrative, production factors, and marketing and selling costs that make some customers more or less valuable to the business and then to use those variables to develop strategies to find and target prospective companies that match the desirable variables.

The sales manager for hypothetical ABC, Inc., can now direct his sales force to prospective customers that match the firm's MVC profiles. For example, he can direct his sales force to companies that match SIC/NAICS and employment designations and their locations. Further, having determined the number and location of these companies using marketing databases, he can prioritize sales call schedules and prepare a sales and marketing budget to cover travel, lodging, and promotional expenses. He has sharpened his market definitions.

While not a failsafe methodology, customer profiling is a practicable and inexpensive way to begin to define customers and markets and to evaluate preliminary strategic options. However, the "customer" must first be identified as either the end-use customer or the sales channel member because of the varying strategic ramifications of selling through reps, distributors, and dealers; there are differences in costs, relationships, and issues with each. Growth strategies that involve selling through reps, distributors, dealers, and so forth, are much different from strategies where the SMM sells directly to end-customers with its own company-employed sales force.

Who Is the Customer?

In most cases, the "customer" is the end-use buyer of the product or service, and generally when we speak of customers this is to whom we refer. But, in other situations, the channel member (rep, agent, dealer, distributor, and so forth) is the customer when it takes "possession and control" of the product until it is sold to the end-user, such as with dealers and distributors.

The first step in answering, "Who is the customer?" must consider the following possibilities. The customer could be the end-user that the SMM sells directly to through its own sales personnel, or through reps, dealers, or distributors that own or manage the customer. Growth strategy in the first case should be straightforward—simply have the sales force go out and sell more products and services to existing customers; the customer relationship is usually stronger and the company has more influence over and information about the customer. Where the sales channel is more influential or controls the customer relationship, as with reps, dealers, and distributors, the SMM and channel partner must collaborate on determining the best customers or type of customers to target for growth.

SMMs frequently use reps, dealers, and distributors to sell products and services, mostly in conjunction with inside and outside company-employed sales personnel: 71 of the 126 firms in the questionnaire reported using them. Only 10 reported using reps, dealers, and distributors

Table 18. Use of Reps, Dealers, and Distributors

	Use reps, dealers, distributors		
Use company-employed sales	**Don't use reps, dealers, distributors**	**Do use reps, dealers, distributors**	**%**
Use only inside company sales	17	21	31%
Use only outside company sales	7	2	7%
Use both inside and outside	27	38	52%
Use neither inside nor outside company sales	2	10	10%
Total	53	71	100%
	43%	57%	

exclusively—using neither inside nor outside sales. Thirty-eight reported using both inside and outside company-employed sales personnel in conjunction with some form of distribution, Table 18.

The number of customers is also an issue where thousands of customers are involved, as Table 19 shows.

It shows the 12 companies from the questionnaire with the largest number of customers by type, sales, market orientation, employees, and sales channel configurations sorted in descending number of customers. Noticeably, an SMM's number of customers is limited neither by its employment size or sales nor by its market orientation (consumer, industrial, or both). The smaller Type 1 and Type 2 firms can have as many customers as Type 3 firms and deploy company sales personnel as well as a combination of reps, dealers, and distributors. Obviously, the task of answering, "Who is the customer?" can be daunting where hundreds of customers are involved and where the firm uses inside and outside company sales and reps, dealers, and distributors.

The answer, therefore, can significantly affect all facets of strategy development, including product management and new product development, pricing, promotion, sales coverage, and the size and composition of the sales organization and sales channel. A decision to "grow with existing customers" where there are many customers is not just a matter of intuitively choosing winners and losers in the customer base or listing sales and margin by customer and choosing MVCs and directing the sales force to make it happen. That situation requires a more rigorous analysis and collaboration between the company, its sales force, and its channel network to decide how best to grow with existing customers.

When the Sales Channel Is the Customer

Strategies to diversify the customer base and customer mix may not be practicable where a company sells directly to the sales channel and not to the end-user. In this situation, the SMM does not have data showing sales, profit, SIC/NAICS, or employment size of its end-user customers. SMMs' approach to answering and defining "Who is the customer?" and to developing customer classifications (A, B, C, etc.) must be different

Table 19. Number of Customers

Company	Type	Sales ($1,000's)	Market	No. empl.	No. cust.	Company employed sales force		Reps, distributors, dealers, etc.	
						Inside	Outside	No.	% of sales
A	3J	$27,900	Both	400	3,500	0	27	n/a	n/a
B	2J	790	Both	15	1,500	1	0	50 (R)	50%
C	2P	8,000	Industrial	50	1,400	2.5	2.5	6 (R) 10 (D)	n/a
D	2P	4,000	Consumer	65	1,385	3	8	5 (R) 160 (D)	84%
E	2J	4,200	Industrial	30	1,300	3	5	0	0%
F	2P	34,000	Consumer	82	1,200	20	0	0	0%
G	3P	28,800	Industrial	125	1,200	0	0	100 (R)	100%
H	2P	1,000	Consumer	10	1,000	0	0	20 (R) 1,000+ (D)	n/a
I	3J	8,200	Industrial	77	800	4	6	100 (R) 200 (D)	50%
J	3P	10,000	Industrial	79	700	6	2	700 (D)	95%
K	3P	12,900	Industrial	115	602	7	1	500 (D) 35 (R)	46%
L	1P	2,500	Industrial	17	600	2	1	0	0%

Source: R = no. of raps; D = no. of dealers of distributors. % of Sales = percentage of sales by R and D.

where reps, dealers, distributors, and others make up the primary sales channel, and the company does not have direct contact with or is not in control of the end-user customer. Two strategic situations arise from this.

Where the SMM considers the channel member as the end-customer, the focus is on the channel member, not the end-user. The primary goal should be to strengthen channel relationships and to collaborate on strategies to move more products through the channel. SMMs, therefore, must understand competitive factors within the channel, such as commission rates and payments, their products' strengths and weaknesses relative to the other companies in the channel, and so forth, that compete for the channel's time and resources. The SMM must strengthen its competitive position within the sales channel, for example, by offering compensation that is more lucrative, better products and services, and support from the factory.

In the second situation, the manufacturer collaborates with the channel but focuses on the end-user. Most information about the end-customer (sales history, contact info, and so forth) resides with the channel member. SMMs most likely will have sales data by rep, dealer, and distributor—but not by the end-customer. The rep, dealer, or distributor will need to provide end-customer data to the SMM, assuming it has these data. In most cases, the rep, dealer, or distributor does not know the end-customer SIC/NAICS code and employment size so the SMM will need to develop this from end-customer data (physical address, phone number, and so forth) supplied by the channel member. The goal of this collaboration is to help the channel prioritize the SMM's customers, via the A, B, C classification, and jointly developing sales, marketing, and promotional strategies. In this sense, the channel becomes the MVC or strategic partner.

This collaboration, however, is very difficult to carry out. Most reps, dealers, and distributors consider information about end-users proprietary and do not want to reveal or share it, assuming they even have it and that it includes sales, profit, SIC/NAICS codes, or employment size by end-customer. The relationship between the SMM and rep, dealer, or distributor must be trustworthy and strategically beneficial to both to be successful.

A, B, and C Customers—A Simple Classification for Segmenting and Prioritizing the Customer Base

After a company has defined its "customer" and established its MVCs, there still remains the task of determining what to do with them as well as with the other customers, which, as shown earlier, can be hundreds. For example, MVCs require specific actions and priorities to ensure their loyalty and continued business. Less valuable customers would not necessitate as much attention and resource allocation. A "back-of-the-envelope" classification using A, B, and C to designate varying levels of attention and priority for different customers simplifies this task.

In general, the classification involves assigning A to MVCs; B customers are valuable but not a priority; and C customers require little, if any, priority. While there is no cast-in-concrete criteria for assigning A, B, and C, a company can create its own guidelines depending on the number of customers, its products and markets, and the composition of the sales organization. Additional designations, such as D, E, and so on, could be used if the customer base is extensive and the sales organization is intricate—composed of inside and outside company personnel, reps, dealers, and distributors, thus justifying additional classifications.

Deciding what to do with the types of customers and how to do it is the big strategic question. For example, should the company attempt to increase sales with its A customers, find more like them, or just maintain them? Because they are A, their business must be maintained and possibly justifying special programs and services to ensure their loyalty. B customers must also be managed but not with the investment in and frequency given to A customers; there might be good potential to sell more to them or convert them to A status. C customers could be low-volume and/ or low-margin who buy occasionally and in shrinking or insignificant markets; justifying less costly selling than face-to-face sales calls, such as e-mail or inexpensive direct mail.

The sales, margin, SIC/NAICS, and employment size information the firm has compiled about its customers now provide an opportunity to develop very clear descriptions about the types of customers to target and pursue as well as markets that might contain potential new business. Figure 21 shows a basic classification of BuzzCo's customers and illustrates the strategic usefulness of this information.

BuzzCo's Customer Classifications

Customer classification	Customers	Guideline/criteria	Market, industry, product	Primary contact, initiative
A	A, D, B, E, Z	Generates margin => 40%, minimum annual revenue > $100,000, pays within 90 days, well-organized with good business systems, is viable long-term, potential to grow.	3600 Electrical and electronic equipment 3400 Fabricated metal products 3700 Transportation equipment	Outside sales and dedicated reps Technical training Direct customer service representative 24-hour emergency service Factory sales calls monthly
B	F, G, I, J, L, M, Y, N, O, Q, R, T, U, W	Margin < 40%, pays within 100 days, annual revenue < $100,000, growth potential.	3600 Electrical and electronic equipment 3400 Fabricated metal products 3700 Transportation equipment 2600 Paper and allied products 3500 Industrial machinery and equipment. 2100 Tobacco manufacturers	Inside sales weekly telephone follow-up Rep factory calls bi-monthly Direct mail program Targeted volume discounts
C	H, S, V, P, K, C, X	Annual revenue <$50,000, pays within 100 days, no growth potential.	N/A	Inside sales weekly telephone follow-up Rep factory calls as needed Direct mail program

Figure 21. BuzzCo's customer classifications.

Preliminary goals and strategies for BuzzCo's A, B, and C customers are explained as follows:

- BuzzCo adopted profit margin, minimum sales revenue, invoice payments, the efficiency of the customer's business systems and communications, and its long-term viability as primary criteria for A customers. Insight of customers' business systems and communications is discernible by routine contact via inside sales and other BuzzCo personnel. Long-term viability can be determined via credit reports, publicly available data, and by observing customer operations during factory sales visits. SIC/NIACS compilations led BuzzCo to research 3400, 3600, and 3700 industries and learned they were forecasted to grow, thus prioritizing them and allocating more sales and marketing resources to the five A customers, who will receive in-factory training, more frequent face-to-face sales calls, and dedicated emergency service.

- A customers, or at least some, could be considered "*strategic partners*"—loyal, possessing solid growth potential, suitable for collaboration on new product development and new services (in the case of job shops and machine companies) that could be marketed to other existing or new customers.

- B customers generate less revenue and profit for BuzzCo, and although they operate in the same industries as A customers, are not perceived to be as well-managed or to have sufficient growth potential. There is no justification for the more expensive face-to-face or frequent sales calls, and B customers will be managed using telephone and direct mail. Some will be offered volume discounts to entice them to increase volume and possibly move up to A status. *However, this preliminary assessment of B customers could change with additional research and analysis of overall market potential.*

- C customers infrequently place orders, are not sizeable enough in their industries to be considered growth potential, and will be managed with minimal contact.

- Specific actions pertaining to customer relations and management, as indicated under <u>Primary Contact, Initiative</u> in the right column, are termed "*account management strategies*," and should clearly describe what the firm intends to do with the customer and how it will happen. This is particularly important to company employees who have regular and routine contact with customers, such as sales, customer service and support, and accounting.

Here are five steps to establishing customer profiles, classifications, and account management strategies. Refer to Tables 12-17 and Figure 21.

1. Find customers' SIC/NAICS codes.
   - Call them (sometimes even customers do not know their SIC/NAICS codes).
   - Google them, which sometimes results in links to business reports showing their SIC/NAICS codes.
   - Enter a description of their products from the website at *www.osha.gov* that will produce the firm's SIC/NAICS code.

2. Determine customers' employment size.
3. Enter SIC/NAICS codes and employment data for each customer in the list previously compiled with their sales and margin data, preferably to the right of these data. Table 14.
4. Sort these data to look for groups or patterns:
   - Descending sales, profit dollars, and margin percent—the high-volume and profitable customers will be at the top, suggesting the SIC/NAICS and employment sizes that produce the most profit for your business. Tables 12 and 13.
   - Group by SIC/NAICS and by employment size and re-sort by sales, profit dollars, and margin percent. This will show, within SIC/NAICS and employment groups, specific better-performing customers. These should be the firm's MVCs, as identified in the previous exercise with sales and margin data, and provide preliminary "customer profiles" that can be later used to search for prospective customers who match that profile. Tables 14–17.

5. Using MVC criteria, SIC/NAICS codes, and employment sizes, classify customers using 'A', 'B', 'C', and so on to prioritize them for account management strategies. Figure 21.

- A customers represent the ones the firm wants to grow with and who should get VIP treatment. Some could be "strategic partners" the firm could collaborate with on new products and services that could be marketed to other existing and/or new customers. A customer profile should be used to locate prospective new customers that match the profile.

- The firm will want to maintain B customers, but develop less costly and time-consuming account management strategies to do so, although some B customers will have the potential to become A customers.

- C customers generally are low-volume, low-margin customers the firm should manage with minimal cost, such as a periodic telephone contact, direct mail, and fax.

- After the classifications are determined, enter them in a column to the left of the customer's name and sort them in descending order of classification to see the number of customers in each classification. See Table 20 showing the number of BuzzCo's 26 customers in each classification.

- List customers by their classification and write down the specific actions the firm will take to manage them. For example, A customers will receive more frequent sales and promotional contact, better customer service, and tailored services. B customers will be contacted less frequently and with less costly sales, marketing, and promotional initiatives; however, some that are considered potential A status could receive more attention. C customers might receive only occasional follow-up since they are unlikely to justify additional investment.

The actions that are specified or listed by classification, or specific to certain customers, are "*account management strategies*." See the last column in Figure 21 for examples.

Of the 126 companies in the questionnaire, only 10 reported using only reps, dealers, and distributors, indicating the majority of firms use

Table 20. BuzzCo's Classifications

	No. of customers			
	Customer classification			
SIC Code	A	B	C	Grand total
3700	4	4	1	9
3000	1	2	2	5
3600		2	2	4
3500		2		2
2100		1		1
2200			1	1
2300		1		1
2600		1		1
2900			1	1
3400		1		1
Total	5	14	7	26

a combination of company-employed sales personnel and sales channels. Accordingly, most firms can use the steps presented in this chapter to prioritize customers as well as the two courses of action discussed earlier to help their channels move more of their products and services.

The Customer Database as a Strategic Asset

Data on customer sales and margin, SIC/NAICS codes, and employment size, when summarized, formatted as previously illustrated, and readily available, can greatly simplify the process of deciding where and how to grow. Unfortunately, most SMMs do not maintain these basic data, as stated in "*Operating in the dark*" in Chapter 1.

Ideally, customer databases populated with sales, costs, and margins, by product and customer, SIC/NAICS, customer employment size, and so forth would greatly reduce the time and effort to make this information available for growth planning sessions as well as reviewing and evaluating strategy implementation/execution. Electronic spreadsheets can sort, crunch, analyze, and summarize data quickly.

Since many SMMs are spreadsheet-conversant, using spreadsheets at the start of a strategy development project to compile customer information—sales and margin data (including products and services), SIC/NAICS codes, employment size, and other pertinent data depending on the situation—keeps the process simple and timely and provides residual value for subsequent review of strategy implementation. The subsequent presentation of these data, when analyzed and summarized, graphed, and charted by customer, product, SIC/NAICS code, market, and employment size, often gives management a new and insightful view of its current situation that clarifies preliminary strategic issues and options early in the project.

Spreadsheet customer databases, populated with this information, become vital strategic assets. Management will have at its fingertips information needed to make decisions about existing account management strategies, new customer development requirements, identifying and prioritizing target markets, and sales coverage and channel management. By providing insights about preliminary strategic alternatives, it will greatly simplify the process of growth strategy development.

The following list includes data that could be used in a spreadsheet-based customer database in addition to typical contact information.

Note: If the company sells exclusively through distribution, it might not need a customer database as described in this section because the distributor most likely is the customer.

Sales

- Dollar sales and unit sales by customer for current period, year-to-day, and for past two fiscal years. Cross-referenced to products.
- Dollar sales and unit sales by product, model, unit, (for job shops: machining centers, process, etc.) for current period, year-to-day, and for past two fiscal years. Including unit prices and discount history. Cross-referenced to customers.

Demographics for Market and Size (other criteria as needed)

- SIC/NAICS (or other market or market segment designation the company has defined), and employment sizes by customer.

Sales Personnel/Channel

- Sales by company sales person, rep, distributor, and others. Cross-referenced by customer and product (and market if applicable and possible).

Quotation History (will also be covered in Chapter 4—Bids and Quotations)

- Dollar amount and number of quotes submitted to customers, quote status (won, lost, pending, and withdrawn), won versus lost analysis.

Competition (will also be covered in Chapter 6—Marketing Research and Competitor Information)

- List of direct competitors by customer, market, product, and so forth (competitors could be different from market to market if the firm sells into multiple markets).

Summary

This chapter discussed the **C**ustomer component of *C-P-M*™ and illustrated the value of first looking into the firm's customer base from a strategic point of view before pursuing a growth strategy. Customer analysis can reveal circumstances that could hinder an SMM's prospects for successful long-term growth—such as too much business concentrated in too few customers—and can identify the MVCs around which a company should create special programs and services to keep their business. It presented several steps showing how to identify winners and losers because not all customers are equally valuable or important to the SMM, how to prioritize customers and manage them more effectively and efficiently using account management strategies, and it introduced customer profiling as means to sharpen market descriptions and definitions and identify prospective new customers.

Without a reasoned basis for picking winners and losers among customers and without developing profiles to target prospective new customers, SMMs resort to shotgun marketing that does not differentiate customers and where any new customer is a good one as long as it brings in revenue. Shotgun marketing result in diluted profits, low repeat business, and problems with customer service and satisfaction because of diverse customers' needs and requirements.

Customer analysis should lead to penetrating questions about the viability of the firm's customer base relative to the long-term growth goals of the business and answer the question, "Can existing customers provide the desired long-term growth and profit?"

Additional critical strategic questions that arise from customer analysis:

- What is the impact on cash flow and working capital of high-volume customers with relatively low margins?
- What can be done with existing customers to improve their profitability and cash flow?
- Who are the firm's most valuable customers and can the business find more like them?
- Are current customers going to provide the long-term growth the firm seeks or will additional customers/products be needed and where will the firm get them?

Graph 3 illustrates the implication of these questions. After analyzing its customer base and getting answers to the questions posed earlier, the firm

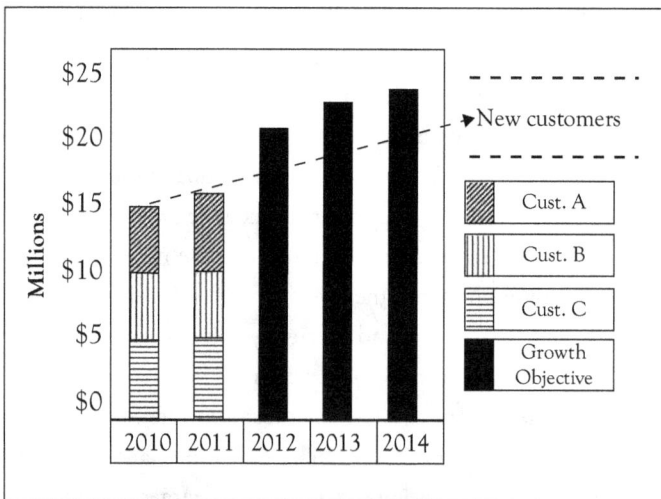

Graph 3. *High-level strategic question about customers.*

concluded that existing customers who generated about $15 million in sales in 2010–2011 could not support growth beyond $20 million that the company wanted and that additional customers would be needed—the trajectory of the arrow.

If an SMM determines it cannot gain more business from existing customers with existing products, the strategic options are immediately clear—develop new products and services for existing customers, find new customers for existing products and services, and/or develop new products and services for new customers. Selling more of current products and services to existing customers will not close the growth gap.

The steps outlined in this chapter are intended to help SMMs make that determination by the following steps:

- Answering the question, "Who is the customer?"
- Identifying MVC, A, B, and C customers and creating account management strategies to sustain existing customers and to attempt to increase sales to them.
- Developing customer profiling using SIC/NAICS and employment size to locate prospective new customers that match the profile of the firm's best customers.

Customer analysis requires sales, margin, and other pertinent data by customer, such as accounts receivable, but most SMMs do not organize these data into one central database. Such data typically reside disparately in electronic format or hard copy in multiple places, thus making difficult the task of compiling them for strategy development. However, when compiled and maintained in a spreadsheet or database, management will find it strategically valuable in gaining insights about customers, products, and markets and that it facilitates growth planning.

CHAPTER 4

Quotation Analysis to Improve Competitiveness

Many SMMs use quotations to generate sales, but like customer information in the last chapter, they generally do not use the information generated by quotes to their advantage. Rather than utilizing quotes to learn why they win business or lose it—a strategic application—they use quotes as just a way to increase sales—a tactical measure. There is a wealth of insight that businesses can acquire at little cost about why they win or lose sales, about competitors, and about market conditions.

Most of the 126 firms in the questionnaire reported preparing quotes as a means of generating sales. Not surprisingly, all 54 job shops and machine companies reported preparing quotes and 57 of the 71 product companies reported using quotes, totaling 111 of 125 (Table 21). Although most businesses at some point use quotes to generate business, it seems more connected to industrial products firms than to those selling into consumer markets, and surely with respect to job shops and machine companies preparing quotes is a primary selling strategy.

Table 22 shows that while most firms use quotes and have a quote management system, they don't track reasons for losing quotes and few—only 15 of the 111—use those reasons to strengthen their competitive situation by changing sales, marketing, and promotional strategies, products and services, prices, customer and technical support, and quality.

Without knowing why it loses sales a company cannot know what to do to increase sales. Getting feedback on why quotes are not won and subsequently changing sales, marketing, and promotional strategies, products, pricing, quality, customer service, and support based on that feedback is a fundamental tenet of B2B industrial marketing.

Table 21. No. of Firms Using Quotes

	Job shop				Product				Total
	1	**2**	**3**	**Total**	**1**	**2**	**3**	**Total**	**Total**
Total Firms	12	26	16	54	14	36	21	71	125
No	0	0	0	0	6	8	0	14	14
Yes	12	26	16	54	8	28	21	57	111

Market										
Industrial	9	21	15	45	8	24	20	52	97	100%
No	0	0	0	0	3	3	0	6	6	6%
Yes	9	21	15	45	5	21	20	46	91	94%
Consumer	0	1	0	1	4	8	1	13	14	100%
No	0	0	0	0	2	4	0	6	6	43%
Yes	0	1	0	1	2	4	1	7	8	57%
Both	3	4	1	8	2	4	0	6	14	100%
No	0	0	0	0	1	1	0	2	2	14%
Yes	3	4	1	8	1	3	0	4	12	86%

Quotation Management—A Fundamental Tenet of B2B Industrial Marketing

There are five basic elements of a good quote management system:

1. Number of quotes produced.
2. Cost to prepare a quote.
3. Hit rate—the percentage of quotes won of total prepared and submitted.
4. Reasons for not winning quotes.
5. A record of quotes submitted, pending (still active and being evaluated), cancelled, won, and lost.

The number of quotes produced is a measure of a business' success in advertising and promotion and of its sales force generating and converting inquiries into quotes. The companies reported as few as a couple dozen quotes per year to over 2,500. Three of the four top quote producers that indicated producing more than 2,500 quotes annually are envelope printers—businesses that usually have automated quoting systems whose cost per quote is low. Nearly two-thirds of the 81 SMMs who reported knowing the number of quotes produced averaged about 300 per year and 38 estimated their cost per quote at less than $100. However, my experience suggests the cost to prepare a quote to be higher, particularly where sales, production, and quality, and engineering team up. Although companies might know quote production and track reasons for losing quotes, they typically don't record the time spent on quote preparation— it's considered just a cost of doing business and winds up in overhead. I think companies would be surprised at the cost per quote should they actually track it.

Sixty-six firms reported knowing their hit rates, which is a very significant number because it is the key indicator of a company's competitiveness and effectiveness in targeting customers and markets interested in its products and services. Companies that don't have good definitions of markets and don't have clear MVC profiles likely experience low hit rates. Judging from Table 22, firms that have quote systems keep track of their hit rates but do not necessarily follow-up on reasons for not winning them.

Table 22. Track Reasons, Change Strategies, and Know Hit Rate

	Job shop				Product				Type			
	1	2	3	Total	1	2	3	Total	1	2	3	Total
Use quotes	12	26	16	54	8	28	21	57	20	54	37	111
Have quote system	5	16	9	30	4	15	16	35	9	31	25	65
No quote system	7	10	7	24	4	13	5	22	11	23	12	46
Track Reasons												
Have system and track reasons	0	4	2	6	1	6	8	15	1	10	10	21
Change Strategies												
Have quote system and track reasons and change strategies	0	3	1	4	0	5	6	11	0	8	7	15
Know hit rate	5	15	9	29	5	15	17	37	10	30	26	66

Low Hit Rates, High Hit Rates, and Pricing Problems are Canaries in the Mineshaft

Of the 111 firms using quotes, 70 reported hit rates shown in Table 23. Note that almost two-thirds have hit rates of 30% or below. Although there is no standard specifying a good or bad hit rate percentage, percentages below 30% and over 65–70% should indicate problems. For example, a low percentage could indicate a very competitive market—or weak competitive position—and a very high percentage can indicate the firm is "buying" the business—leaving money on the table by too low a price. Either situation calls for an explanation because it could be an early warning of competitive problems.

A key indicator of a competitive market or that an SMM might not have a competitive edge is losing quotes due to pricing, particularly where its hit rate is low. Responses to questions about firms' pricing resulted in *"meet competitors' pricing," "whatever the customer will pay,"* or *"pull a number out of the air,"* indicating pricing problems stemming from a lack of adequate costing and pricing procedures and lack of knowledge of competition. Of the 111 firms using quotes, 74 acknowledged pricing problems—not being able to win quotes at the quoted price because it was too high, shown in Table 24. Twenty-nine either didn't know if they had pricing problems or didn't answer the question, and another 29 who reported pricing problems had hit rates below 30%.

Companies listed various reasons for quoting high, but over half, 53 of 74, reported these three reasons most often, see Table 25:

- Costs were unknown and the companies priced high as a cautionary measure
- Not having competitive advantage, priced at "market," and
- Not knowing competitors' pricing.

Table 26 further illustrates the connection between knowing costs, pricing, and hit rate. Of the 74 companies reporting pricing problems, only 28—less than 40%—knew both direct material and direct labor costs. Companies wanting to grow will need to know their costs and competitors' and market pricing to win more business, which is evidenced by higher hit rates.

Table 23. Quote Hit Rate

Hit Rate	Job shop				Product				Type				% of Total	Cum %
	1	2	3	Total	1	2	3	Total	1	2	3	Total		
Up to 10%	1	3	5	9	3	4	2	9	4	7	7	18	26%	26%
11% to 20%	0	3	1	4	1	2	6	9	1	5	7	13	19%	44%
21% to 30%	0	4	2	6	1	2	4	7	1	6	6	13	19%	63%
31% to 40%	1	1	0	2	1	2	3	6	2	3	3	8	11%	74%
41% to 50%	0	2	1	3	0	3	2	5	0	5	3	8	11%	86%
51% to 60%	1	1	0	2	0	1	0	1	1	2	0	3	4%	90%
61% to 70%	0	1	0	1	0	0	0	0	0	1	0	1	1%	91%
71% to 80%	2	0	0	2	0	0	0	0	0	0	0	2	3%	94%
81% to 90%	0	0	0	0	1	1	1	2	0	1	1	2	3%	97%
90% to 100%	0	0	0	0	1	1	0	2	1	1	0	2	3%	100%
Total	5	15	9	29	7	16	18	41	10	31	27	70	100%	

Average hit rate = 31%

Table 24. Seventy-four Companies with Pricing Problems

Hit rate	Job shop				Product				Type			
	1	2	3	Total	1	2	3	Total	1	2	3	Total
Up to 10%	1	2	4	7	2	3	2	7	3	5	6	14
11% to 20%	0	3	0	3	0	1	4	5	0	4	4	8
21% to 30%	0	3	1	4	0	2	1	3	0	5	2	7
31% to 40%	1	0	0	1	1	1	2	4	2	1	2	5
41% to 50%	0	1	1	2	0	2	2	4	0	3	3	6
51% to 60%	0	0	0	0	0	1	0	1	0	1	0	1
61% to 70%	0	1	0	1	0	0	0	0	0	1	0	1
71% to 80%	1	0	0	1	0	0	0	0	1	0	0	1
81% to 90%	0	0	0	0	0	0	1	1	0	0	1	1
90% to 100%	0	0	0	0	0	1	0	1	0	1	0	1
DK/NA	6	6	6	18	1	7	3	11	7	13	9	29
Total	9	16	12	37	4	18	15	37	13	34	27	74

Table 25. Reasons for Pricing Problems

Pricing problem	Job shop				Product				Type			
	1	2	3	Total	1	2	3	Total	1	2	3	Total
Yes	9	16	12	37	4	18	15	37	13	34	27	74
No	3	8	4	15	4	10	6	20	7	18	10	35
Don't know	0	2	0	2	0	0	0	0	0	2	0	2
Total	12	26	16	54	7	26	20	57	19	52	36	111
No costs, no competitor pricing, no competitive advantage	8	9	9	26	2	11	14	27	10	20	23	53

Table 26. Pricing Problems and Knowing Costs

Know costs	Job shop				Product				Type			
	1	2	3	Total	1	2	3	Total	1	2	3	Total
Both M and L	2	7	5	14	0	7	7	14	2	14	12	28
Neither M or L	4	4	2	10	0	7	6	13	4	11	8	23
Material only	3	5	5	13	1	3	2	6	4	8	7	19
Labor only	0	0	0	0	0	1	0	1	0	1	0	1
Not asked	0	0	0	0	3	0	0	3	3	0	0	3
Total	9	16	12	37	4	18	15	37	13	34	27	74

Quotation and Lost Order Analysis—The Market Link to Continuous Improvement, Gaining Competitive Advantage, and to Increasing Sales and Profit

There is considerable potential for an SMM to strengthen its sales and marketing strategies, improve its strategic and competitive situation, and increase both sales and profit using data and feedback from its quote management system. Lost order analysis involves asking customers and prospects why they did not award a quote and which competitor got the business. This is the only way a company will know why it is winning or losing business.

Table 27, an excellent format for looking at quote performance, illustrates BuzzCo's 2010 summary of quotes won and lost compiled

Table 27. Buzz Co's 2010 Quote Analysis

					Quotation won / lost analysis 2010					
	Won					Lost				
Dollar range of bid	Total $	% of Sales	CM%	No. won	% of Total	Total $	CM%	No. lost	% of Total	Ratio lost to won
$0 — 100	358	0%	47%	5	1%	1,083	26%	14	2%	2.8
$101 — 500	47,634	2%	60%	155	27%	49,481	50%	150	24%	1.0
$501 — 1,000	99,595	4%	61%	138	24%	89,527	52%	123	19%	0.9
$1,001 — 2,000	203,344	9%	60%	156	27%	158,037	47%	113	18%	0.7
$2,001 — 3,000	122,255	5%	55%	50	9%	126,070	52%	50	8%	1.0
$3,001 — 10,000	248,478	10%	50%	47	8%	518,507	51%	102	16%	2.2
$10,001 — 50,000	180,726	8%	53%	11	2%	1,599,609	45%	60	9%	5.5
$50,001 — 100,000	156,152	7%	57%	3	1%	1,285,733	43%	20	3%	6.7
$100,001 — 250,000	377,490	16%	52%	3	1%	577,875	43%	5	1%	1.7
$250,001 — 600,000	952,000	40%	54%	2	0%	0	0%	0	0%	0.0
Total	$2,388,032	100%	54%	570	100%	$4,405,921	43%	637	100%	
		Hit rate =	47%							

from its spreadsheet of 1,207 quotes submitted, segregated by their dollar range, total quotes submitted, quotes won and lost, contribution margin, and other metrics that can be used to inform sales and marketing strategies.

BuzzCo's hit rate (570 won versus 1,207 submitted), at 47% is good, winning almost half of quotes submitted. Overall quote production of 1,207 might be good or bad, depending on the firm's sales history and growth goals. For example, if the firm submitted much fewer quotes in past years then 1,207 could indicate good sales effort and marketing. However, if the growth target were $3 million in sales, then the quote volume fell short because it produced only $2.4 million. The BuzzCo sales team would have needed to generate 1,523 quotes, at its 47% hit rate, at an average successful quote dollar amount of $4,190 ($3,000,000 ÷ $4,190 ÷ 47%) to produce that revenue.

The dollar ranges of the quotes show where BuzzCo is most competitive; three-quarters of its successful quotes (449) were between $101 and $2,000 in price, and at good margins—in the low 60% range, as indicated by the ratio of lost quotes to won quotes (a lower ratio is better). Note that although the firm generally lost quotes in the higher dollar ranges, it did win 5 in the $100,000 to $600,000 range totaling 56% of the firm's revenue. But generally it is not competitive at higher-priced quotes (higher ratio of lost to won @ 6.7) above $10,000; it lost 85 of 104 quotes in that range at a 18% hit rate. If BuzzCo wanted to be more successful on larger jobs it would need to learn from the prospects and customers why it didn't get those orders—it would need to conduct lost order analysis. Table 28 summarizes BuzzCo's analysis and evaluation of lost quotes.

After asking customers who won the quotes and why, BuzzCo determined there were seven primary direct competitors and several unknown companies involved with the 637 lost quotes. Customers generally reported three competitive factors—price, delivery, and tolerance—as evaluation criteria for awarding work. BuzzCo apparently needs to reconsider its pricing since price accounted for most of the rejected quotes—350 of the 637. The company's 54% contribution margin, which is good, allows some room to lower price. However, this will be done on a case-by-case basis since the firm wants to avoid "buying the business."

Table 28. *BuzzCo's Lost Order Analysis*

Winning competitor	1 = Price		2 = Delivery		3 = Tolerance		4 = Kept In-House		Total	
	No.	$	No.	$	No.	$	No.	$	No.	$
A	33	218,769	21	67,766	4	10,216	7	157,302	65	454,053
B	18	196,503	4	167,092	5	24,256	4	5,418	31	393,269
C	12	145,487					6	6,967	18	152,454
D	16	142,644							16	142,644
E	23	114,685	3	13,218	1	90	2	10,798	29	138,791
F	16	24,731							16	24,731
G	9	14,784							9	14,784
Unknown	221	1,902,551	69	281,490	153	836,871	10	64,283	453	3,085,195
Total	350	2,778,604	97	529,566	163	871,433	29	244,768	637	4,405,921
% of Bids	55%		15%		26%		5%		100%	
% of Dollar Amount of Bids		63%		12%		20%		6%		100%
Avg. Price	7,939		5,459		5,346		8,440		6,917	
Cost of Lost Bids	$37,842		$10,488		$17,623		$3,135		$68,872	

Competitively, with respect to competitors A, B, and E, BuzzCo must improve delivery and improve tolerance when competing one on one against them. BuzzCo management has known for some time that delivery and tolerance have been problematic. Its reputation on delivery and tolerance, beyond just affecting its overall competitive position relative to direct competitors, also played a role in not winning larger jobs. With customers' feedback on its performance relative to direct competitors, BuzzCo has more information by which to justify capital expenditures to make operational improvements to strengthen its competitive position. It anticipates that operational improvements will also result in lower costs to allow lower pricing.

These findings present the following strategic issues, implications, and questions assuming BuzzCo desires to increase sales.

- Focus on larger jobs that generate more volume and margin (it has penetration in the higher dollar quote range and was asked to quote on 10 and won 5). Not only will it need to invest in improving delivery and tolerance, but it will also need to change its sales, marketing, and promotional strategies to target businesses with higher volume and margin potential. This could include existing as well as new customers.
- Improve operational performance. The 637 lost quotes totaling $4.4 million come from businesses that already know about BuzzCo. After improving delivery and tolerance performance and using some of the firm's healthy contribution margin to negotiate price, the firm will be positioned to solicit repeat quotes from these known customers and prospects at minimal incremental sales and marketing costs. Just getting 10% of this business would add $400,000, to sales, albeit possibly with some lower margin.

The firm might also consider not soliciting or accepting smaller jobs. The $0 to $2,000 range averaged $745 and 49% in margin compared with overall company range of $4,190 and 54%, respectively. Considering the costs to solicit this low-revenue business, at an average of $108 (see calculation, Figure 22), customer services and support, and invoicing, sacrificing this segment could be a reasonable trade-off to higher volume and more profitable business.

Lost order analysis also involves looking at individual customer's history of quotes won and lost, shown in Table 29. A sample from BuzzCo's quote management system shows the number of quotes by customer, total dollars, and margin percent by won or lost.

This information provides another criterion by which to evaluate the results of doing business with certain customers as well as the company's efforts to generate business. It can also be used as input into the design of account management strategies, introduced in the last chapter, that describe how the firm intends to manage A, B, and C customers. For example, customer K could be classified an A customer who justifies MVC status because it awards BuzzCo good business, whereas customers C, Q, R, S, T, and U could be classified as C customers, deserving less attention and fewer resources.

	Bid Range			
	$0 to $2,000	Company Average		
Avg. revenue/job	$745	$4,190		
Average CM%	49%	54%		
	% On Quotation	Salary	Quote Cost	
Owner	25%	$100,000	$25,000	
Design Engineer	50%	$51,000	$25,500	
Plant Manager	50%	$70,000	$35,000	
Quotation & Customer Service	100%	$45,000	$45,000	
Total Payroll to Quote			$130,500	
Total Quotes Prepared			1,207	
Cost per Quote			$108	

Figure 22. BuzzCo's cost to prepare a quote.

The following four examples—Metro Plastics, Inc., Peachstate Construction, Inc., Conveyor Specialty, and Rooftop Industries—illustrate the benefits of using and the consequences of not using lost order and quote analysis.

Table 29. BuzzCo's Quote Summary by Customer 2010

	Won			Lost		
Cust.	Quotes	Total $	Margin %	Quotes	Total $	Margin %
A				1	39,458	43%
B	5	2,434	58%	1	470	35%
C				7	107,222	46%
D				1	390	69%
E	1	433	70%			
F	1	1,650	53%			
G				2	7,515	68%
H				5	4,069	35%
I				2	4,326	57%
J	5	12,324	67%			
K	5	1,130,953	53%			
L	2	4,896	75%			
M				2	8,439	58%
N				1	3,634	41%
O	5	8,765	49%			
P	5	12,305	59%	3	841	53%
Q				4	1,883	41%
R				1	2,568	49%
S				1	313	56%
T				1	675	65%
U				7	47,107	53%
V	2	700	63%			
W	12	45,203	49%	12	97,190	47%

Metro Plastics, Inc., a Type 2 plastics company, calculated a 3% hit rate on about 450 annual quotes costing about $190,000 to prepare quotes (management salaries to prepare quotes divided by the number of quotes), indicating a cost of lost quotes of $184,300 ($190,000 divided by [97% = 100% minus 3%]). Metro's owner felt the $184,300 could be redirected to prospects matching his MVC profile rather than respond to inquirers only interested in price (termed "bottom feeders" by Metro's owner), and not in its value-added mold design and engineering services. The owner subsequently screened inquirers before committing to a quote and referred bottom-feeders to his competitors. His quotation and lost order analysis resulted in a 66% increase in sales and commensurate margin by redirecting its sales, marketing, and promotional strategies, and implementing customer profiling.

Peachstate Construction, Inc., a metals fabrication company specializing in pre-engineered steel buildings, selling to over 200 industrial and individual private-party customers comprising 22 market segments and using quotes as its sole selling strategy, reported the following 3-year quote data, Table 30.

Based on quote dollar volume, management estimated its market potential at about $90,000,000 and wanted to grow the business to about $25,000,000 within 5 years. The executive VP said the high number of quotes being generated had lulled the company into thinking it was doing really well until he saw this summary. Management thought the sheer amount of quoted business indicated the company was doing really well, but quote analysis and other data showed the firm was not positioned for growth.

During 2005–2007, the firm's hit rate, based on sales as a percentage of quote dollars, averaged about 11%. Quote production increased 57% but sales increased only 4%—just about the same as inflation. While the 11% hit rate itself was not particularly significant at the time (since hit rates vary depending on circumstances), the lack of conversion to orders following such a big increase in quotes volume should have been a red flag.

Table 30. Peachstate Quote Analysis

	2005	2006	2007
Quotes	1,478	1,646	2,264
$ Value of Quotes	$80,530,273	$90,197,570	$127,397,561
Sales	$10,718,000	$11,608,339	$11,125,128
Avg. $ per Quote	$54,486	$54,798	$56,271
Hit Rate	13%	13%	9%

Additionally, the firm incurred a lot of debt in 2006 to improve operations, increasing its debt-to-equity ratio from 1.6 in 2006 to 12.9 in 2007, and working capital and liquidity ratios were low. Further, gross profit came in at 8% and 7% respectively, and contribution margin decreased from 30% to 20%. The hit rate and failure to convert quotes to sales, weak financial situation, and low profitability should have been sufficient to alert management to impending problems. However, the company had not conducted any lost order analysis. In the first 6 months of 2008, the firm produced 1,171 quotes totaling $99,334,727; by summer it idled the plant due to no orders. Lost order analysis in 2006 and 2007 might have alerted the company to the housing and construction collapse beginning in 2008.

Conveyor Specialty, Inc., producing highly engineered and computerized palletizing equipment, mentioned in Chapter 3, made significant changes to pricing, parts replacement strategy, inside sales responsibilities, and sales coverage based on lost order analysis.

- The firm found competitors' pricing about 15% lower on certain add-ons and decided to meet market pricing.
- It implemented a field stocking strategy for parts to reduce replacement time resulting in better customer service.
- It charged inside sales personnel with increasing the number of leads by 1,000 per year.
- It hired more factory sales personnel and doubled the time in the field for all factory sales people. This was intended to increase the firm's hit rate from 12% to 40% and unit sales from 70 per year to 100.

The analysis also revealed the 2006 palletizing market to be $116 million, based on total quotes submitted, but the company was only winning quotes for $14.3 million, 12% of the market. By offering market pricing, stocking more parts inventory, and increasing sales coverage the firm estimated it could increase its sales forecast to 100 units annually.

Rooftop Industries, Inc., a 150-employee Type 3 manufacturer of commercial rooftop HVAC, wanted to find new markets because it believed it had fully penetrated K-12 schools, its primary market. A review of its 2007–2008 sales and marketing activities, which included quote production and analysis, resulted in the following.

- It sold primarily through 84 reps and dealers who also sold competitors' products. Although 30% of reps accounted for 80% of sales, which indicated a good distribution of sales throughout the network, one rep accounted for 13% of sales and the next highest producer accounted for 6%; many reps were not producing according to their market's potential.
- This was a case where the sales distribution channel was the primary contact with the end-user and a major influence in the end-user/manufacturer interface, although the company maintained control over contract negotiations, post-sale terms, conditions, and warranties, and final selling price. Rooftop provided some national advertising and lead generation, but the sales channel primarily was responsible for finding prospects and initiating sales presentations.
- Quote analysis showed that in spite of a significant increase in quote production due to adding reps, the hit rate dropped off from 25% in 2007 to 18% in 2008 (Table 31). Rooftop management attributed some of this to the general seasonality of the HVAC market. But, with respect to the education

Table 31. Rooftop's Two-Year Quote Analysis

	Submitted		Sold		Hit rate	
Market	**2007**	**2008**	**2007**	**2008**	**2007**	**2008**
School	94	267	31	78	33%	29%
Government	1	15	1	4	100%	27%
Industrial	22	39	5	5	23%	13%
Commercial	117	315	23	36	20%	11%
Other	30	50	6	4	20%	8%
Hospital	25	46	7	2	28%	4%
Total	289	732	73	129	25%	18%

market, the school budgeting and purchasing process further extended the selling cycle; hence, there were 523 open quotes at the end of 2008, some of which were expected to be awarded in FY 2009. Had some of these quotes been awarded to Rooftop in 2008 its hit rate obviously would have been higher.

The relevant observation, however, regarding the issue of the company's penetration of the school market was the 361 quotes submitted for the 2 years. Preliminary market research found over 14,000 school districts comprising more than 90,000 K-12 schools. A comparison of the 361 quotes to the number of districts and schools indicated that the company's reps were not anywhere close to fully penetrating that market.

In conjunction with summarizing quote performance, Rooftop's cost to prepare and submit quotes was estimated at about $246,000 using annual salaries and estimated time employees spent on quotes (Table 32). With about 80% of quotes either lost, on hold, or carried over, Rooftop was spending about $196,800 per year on quote activity that did not result in sales. However, management believed the 20% hit rate was typical of the industry and that its quote costs were just part of doing business. It acknowledged that the high number of quotes was straining engineers' workloads, in addition to their other duties and responsibilities, and led them to investigate ways to streamline the quoting process to reduce the number of days to prepare a quote. Reps had complained that 45 days to turnaround a quote was too long.

Table 32. Rooftop's Cost per Quote

Position	% on Quotes	Salary	Quote cost
Sales manager	40%	$85,000	$34,000
Inside sales	40%	30,000	12,000
8 engineers	50%	50,000	200,000
			$246,000
Average annual quote production			500
Avg. cost per quote			$492
Average annual cost of lost quotes @ 80%			$196,800

Quote analysis showed that the education market was not fully penetrated as believed and also revealed performance problems in the sales channel. This convinced Rooftop to improve its rep factory programs, such as training on HVAC technology and impending product innovations, EPA regulations affecting the industry, company promotional strategies, and customer relations. Rooftop Industries, Inc. exemplifies the situation discussed in Chapter 3 where the channel is the end-user, or at least where it is a major determinant or influencer of sales volume, and where the company and the sales channel must collaborate and strengthen the relationship.

BuzzCo, Metro Plastics, Specialty Conveyor, and Rooftop used quotation and lost order analyses to gain insight into their competitive situations and to evaluate strategic issues involving changes to products, services, pricing, sales, marketing, and promotional strategies and their sales organizations. As is often the case, these analyses lead to unexpected insights into why business is won or lost and can shake up strategic paradigms previously held by management, as with Rooftop's belief that the education market was fully penetrated. Peachstate Construction was not as fortunate, however, because it was too late to reverse the trends indicated by the preliminary quote analysis. It might not have idled production had it investigated why so many quotes were not converting to sales.

Prior to their analyses, none of the five companies had ever reviewed or evaluated their quoting practices and results and did not have quote management systems. Their examples illustrate the insights to be gained from lost order and quotation analysis:

- Learning why a company wins or loses sales and the changes to products and services, pricing, customer service, quality, delivery, sales force and sales channel, factory operations, and factory relations needed to increase sales.
- Identifying the cost of responding to or pursuing business that is likely to be unprofitable.
- Gaining better insight into the potential to further penetrate existing markets and to increase sales.

	Annual Sales	Amount of Annual Quotes
	($millions)	
BuzzCo	$2.4	$4.4
Peachstate Construction	$11.5	$90 to $127
Conveyor Specialties	$30.0	$116.0
Rooftop Industries	$20.0	$120.0

Figure 23. New sales potential from quote analysis.

Inferring Market Potential from Quotations; a Source of New Business Without Incurring Additional Selling Costs

Information from quote management and lost order analysis can lead to practical estimates of market potential—something B2B manufacturers struggle with since many do not conduct marketing research and don't know the number of prospects in their target markets.

Quote summaries for BuzzCo, Peachstate Construction, Conveyor Specialty, and Rooftop Industries illustrate the potential to increase sales relative to their annual sales. Figure 23 shows the dollar amount of quotes the four companies prepared compared with their annual sales. Since quotations result from existing customers and prospects that already know about a company, they represent potential increased business simply by winning more quotes—just by increasing the hit rate. The incremental cost of increasing sales is minimal compared with growth strategies calling for new customers. By just improving their competitive situations—via quotation and lost order analysis—and therefore their hit rates, these firms could add sales at relatively no incremental cost—it is a low hanging fruit.

Using Quote Status to Bolster the Sales Forecast

Of the 111 companies that use quotes, 66 prepare a sales forecast and 34 update it during the business year with actual sales, see Table 33. Since business practitioners say that preparing a sales forecast is a fundamental good business practice you would expect more companies preparing a forecast.

Table 33. Using Quotes and Sales Forecasting

	Job shop				Product				Type			
	1	2	3	Total	1	2	3	Total	1	2	3	Total
Use quotes/bids	0	0	0	0	0	0	0	0	0	0	0	0
Prepare forecast	3	15	13	31	2	16	17	35	5	31	30	66
No forecast	9	11	3	23	5	12	4	21	14	23	7	44
Not asked	0	0	0	0	1	0	0	1	1	0	0	1
Update to Actual	0	4	10	14	1	5	14	20	1	9	24	34

Where sales forecasting exists, a quote management system offers the potential to augment the forecast just by using historical quote production, average dollar per quote won, and hit rate. BuzzCo could forecast an increase in sales from $2.4 million to $3 million by using quote metrics to calculate the number of quotes needed to generate that forecast. It would need 1,523 quotes, at its 47% hit rate, at average quote dollar amount of $4,190 to produce that revenue ($3,000,000 ÷ $4,190 ÷ 47% = $1,523). It would need to increase the number of quotes from its 2010 level of 1,207 to 1,523—a 26% increase. It must decide whether to get the increase from existing customers, new customers, or both—and then task the sales force to make it happen. But remember, most SMMs don't conduct marketing research or know where to get new customers. This is a good reminder of customer profiling and use of marketing databases, discussed in Chapter 3, to find new customers. This "back-of-the-envelope" approach is a pragmatic first step to preparing a sales forecast that calls for growth.

In addition to providing input into a sales forecast, a quote management system, through lost order analysis and updates on quote status, can help management updating the forecast with real-time customer and market data by assigning a status code to each quote.

The following five descriptions are good examples of how to update a sales forecast with real-time customer and market conditions:

1. Won—The quote is won and can be entered as "actual" against the forecast.
2. Still open or pending—The customer or prospect has not made a decision and the quote is still viable. The dollar value of the quote should remain in the sales forecast although some companies apply a probability of success to the dollar amount to "normalize" the forecast.

Table 34. BuzzCo's Quote Status

Customer or prospect	Quote amount	Status		Competitor
		Won, pending, lost, delayed, cancelled	Coded reason for lost	
A	$10,000	W		
B	$5,000	P		
C	$15,000	L	2 = Delivery	Peach State
D	$6,000	D		
E	$12,500	C		

3. Lost—The quote was awarded to a competitor. Delete the dollar amount of the quote from the forecast and update the lost order report with who got the quote and why.

4. Delayed—The customer or prospect intends to make a decision but at a later date. The dollar amount of the quote is flagged and noted. Management discretion should be used to determine if the forecast is to be modified because the timing of the "sale" can affect profit and cash flow.

5. Cancelled—The customer or prospect decided not to proceed with the purchase and the dollar amount of the quote is removed from the forecast.

Table 34 illustrates BuzzCo's quote status report. Customer C's quote was awarded to Peach State, one of BuzzCo's competitors, who was able to deliver sooner (lost code 2). In addition, other codes can be customized to the company's situation (for example, 1 = price, 2 = delivery, 3 = specifications or tolerance and so forth.

Using Quote Production and Hit Rate to Strengthen Sales Management

Where a firm knows the number of customers and prospects in the markets it wants to target, the number of quotes generated (by customer, prospect, market, market segment, etc.) will indicate the business' success in attaining desired sales coverage and market penetration. The hit rate tells the firm its success in converting inquiries into orders both at the company level and at the individual sales person level. If a sales territory possesses good sales potential but the assigned sales person does not generate a sufficient number of quotes, his ability to develop leads and generate quotes will become suspect. Similarly, if quotes are not won the salesperson's ability to "close the deal" will be suspect—assuming there are no competitive reasons for losing an order beyond the salesperson's expertise. Quote production and hit rate can be excellent components of sales and incentive compensation schemes and evaluation criteria.

Summary

Quotation management and lost order analysis are critical elements of B2B industrial marketing that most manufacturers overlook or do not manage effectively. However, when properly designed and used, they are an excellent means by which a company can keep tabs on market activity, its competitive situation, and its success in planning, executing, and evaluating company and sales force performance and growth strategies.

The absence of a good quote management system or lack of quote analysis and lost orders is a major impediment to developing and executing effective growth strategies. Even where a quote management system exists, few SMMs use them to obtain market intelligence to improve sales or gain competitive advantage. Table 35 shows in descending occurrence SMMs' use of various aspects of a quote management system. The most valuable but least used are understanding why they win or lose business and to make constructive changes to products, services, and strategies; the two at the bottom of the list. Less than a third of the 111 who use quotes track the reasons for lost business or make changes to improve their competitive position.

High quote production, generally considered a good barometer of sales and marketing success, can disguise poor sales management and a weak competitive situation. If a company prepares many quotes and is not winning a reasonable percentage you could conclude that something is wrong—and most likely there is. The company likely is a shotgun marketer, not focused on the customers and markets that are a good match for its products and services, and probably does not possess a competitive advantage.

Table 35. Summary of Quote Management Findings

Measurement	Job shop				Product				Type			
	1	2	3	Total	1	2	3	Total	1	2	3	Total
No. of firms preparing quotes	12	26	16	54	8	27	22	57	20	53	38	111
Know number of quotes	8	20	10	38	6	22	15	43	14	42	25	81
Have pricing problems	9	16	12	37	4	18	15	37	13	34	27	74
Know hit rate	5	15	9	29	7	16	18	41	12	31	27	70
Have quote management system	5	16	9	30	4	15	16	35	9	31	25	65
Obtain competitor intelligence	2	7	6	15	3	20	15	38	5	27	21	53
Know direct material and labor costs	2	13	6	21	1	10	10	21	3	23	16	42
Know cost of quote	1	6	5	12	4	12	11	27	4	18	16	38
Change strategies	0	9	5	14	0	9	13	22	0	18	18	36
Track reasons for lost bids	0	4	3	7	1	7	9	17	1	11	12	24

Feedback on lost orders can lead to continuous improvement, changes to existing products and ideas for new products and product development, customer service, delivery and shipping performance, pricing, sales coverage and sales distribution channels, and advertising and promotional strategies—all of which can improve competitive advantage.

Like customer analysis and profiling in the previous chapter, it derives most information and insight from information already compiled and recorded in the company. It further builds on the 'C' part of *C-P-M*™.

CHAPTER 5

Using Customer Feedback to Inform Strategy

The previous two chapters dealt with generating and using information about existing customers and from quoting outcomes that can help SMMs find new customers and markets—the latter involving direct feedback from customers and prospects about the company's competitive situation. This chapter supplements that idea with practical steps on how to get even better, more detailed feedback from customers to improve its competitive situation and involves soliciting direct feedback from them, specifically:

1. Factors that customers consider important when selecting suppliers,
2. The company's performance on those factors, and
3. Competitors' performance also on those factors.

Getting feedback from customers is a sensible business practice available to SMMs to learn about changes to products and services and sales, marketing, and promotional strategies that can improve their competitive situation and inform growth strategies. But questionnaire responses indicate that most manufacturers do not formally discuss these issues with customers and communication usually involves addressing and solving the crisis *du jour*. Only 16 used formal feedback for long-term strategy development: Fifty-eight said they used only informal communication to monitor feedback and customers' satisfaction. As with customer databases and quote management systems, SMMs do not appear to be inclined to invest resources to track and monitor customer feedback about their performance in satisfying customers and how they are doing relative to competition. The following customer satisfaction survey is designed to simplify getting good feedback from customers at a nominal cost.

The "3 *fer*" Is Not Consumer Research or Surveying

The *3-fer* is a customer satisfaction survey specifically intended for B2B companies that combines:

1. Identification of the customer's buying decision criteria
2. A rating of the company's ability to satisfy the customer on those criteria, and
3. Identification of competitors and their performance on satisfying the customer on the criteria.

It incorporates the MVC, A, B, and C customer classifications introduced in Chapter 3, is designed to solicit feedback only from customers that matter, and provides a scaled-down, practicable, "back-of-the-envelop" approach tailored to the company's customer base, products and services, and budget that provides insightful and useful information. It can be adapted by both job shops and machine companies.

Getting Strategically Important Information from Customers

It uses the customer classifications to segment the customer base so that MVC and A customers get the "red carpet" treatment while B, C, and former customers are contacted using less expensive methods, such as direct mail, e-mail or fax.

MVCs get preferential treatment; for example, taken to lunch or dinner and asked about the information solicited in the survey. This is a good opportunity to learn more about the customer's business so that the manufacturer can determine if the customer will be good for long-term growth and also for getting ideas for new products and services the customer might want. (Numerous studies show that customers are one of the best sources of ideas for new products and services.)

B customers, who are good customers but not as critical as MVCs, should be contacted personally by a sales employee, via telephone or face to face, and asked to participate in a short survey. (A customer who declines should be flagged for follow-up by senior management because there might be a problem or situation unknown to the company that needs to be aired out.) Keep in mind that the customer to contact should be the person who is responsible for making the purchase decision or who can speak authoritatively about the company and its products and services. Usually, this is the sales person's primary contact in the customer's organization. (Feedback provided by the customer's receptionist might not be as insightful as desired.)

While getting feedback from as many customers as possible is ideal, C customers might not justify the expense of a face-to-face meeting, unless the sales person happens to be in the area, or other circumstances warrant the cost. Fortunately, there are less costly methods available for getting C customers' input. Before the advent of web-based survey software, faxes were the convenient and low-cost method for B and C customers to transmit their responses. Now, the convenience, flexibility, and economy of web-based surveying surpass the fax.

Customers who have not ordered for a long time or who are considered "former" customers should also be included in the survey for two reasons. First, if they defected to a competitor or had a bad experience with the firm's products and services, their feedback would help identify problems and situations the company might not know. Second, as an opportunity to regain the business if considered an "important" former customer, a sales person or senior manager should contact them.

Whether using web-based software or fax, the goal is to tailor the delivery and administration of the survey to the classification of customer so that more costly feedback (e.g., lunch, dinner with MVCs) is limited and methods that are more economical are used for B, C, and former customers.

A sample budget, Figure 24, illustrates how a company can segment customers by classification to minimize the cost of the survey project.

The amounts shown for Qty./Cost represent (a) the number of customers across, (b) the cost estimates for meeting with A customers; direct phone or F-T-F (face-to-face) with B customers; and less costly contact with C and former customers; and (c) the cost to compile and analyze survey results down the column.

For simplicity, this example uses 89 customers who are presumed end-use customers. The budget for a survey comprising hundreds of customers or more, and involving sales through distribution, would obviously be more involved and would require, as discussed in Chapter 3, determining

	Qty./ Cost	Customer type					Total Budget
		A	B	C	Former	Total	
		10	47	20	12	89	
Design survey							$250
Administration							
Owner or manager, F-T-F meetings	$100	$1,000					$1,000
Sales person, F-T-F, other	$75		$3,525				$3,525
Inside sales, customer service: fax or Internet	$15			$300	$180		$480
Compilation and analysis	$15	$150	$705	$300			$1,155
					Total project cost		$6,410
					Cost per customer survey		$72

Figure 24. Sample survey budget.

who the customer is. That situation would require different surveys for end-use customers and for channel members.

The recommended approach for contacting customers to invite them to participate in the survey involves the owner or senior manager(s) contacting A customers, and sales personnel (inside, outside, or reps) contacting their primary person in B and C customers. Customers should be advised that the company seeks candid feedback, that they are invited to participate in the survey, that the company intends to take action on the feedback, and will share the results if asked. This signals the company's intent about improving its products and services and that it sincerely desires feedback from its customers.

A sample *3-fer* survey for a product company is shown in Figure 25.

The introductory paragraph of the survey should identify the type of products and services the company offers (for example, preengineered metal buildings) and the factors must be tailored to the company's product and service offering.

Factor pertains to the competitive criteria that prospects and customers use to evaluate the merits of the company and its products

Customer Satisfaction Survey (Product)

Please help us understand how we can better serve our customers by providing the following information. We are interested in learning what is important to our customers in selecting producers of pre-engineered metal buildings.

| Please rate each factor on its importance in your selection of a supplier using a 1–5 scale:

Importance Scale
1 = Not important, can do without.

2 = Somewhat important, would like to have.

3 = Important.

4 = Very important.

5 = Critical, non-negotiable, must have.

Please rate <u>Company</u> and up to 3 other suppliers you use of know of, using the following 1–5 scale:

Performance Scale
1 = Must improve.

2 = Performs below average.

3 = Performs average.

4 = Performs above average.

5 = Performance exceeds specs or requirements. | **Price only.** Comparing the Company's products to competitive products perceived as having the same economic value or benefit.

1 = Pricing is high compared to competing products or economic benefit\value.

2 = Pricing is somewhat higher compared to competing products or economic benefit\value.

2 = Pricing is OK, average, or in-line compared to competing products or economic benefit\value.

4 = Price is somewhat lower compared to competing products or economic benefit\value.

5 = Price is very low compared to competing products or economic benefit\value.

Please enter the name of the other suppliers in the boxes below and rate all companies on all factors. |

Importance Rating	Factor	Company Performance Rating	1st Supplier:	2nd Supplier:	3rd Supplier:
	Customer/tech service factors.				
	Production, delivery, quality factors.				
	Price factors.				
	Engineering/design factors.				
	Sales personnel contact, visits, etc.				

Please comment on any particular issues\problems you have experienced in the past two years.

Figure 25. Sample product survey.

and services. In most cases, the company will have some ideas about the factors to list in this column. *However, if the firm uses quotes and conducts lost order analysis, the reasons given for losing orders represent an excellent source of items that customers and prospects consider important to the purchase decision.* Though there are four factors shown in the example survey, an alternative format could have sub-items listed under a main item where there are blank lines. For example, under Customer/tech service factors, sub-items could include knowledge of product, speed of solution or response, and accuracy of solution. Sub-items add definition and detail to the factor so that more insight can be gained from a customer's responses.

Product factors might include: reliable operation, quality meets or exceeds specifications, low maintenance cost, and ease of installation.

Sales personnel factors might include: knowledge of product line, knowledge of customer needs, response to inquiries, and communication skills.

Importance Scale signifies the degree of importance in the buying decision on a 1–5 scale where **1** = Not important, can do without; **2** = Somewhat important, would like to have; **3** = Important; **4** = Very important; and **5** = Critical, nonnegotiable, must have.

Customers then rate the company using the same 1–5 scale for **Performance** where:

1 = Must improve
2 = Performs below average
3 = Performs average
4 = Performs above average
5 = Performance exceeds specs/requirements.

The wording for **Rating** and **Performance** scales can be modified or adapted to company or industry language as long as sufficient differentiation remains between the low and high ratings.

Customers then are asked to name up to three suppliers (the company's competitors) they use or know who supply the same product or product line and to rate them similarly **1–5** on performance. This gives the company a one-to-one, apples-to-apples direct comparison to competitors.

Questionnaire findings showed that although 90 of 126 firms say they can name direct competitors, only 61 could make an "apples-to-apples" comparison to competitors' products and services. This aspect of the *3-fer* helps get information about competitors that is not publicly available. Some customers will not want to identify competitors, but this information should be obtainable with enough customers participating.

Customers' comments in the bottom section provide "off-line" comments that could be very informative since the factors and rating scheme cannot address and quantify all situations and issues. In some cases, customers provide very good nuggets of information that otherwise would never have been disclosed. Management should follow-up on 1 and 5 ratings because they are the extreme good and bad ratings and also follow-up on particularly significant or unusual comments.

The 1–5 rating scheme for "importance" and "performance" affords easy compilation and graphical depiction using electronic spreadsheets, other databases, or web-based software for sorting, analysis, and summarization. The sample data in Table 36 illustrate the responses of a company's customers using the importance–performance scheme on seven factors:

1. Replacement parts
2. Price
3. Quality
4. Customer service
5. Technical materials
6. Technical support
7. Delivery time

Responses by three customers A, B, and C (not to be confused with customer classifications in Chapter 3) generated this information, which the company compiled and summarized from their individual surveys. Average Importance ratings are at the bottom along with customers' average rating of the company on the seven factors. Note that Importance Average is sorted left to right in ascending order to show the least important factor at the left (Replacement Parts) and the most important at the right (Delivery Time), which facilitates graphic depiction. Competitor ratings on each factor are also averaged at the bottom.

Table 36. Sample Compiled Survey Results

Customer	Competitor	Replacement parts	Quality	Price	Performance Customer service	Technical materials	Technical support	Delivery time
					Survey data by customer, by factor			
A	Importance	2	4	4	4	5	5	5
	Company	4	2	4	5	1	5	4
	Competitor 1	3	2	3	4	4	2	2
	Competitor 2	3	1	3	4	2	2	2
	Competitor 3	1	4	3	2	5	5	3
B	Importance	3	3	4	3	4	5	5
	Company	4	2	4	5	1	5	4
	Competitor 1	3	2	4	2	2	2	4
	Competitor 2	3	1	3	4	2	2	5
	Competitor 3	1	4	3	2	5	5	3

	Importance	5	4	4	5	3	3	3
	Company	4	5	1	5	4	2	3
C	Competitor 1	4	2	2	2	4	2	3
	Competitor 2	5	4	2	4	3	1	1
	Competitor 3	3	3	5	2	3	3	
Importance Average		5.0	4.7	4.3	4.0	3.7	3.3	2.7
Company Performance–Average		4.0	5.0	1.0	5.0	4.0	2.0	3.7
Competitor 1–Average Performance		3.3	2.0	2.7	2.7	3.7	2.0	3.0
Competitor 2–Average Performance		4.0	2.7	2.0	4.0	3.0	1.0	3.0
Competitor 3–Average Performance		3.0	4.3	5.0	2.0	3.0	3.7	1.0

Individual ratings of '1' should be flagged for follow-up and discussion by sales or senior management because they represent a potential serious problem that needs immediate corrective action. For example, all three customers rated Technical Materials a '1.' The underlying reasons for customers awarding a '5' rating for Technical Support could indicate a competitive strength that could be exploited for competitive advantage.

While this format provides a good summary overview of the company and competitors' performances on the factors, it does not readily portray performance relative to factors considered important in the buying decision.

Graph 4 illustrates the *3-fer's* most beneficial feature—combining three elements into one to portray a company's competitive position:

1. Factors that customers consider important when selecting suppliers,
2. The company's performance on those factors, and
3. Competitors' performance on those factors.

The seven competitive factors used by customers in this market to evaluate the performance of competing suppliers' products and services are

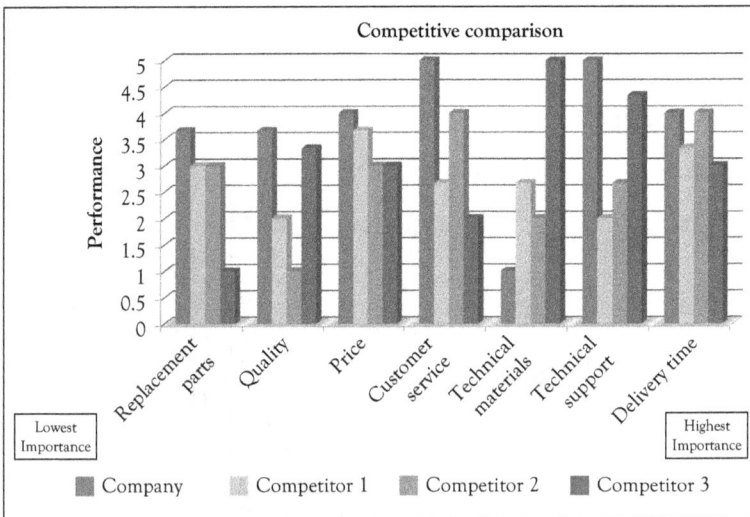

Graph 4. Survey competitive comparison.

now ranked in the order of importance—left (least important) to right (most important). The company—the left bar in each factor—not only sees how it performs on those factors, but also sees how it matches up "apples-to-apples" to direct competitors.

Table 37 shows the rating numbers depicted in Graph 4. Delivery Time, Technical Support, and Technical Materials are rated most important; less important are Replacement Parts, and Quality. Price and Customer Service are in the middle. The company's performance on Tech Materials rated at "1" indicates it needs to improve this factor to be more competitive. Its performance on the two other important factors, Delivery Time and Technical Support—in the "4" to "5" range—indicates a favorable competitive situation that could be exploited. Its performance on Replacement Parts, Quality, and Customer Service, while better than competitors, might not be that significant since customers rank the importance of those as average. Lastly, its "4" Price rating indicates its prices tend to be on the low side.

The strategic choices the company makes based on this feedback would depend on other factors, such as its financial situation, industry and market trends and conditions, and long-term goals. Initial observations could include deciding to raise prices to exploit its favorable positions in the important factors, Technical Support and Delivery Time, or improving Technical Materials since that might not entail much investment. Improving Replacement Parts and Quality, conversely, might require considerably more cost at marginal benefit, as those factors are rated less important.

Consider also that this example, purposefully kept simple to illustrate how the three types of data can be applied graphically to demonstrate competitive position, included neither different customer types nor multiple product lines, which would have made interpreting the feedback and deciding on strategic actions significantly more complex. Companies with multiple product lines, selling into more than one market or with a very diverse set of customers could justify different surveys to accommodate those differences. While the costs associated with design, administration, compilation, and analysis would increase, there also should be a commensurate increase in the value of customer feedback.

Table 37. Rating Summary

Performance								
		Replacement parts	Quality	Price	Customer service	Technical materials	Technical support	Delivery time
	Importance average	2.67	3.33	3.67	4.00	4.33	4.67	5.00
Performance	Company	3.67	3.67	4.00	5.00	1.00	5.00	4.00
	Competitor 1	3.00	2.00	3.67	2.67	2.67	2.00	3.33
	Competitor 2	3.00	1.00	3.00	4.00	2.00	2.67	4.00
	Competitor3	1.00	3.33	3.00	2.00	5.00	4.33	3.00

Specialty Conveyor, Inc., a Type 3 company mentioned previously that makes and sells highly engineered automated material handling and conveyor systems, designed its survey around four aspects of its product and services offering:

1. Product quality
2. Dependable service
3. Dependable parts support
4. Equipment modifications

Each of the four categories was broken down into sub-items and rated by customers shown in Graph 5.

The firm's customers, which are capital-intensive, characterize a homogeneous market where needs for material handling and packaging are very

Customer satisfaction scores

Product quality		0	0.5	1.0	1.5	2.0	2.5	3.0	3.5	4.0	4.5	5.0
Equip. and parts complete and tested	4.5											
Reliability and durability	4.1											
Factory test procedure	3.8											
Warranty fair and adequate	3.2											
Manuuals correct and readable	2.1											
Average	3.5											
Dependable service												
Respond quickly	3.9											
Technical knowledge	3.7											
Problems resolved quickly	3.0											
Cust. training for operator/maintenance	2.9											
Timely programming updates	2.3											
Average	3.2											
Dependable parts support												
Good product knowledge	4.6											
Accurate shipments	4.2											
On-time shipments	4.2											
Adequate documentation	2.7											
Quick response to downtime	2.3											
Competitive prices for parts	1.8											
Average	3.3											
Equipment modifications												
Quotations prompt/complete	4.7											
Responsive solutions	4.4											
Delivery times meet needs	3.6											
Shipments accurate/on-time	2.3											
Price competitive	1.7											
Average	3.3											

Graph 5. Specialty Conveyor, Inc.'s scores.

similar. They comprise businesses that move high volumes of packaged goods from inventory storage to automated packaging stations. Although competing material handling and conveyors models differ in design and specifications the primary function is to move product, automate packaging, and stack. Consequently, the competing factors are few (see Table 38) and there is little variation in their relative importance—all are rated **4** = very important or **5** = critical, nonnegotiable—averaging between 4.2 and 4.8–with Dependable Service at 4.2 on the left (least important) and Equipment Modifications at 4.8 on the right (most important). This market requires quality, dependable service, uptime, and parts support, and ability to modify equipment as customers' product lines, quantities, size, and seasonality change.

The firm concluded that its documentation and updates need to be improved and that its pricing might be too high relative to the better showing of competitors in Parts Support and Equipment Modifications. Sub-items of 'Manuals correct and readable' (Product Quality) and 'Timely programming updates' (Dependable Service) decreased these two factor's average ratings. 'Competitive prices for parts' and 'Price competitive' in Parts Support' similarly brought down the average ratings for Parts Support and Equipment Modifications.

Graph 6 shows the resulting competitive comparison and Table 38 shows the rating summary.

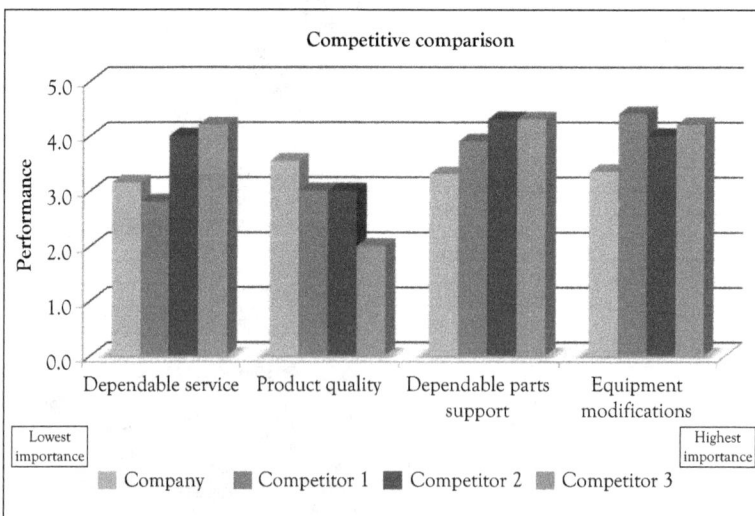

Graph 6. Specialty Conveyor, Inc.'s competitive comparison.

Table 38. Specialty Conveyor, Inc.'s Competitive Comparison

	Company/ competitor	Performance			
		Dependable service	Product quality	Dependable parts support	Equipment modifications
	Importance	4.2	4.6	4.6	4.8
Performance	Company	3.2	3.5	3.3	3.3
	Competitor 1	2.8	3.0	3.9	4.4
	Competitor 2	4.0	3.0	4.3	4.0
	Competitor 3	4.2	2.0	4.3	4.2

The company talked to key customers about some of the weaker ratings and learned two things that fell under the survey's radar and were not picked up in the ratings. Because a key competitor had laid off service tech employees, customers expected a drop in customer service and support. There was also some concern about competitors' warranties, in general, living up to commitments.

Specialty Conveyor, Inc. decided on the following actions:

- Explore hiring degreed engineers to:
  - Further strengthen technical knowledge and to improve 'Customer training for operator/maintenance' (Dependable Service)
  - Gain competitive advantage:
    - In light of the (a) firm's favorable ratings in 'Equip. and parts complete and tested' (Product Quality) and in 'Respond quickly' (Dependable Service) and
    - (b) competitors' impending faltering in customer service and tech support and customers' concerns about warranties. Confirm via field intelligence the situation with competitors' warranties.
- Improve the firm's customer database for programming update notifications.
- Improve technical and maintenance manuals. Upgrade software to create and publish the manuals and supporting documents, graphics, and so forth.

- Review costing procedures to verify accuracy, update product costing sheets, and confirm competitors' parts pricing. Forecast impact on profit/cash flow of marketing pricing rather than cost-plus pricing.
- Try to educate customers on the benefits of carrying spare parts.

Customer satisfaction surveys for job shops and machine shops can be designed similarly to product company surveys but with different competitive factors, typically quality, on-time completion and delivery, quoting timeliness, engineering and design, tolerance, invoicing accuracy and timeliness, customer service and technical support, and machining capabilities and can use the same rating scales for importance and performance.

- Dan's Machine Shop, a 10-employee company, learned that although customers gave him high marks on customer service and pricing, his machining capabilities did not match up to competitors, two of which he did not know about until customers listed them on the survey. Dan was not in a position to update equipment to match competition because 18 months earlier he had borrowed to construct a new building and purchase equipment. He might have revised plans for equipment and capital improvements if he had had information about customers' needs and about competition before making major improvements.

The Acid Test

It's natural for employees to think they are doing all they can to keep customers happy and satisfied and there is a simple reality check to verify the accuracy of their belief. The acid test involves having employees fill out the survey as if a customer were filling it out and later comparing actual customer responses to the employees' responses.

Employee's average ratings (bottom line of each category) shown in Graph 7 on the next page on 'Product Quality' and 'Equipment

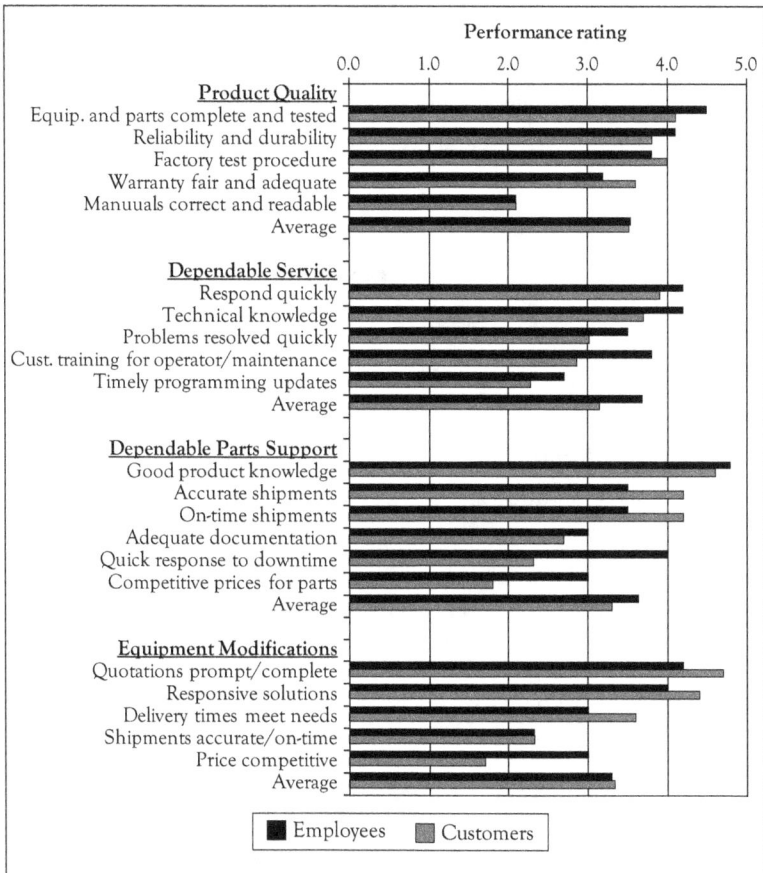

Graph 7. Sample acid test.

Modifications' match customers' responses, indicating they are reason-ably attuned to customers' satisfaction on those factors. There is some difference, however, in the ratings for 'Dependable Service' in total and one sub-item under 'Parts Support,'–'Quick response to downtime' where employees rated the company better than customers. This coin-cides with the findings mentioned earlier on Specialty Conveyor Inc.'s lower customer ratings that resulted in its decision to hire degreed engi-neers to shore up these areas. In addition to engineering and techni-cal training for service and support employees, the company provided training in communicationskills and increased the number of employ-ees participating in management meetings that cover customer service, support, maintenance, and repair.

Bigger differences between employees' ratings and customers' ratings should raise concern that employees might not be attuned to customer issues or that management is not effectively communicating the importance of customer relations and account management, particularly where there is direct contact with customers.

Summary

SMMs need customer feedback to alert them to problems that could cause loss of customers and jeopardize their businesses, but according to questionnaire responses few formally solicit customers to learn about their performance in keeping customers satisfied and how to make changes to products and services and sales, marketing, and promotional strategies that can improve their competitive situation and inform growth strategies.

In particular, they should get information about three things:

1. Customer's decision criteria for selecting suppliers of the types of products and services the SMM offers,
2. How the SMM is performing on those criteria, and
3. How competitors are also performing on those criteria.

The *3-fer* customer satisfaction format combines these items in a one- or two-page document whose data are easily compiled and summarized and done at relatively low cost. Surveying customers using the *3-fer* amplifies information gained from customer analysis and customer profiling, and in addition to lost order analysis it delivers a snapshot of competitors' products and performance directly related to the market place that is not available from D&B, websites, or other public information.

Formal customer surveying, well planned and executed, in preparation for taking on a growth strategy project, greatly improves the odds that products, services, and sales and promotional strategies will produce the desired outcomes.

CHAPTER 6

Product Analysis and Product Management

Products and product management were the fifth most-cited sales and marketing problem of the 126 companies following (1) marketing, marketing research, analysis, and knowledge; (2) sales force capabilities, performance, and sales coverage; (3) competitor intelligence, differentiation, and competitive advantage; (4) and prospect and lead generation. Some of the companies' comments pertaining to products and product management included:

- Limited market knowledge, foreign competition, poor customer awareness of company's capabilities, lack of quality leads, declining market share, limited sales personnel, insufficient product capabilities;
- Lack of products with a universal application and appeal;
- Unknown focus of what our core competencies are and where best to market our core competencies;
- Need to identify areas of higher profits from current product lines;
- Using more differentiation from competition;
- Reducing margins to get business;
- Lack of pricing power with existing customers;
- Need to expand new products and materials to sell;
- Cost of products;
- Increasing cost to develop and deliver products relative to prices that customers will accept; and
- Customers finding other solutions to services we provide.

These comments overlap several areas and indicate the inter-connectedness to them all: market and competitor knowledge, competitive position and competitive advantage, profitability, costing and pricing, and customer relations—areas already mentioned in previous chapters. As with customer analysis, the starting point for assessing long-term value of the products to the company and identifying winners and losers begins with sales volume and margin analysis.

This chapter deals with the strategic question presented in Chapter 2, "Which products and services (production and machining capabilities for jobs shops and machine companies) are profitable; can they be improved, if not profitable; and does the firm need to increase its product offering by developing new products or acquiring others to support long-term growth?" It addresses the P in C-P-M™.

Evaluating Product Performance—Finding Winners and Losers

Showing the sales history of products over 3–5 years gives a good snapshot of their relative performance. This graph illustrates performance of three products over 5 years and shows that Product B's sales volume has

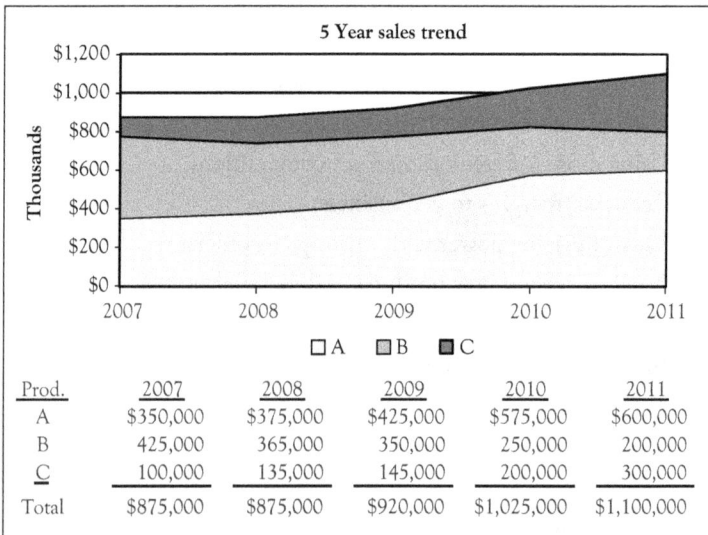

Prod.	2007	2008	2009	2010	2011
A	$350,000	$375,000	$425,000	$575,000	$600,000
B	425,000	365,000	350,000	250,000	200,000
C	100,000	135,000	145,000	200,000	300,000
Total	$875,000	$875,000	$920,000	$1,025,000	$1,100,000

Graph 8. 5 Year product sales trend.

decreased and that of Products A and C have increased. In 2007, Product B was the big seller; in 2011 Product A has the highest sales.

Such changes in the relative performance of products require explanation when a company decides to grow beyond "business as usual"—just keeping up with inflation or moderate growth—because diminishing performance of any of its products will be a drag on growth unless the reasons for the declining performance are understood. Weakening products can consume operational, financial, and sales and marketing resources that otherwise could have been put to better use. Before deciding the fate of Product B, however, management should look at its profit and cash flow performance, not just at its sales.

Since sales reports might not show product profitability, a modified income statement is needed that breaks out product sales and associated expenses so that their profitability can be assessed. The segmented income statement, which uses the cost accounting format to show revenue and variable expenses and fixed costs, provides excellent insight into product sales and profitability (see Table 39). It gives much clearer information by which to decide Product B's fate. Where accounting systems do not provide direct material and labor costs at the product level, other data sources can be used to estimate unit product cost, such as accounting standards for material and labor, purchase orders, timesheets, and production reports.

Table 39. Segmented Income Statement

	Total company		Prod A		Prod B		Prod C	
	Segmented income statement format							
% of Sales			55%		18%		27%	
Sales	$1,100,000	100%	$600,000	100%	$200,000	100%	$300,000	100%
Direct Materials	300,000	27%	150,000	25%	70,000	35%	80,000	27%
Direct Labor	169,000	15%	100,000	17%	38,000	19%	31,000	10%
Commissions	35,000	3%	15,000	3%	15,500	8%	4,500	2%
Total Direct Cost	$504,000	46%	$265,000	44%	$123,500	62%	$115,500	39%
Contribution Margin	$596,000	54%	$335,000	56%	$76,500	38%	$184,500	62%
Fixed Costs	$471,000		145,000		175,000		151,000	
Pre-tax Profit	$125,000	11%	$190,000	32%	($98,500)	−49%	$33,500	11%

Product A accounts for 55% of total sales and has a 56% contribution margin, which is very good. Product B accounts for 18% of sales with a 38% contribution margin, which is good, but it consumes the most fixed cost and overhead resulting in a ($98,500) loss. Its contribution margin is okay, but management must find out why it consumes so much overhead, has a higher sales commission at 8%, and is a drag on profit. An initial look at B just using sales trend suggested a possibly weakening product, but its 38% contribution margin indicates it might be viable if management can get its commission more in line with A's and C's as percentage of sales and lower its overhead costs. The segmented format provides a much more detailed statement than does the typical income statement that reports sales only at the company level and not by product. It gives management much more information by which to evaluate products—direct costs (44%, 62%, and 39%, respectively), sales commissions (3%, 8%, and 2%, respectively), and fixed costs and overhead ($145,000, $175,000, and $151,000, respectively).

B's sales and profit performance, in light of the company's intention to grow, calls for looking into its viability and competitiveness. The following questions, which are not all inclusive, need answers from both internal review and external analysis—competitive comparison and market analysis and research specific to product B. Some of the questions management could ask about product B include the following.

- What is the cause of B's sales decline? Lack of selling and marketing effort? Quality, performance problems? Better competing products? Overall decline in demand for this product category? Technological obsolescence?
- Are there operational and production problems to be solved to lower its 62% cost of sales? Is B's pricing too high due to these costs?
- Why are B's commissions higher than A's and C's? Is B getting sufficient attention and sales coverage by company sales personnel and reps?
- Is there a product that can replace the $76,500 contribution margin B generates should a replacement be needed? Can A and C make up the difference in sales and margin? Dropping

B from the product line, at least in the short term, is not advisable since it generates $76,500 in contribution margin.
- Can the overhead that B consumes be reduced?

Another aspect of this format deals with assigning, or allocating fixed costs and overhead to the products, which is difficult to do accurately and can be costly. To simplify this, accountants divide fixed costs and overhead by the estimated amount of direct labor the company will use annually and then allocate fixed costs and overhead according to the labor content of the various products. Since this is not a precise method it can result in over- or underestimating the amount of fixed cost and overhead a product actually consumes and can add to the difficulty of costing and pricing products—particularly where actual direct labor costs are unknown or uncertain.

I approach overhead simply. I start with the manufacturing and SG&A overhead reported on the typical income statement and ask management to estimate the amount of overhead attributable to each product or product line, which is how I showed the fixed cost and overhead in the segmented format example. *Note: This is a very rough approximation to quickly see individual product's profitability and avoids time-consuming and costly overhead analysis.* After management reviews the results—such as product B's $175,000—it can decide whether to pursue a more robust overhead analysis, either just for the one product or across the board. This "back-of-the-envelope" approach works well with smaller companies with few products or product lines that are not too complex. Bigger companies, with expensive products comprising sophisticated subassemblies, such as Conveyor Specialty, Inc.'s computerized packaging machines, need accounting specialists, CPAs, or the chief financial officer to develop the direct and fixed costs and overhead for product profitability analysis.

Product management's role in the development of growth strategies is to help the company choose the products that can support profitable growth and decide if new products—or modifications to existing ones— are needed. Effective product management requires knowledge of and insight into the areas cited earlier: market and competitor knowledge, competitive position and competitive advantage, profitability, costing and pricing, and customer relations. However, responses to questions in the questionnaire indicate most firms do not have a lot of this information and helps explain why many cannot simply "turn on their sales spigot."

Review of Product Management Practices

The widely held notion that manufacturers know their costs and margins and have good information about competitors and insights into their markets is not reflected in the findings about companies' product management practices. The following summary shows that most companies operate without reliable cost data that can inform pricing, that perceptions about competitors most likely derive from anecdote since they do not formally generate information about competitors, and that few know where to go to find new customers.

These findings support the contention in Chapter 1 that many SMMs operate in the dark due to lack of good strategic information about costs, margins, and pricing, about customers, markets, and competition, and that this leads to shot gun marketing.

Responses in Table 40 fell into three categories—Costing and Pricing, Market and Competitor Intelligence, and Sales Forecasting and Reporting—with Costing and Pricing factors the most frequently reported. Issues with pricing, and reasons given for pricing problems, centered on pricing high as a cautionary measure due to uncertainty about costs and lack of competitive advantage, resulting in pricing to "meet competitive prices" or "whatever customers will pay." Most firms have never conducted marketing research, few have good information about competition, and most do not prepare and use sales forecasts and sales reports to the product level.

These results indicate general weaknesses in product management regarding costs and margins, competition, markets, and in the fundamental practice of forecasting and sales reporting.

Factors that Affect SMMs' Ability to Develop Direct Costs

There are several factors affecting SMMs' inclination to have and use reliable cost data, including the size of company (smaller firms tend to have fewer resources), type of company (job shop versus product), type

Table 40. Product Management Practices

	Total companies	Job shop				Product				Type			
		1	2	3	Total	1	2	3	Total	1	2	3	Total
Total companies	126	12	27	16	55	14	36	21	71	26	63	37	126
Costing & pricing — Discount at least 25%	95	6	22	12	40	10	28	17	55	16	50	29	95
Have pricing problems	79	9	17	12	38	5	21	15	41	14	38	27	79
Have target margins	60	1	11	5	17	6	22	15	43	7	33	20	60
Don't know material and labor costs	42	2	13	6	21	1	11	9	21	3	24	15	42
Meet target margins	15	0	2	1	3	2	7	3	12	2	9	4	15
Market & competitor intelligence — Have never conducted marketing research	78	4	19	11	34	2	28	14	44	6	47	25	78
Know number of prospective customers	21	0	2	3	5	0	11	5	16	0	13	8	21
Collect information about competitors at least informally	20	0	3	1	4	1	12	3	16	1	15	4	20
Sales fore-casting & reporting — Report to product level	52	0	6	0	6	5	24	17	46	5	30	17	52
Forecast to product level	35	0	4	1	5	2	15	13	30	2	19	14	35
Compare actual to forecast	19	0	2	0	2	0	5	12	17	0	7	12	19

of product (simple versus complex), and unit production versus process-ing production. Questionnaire data showed that 11% of Type 1 compa-nies reported having actual material and labor costs compared with about 40% for Types 2 and 3 firms. Nearly 40% of Types 2 and 3 job shops reported having material and labor costs compared with about 30% for Types 2 and 3 product companies.

Simple products (jobs or work orders for job shops and machine companies) obviously present less of a challenge to cost than do complex products, and product companies that produce and sell a small number of products have a simpler costing task than do companies with multiple products.

These examples illustrate the challenges and issues companies face in getting to actual unit costs and help explain why multiple pricing methods are used, even when they know actual direct material and labor costs. Forty-two companies who reported knowing both direct material and labor costs, in addition to using "actual cost plus margin"—a very widely used method—also used "meet competitive prices," "estimated cost plus margin," and "whatever customers will pay" and others. No doubt that market and competitive forces, operational issues, product line depth and breadth, and product complexity make difficult the task of accurate costing and pricing and help explain why firms reported pricing problems and were discounting to get the sale.

Table 41. Multiple Pricing Methods

		Job shop				Product				Type			
		1	2	3	Total	1	2	3	Total	1	2	3	Total
	Know both direct material and labor costs	**2**	**13**	**6**	**21**	**1**	**11**	**9**	**21**	**3**	**24**	**15**	**42**
Pricing method	Actual cost plus margin	0	5	4	9	1	6	7	14	1	11	11	23
	Meet competitive prices	1	4	2	7	1	5	8	14	2	9	10	21
	Estimated cost plus margin	1	4	1	6	0	6	7	13	1	10	8	19
	Whatever customers will pay	1	3	1	5	0	4	4	8	1	7	5	13
	Standard cost plus margin	0	4	3	7	0	4	1	5	0	8	4	12
	Below competition	0	0	1	1	0	1	2	3	0	1	3	4
	Target margin	0	0	1	1	0	1	0	1	0	1	1	2
	Time and materials	0	0	1	1	0	0	0	0	0	0	1	1

SMMs must also account for overhead costs, such as rent, depreciation, factory and office salaries and benefits, utility costs, and others in their pricing, which can be difficult to do accurately across all products and services.

"We Keep It in the Product Line Because It Absorbs Overhead"

I've heard, "We keep it in the product line because it absorbs overhead," many times. Technically, any product or service will absorb overhead as long as its selling price exceeds the direct variable costs to produce and sell it. If the SP = $100 and direct costs (usually direct material and direct labor) = $90 the $10 difference (contribution margin) will absorb $10 in fixed overhead. If fixed OH is $100,000 the firm will need to sell 10,000 units to cover overhead just to break even.

Overhead is typically covered by allocating (spreading) its cost over the number of units or services produced. If a company cannot sell the break even volume it cannot cover its overhead. In the previous example, if the firm sold 10,001 units—one past the break even point—it would realize a $10 profit. This is an example of cost accounting, which does not use allocations of overhead per unit to cover overhead but rather the contribution margin and the dollar amount of overhead. Financial accounting, which most businesses use, allocates (spreads) manufacturing overhead dollars over products and services, based on an estimate of the amount of products and services to be sold—the sales forecast. If the business sells less than the forecast, overhead will not be absorbed or covered, thus resulting in loss. Similarly, in the cost accounting example, if 9,999 units are sold the company would have a $10 loss.

Figure 26 is a very basic illustration of the financial accounting method of spreading $500,000 in manufacturing overhead costs over 10,000 units of production, adding $50 ($500,000 / 10,000 units) for manufacturing overhead per unit to $25 of direct costs to arrive at a total unit manufacturing cost of $75. Adding a 33% markup ($75 × 33% = $25) to cover other fixed costs, such as SG&A at $150,000 ($150,000 / 10,000 = $15 to cover SG&A and $10 for profit), and to provide a profit produces a $100 unit selling price, which is the "actual cost plus margin" pricing method.

Mfg OH = rent, depreciation, telephone, insurance, licenses, salaries and benefits, utilities, etc.	$500,000
SG&A OH = office salaries, insurance, licenses, office supplies, other	$150,000
Total unit sales forecasted	10,000
Direct material and labor per unit	$25
Mfg. OH per unit	50
Total unit mfg. cost	$75
SG&A OH per unit @ 33% of mfg. cost	25
Unit selling price	$100

Figure 26. Basic overhead calculation for financial accounting and cost plus pricing.

Financial accounting					
Costing/Pricing			Unit sales volume	8,667	
Selling price	$100	100%	Sales	$866,667	100%
Direct material	15	15%	Direct material	130,000	15%
Direct labor	10	10%	Direct labor	86,667	10%
Mfg. OH	50	50%	Mfg. OH	500,000	58%
Total Mfg. Cost	$75	75%	Gross profit	$150,000	17%
SG&A and profit @ 33% of Cost	$25		SG&A	150,000	17%
			Profit (Loss)	$0	0%

Figure 27. Financial accounting at breakeven.

Figures 27–33 illustrate the effect on profit of not selling enough to cover overhead (under absorbing), of selling at breakeven, and of selling more than forecast, which more than covers overhead (over absorbing). Both the financial and cost accounting formats are illustrated.

Figure 27 shows the previous costing and pricing calculation on the left based on 10,000 units forecasted and on the right a basic income statement at break-even units of 8,667. Note that although the cost plus pricing method arrived at a price of $100 and 25% gross profit ($100 minus $75 total manufacturing cost = $25 gross profit) the actual gross profit of $150,000 at $866,667 in sales is 17 percent. This is because at the less-than-forecasted sales volume (8,667 units versus 10,000) manufacturing overhead accounts for 58% of sales rather than 50%, according to the cost calculation, leaving a smaller gross profit.

Cost accounting					
Costing/Pricing			Unit sales volume	8,667	
Selling price	$100	100%	Sales	$866,667	100%
Direct material	15	15%	Dir. var. costs	216,667	25%
Direct labor	10	10%	Cont. margin	$650,000	75%
			Fixed costs (mfg. and SG&A)	650,000	75%
Contribution Margin	**$75**	**75%**	Profit (Loss)	$0	0%

Figure 28. Cost accounting at breakeven.

Financial accounting					
Costing/Pricing			Unit sales volume	7,000	
Selling price	$100	100%	Sales	$700,000	100%
Direct material	15	15%	Direct material	105,000	15%
Direct labor	10	10%	Direct labor	70,000	10%
Mfg. OH	50	50%	Mfg. OH	500,000	71%
Total Mfg. Cost	$75	75%	Gross profit	$25,000	4%
SG&A and profit @ 33% of Cost	$25		SG&A	150,000	21%
			Profit (Loss)	($125,000)	-18%

Figure 29. Amount under-absorbed.

	Unit volume =	7,000
	Fixed $ to absorb	Actual $ absorbed
Mfg. unit OH @ $50	$500,000	$350,000
SGA	150,000	175,000
	$650,000	$525,000
Amount under-absorbed		($125,000)

Figure 30. Financial accounting at a loss, under-absorbing overhead.

Figure 28 shows the same information in the cost accounting format. Note that while the cost plus pricing method resulted in a 25% gross profit margin, the cost accounting contribution margin is 75 percent, which is a very good margin that could provide significant flexibility in negotiating price discounts, which are discussed in the next section.

Figures 29 to 33 illustrate the effects of lower and higher sales volumes on profit caused by under-absorbing overhead (lower sales volume than forecasted) and by over-absorbing overhead (higher sales volume than forecasted).

Cost accounting					
Costing/Pricing			Unit sales volume	7,000	
Selling price	$100	100%	Sales	$700,000	100%
Direct material	15	15%	Dir. var. costs	175,000	25%
Direct labor	10	10%	Cont. margin	$525,000	75%
Contribution Margin	$75	75%	Fixed costs (mfg. and SG&A)	650,000	93%
			Profit (Loss)	($125,000)	−18%

Figure 31. Cost accounting at a loss.

Financial accounting					
Costing/Pricing			Unit sales volume	10,000	
Selling price	$100	100%	Sales	$1,000,000	100%
Direct material	15	15%	Direct material	150,000	15%
Direct labor	10	10%	Direct labor	100,000	10%
Mfg. OH	50	50%	Mfg. OH	500,000	50%
Total Mfg. Cost	$75	75%	Gross profit	$250,000	25%
SG&A and profit @ 33% of Cost	$25				
			SG&A	150,000	15%
			Profit (Loss)	$100,000	10%

Figure 32. Financial accounting at a profit.

Cost accounting					
Costing/Pricing			Unit sales volume	10,000	
Selling price	$100	100%	Sales	$1,000,000	100%
Direct material	15	15%	Dir. var. costs	250,000	25%
Direct labor	10	10%	Cont. margin	$750,000	75%
Contribution Margin	$75	75%	Fixed costs (mfg. and SG&A)	650,000	65%
			Profit (Loss)	$100,000	10%

Figure 33. Cost accounting at a profit.

Figure 29 shows a loss of $125,000 due to selling less than the fore-casted 10,000 units and Figure 30 shows why. Each unit was allocated $50 to cover the $500,000 in manufacturing OH ($500,000 ÷ 10,000), but since only 7,000 were sold unit sales only covered $350,000 of over-head (7,000 × $50). The SG&A allocation of $15 per unit ($150,000 ÷ 10,000) × 7,000 covered $105,000 and the $10 margin per unit provided $70,000, totaling $175,000, exceeding the $150,000 SG&A by $25,000 (over absorption). But the unabsorbed $150,000 of manufacturing overhead caused an overall profit loss of −$125,000 (−$150,000 unabsorbed Mfg. OH + $125,000 absorbed SGA OH = −$125,000 loss). Figure 31 shows the same loss in the cost accounting format without allocations for overhead—just contribution margin less fixed costs.

Figure 32 illustrates unit sales at the 10,000 unit forecast resulting in a $100,000 profit because manufacturing and SG&A overhead allocations and the $10 profit margin sufficiently covered overhead. Similarly, contribution margin in Figure 33 exceeds fixed costs.

Note: Figures 29 to 33 illustrate variations in profit due to changes in sales volume only. In financial accounting where absorption costing is used, increases and decreases in inventory—which were not illustrated for simplicity—also affect profits.

These examples are not meant as primers in accounting but rather as illustrations of how profit is affected by unit costing, allocations of overhead, the spread between the selling price and direct costs, and sales volume: This is known as the *cost–volume–profit* relationship.

Cost –   As pointed out earlier, many SMMs estimate product costs because they don't know the actual costs. The addition of allocations for manufacturing and SG&A overhead—spread across products based on a production forecast—and an estimated profit margin result in estimated prices. This method of pricing is the common cost-plus-pricing that can lead to discounting when market and competitive factors are encountered.

Volume – Since many SMMS don't conduct marketing research and don't know where to find new customers for more sales, it's difficult for them to forecast sales, which many do only on the company level—not on the product level. Yet pricing derived from allocating overhead is based on production estimates that may not have any relevance to a product sales forecast.

Price –   Table 40 showed that 79 of 126 firms reported pricing problems and 95 reported having to discount at least 25%. Table 41 showed questionnaire results listing several pricing methods in addition to cost-plus—such as meet competitors' prices, whatever the customer will pay, and so on—stemming from not knowing costs or competitors' or market pricing and pricing high as a cautionary measure.

Clearly, establishing prices—even where cost-plus pricing is used—is very problematic for SMMs. It begins with uncertainty about costs, then migrates through overhead allocations based on estimates about production and sales volumes and an estimate for profit, ends with a guess about market pricing, and often is discounted. Product management needs to know product costs to be able to establish accurate pricing, to identify winners and losers, and to cull out those incapable of supporting profitable growth—including those kept in the product line just to absorb overhead.

The owner of BuzzCo Machining, Inc. showed me a curved roof knife blade he produced for a customer because it absorbed overhead. *C-P-M*™ analysis revealed its 11% contribution margin with very low volume. That product obviously could not absorb much overhead. He eventually stopped producing it because, even at low volume, it competed for machining time with more profitable products and consumed finished inventory storage space. This is a good example of why "We keep it in the product line just to absorb overhead," is not such a good rationale for keeping low-margin products. The smaller the contribution margin percent, the less overhead a product will absorb, the less profitable it will be, and the weaker the justification for keeping it. Profit analysis using contribution margin can identify low-margin (low absorbing) products whereas gross profit margin—because it includes an amount for overhead absorption—might obscure a product's true profitability. Sales people, however, will argue in favor of preserving some products to fill out the product offering, to keep some customers happy, or to complement other products. Without good costing, pricing based on insights into market and competitive pricing, and overhead allocations based on a reasonable sales volume forecast, product management is at a disadvantage.

The Price Is Right

Since the 79 firms with pricing problems shown in Table 40 reported actual cost plus margin as their most used pricing method, and the previous material described problems of not knowing actual direct labor in addition to problems using it as a basis for allocating overhead, it is reasonable to say that combining uncertain direct labor cost with approximate overhead allocations makes effective pricing all the more difficult.

Because of the uncertainty of direct costs and overhead allocation practices, SMMs desiring to operate more profitably might not confidently be able to decide whether to accept a discounted price that will lessen profit or to hold onto the price. The decision is often to take the discount because the additional volume will absorb overhead at a minimum. However, because of the uncertainty of direct cost upon which an estimate of overhead is allocated, the company will not know the extent of the discount on profit—only trusting that it can make it up on volume.

Fortunately, the contribution format provides an alternative to absorption costing and pricing SMMs can use to decide whether to "hold'em or fold'em"—stay with the quoted price or take the discount. Again, separating direct costs from fixed and overhead costs is the key. The following material describes three company's analyses of cost, feedback from lost orders, and market information to develop policies and guidelines to address discounting and target margins.

Good business practices call for establishing a budget and sales forecast at the beginning of a planning period, usually the company's fiscal year (FY). Padco Industries, Inc. used its 2011 income statement as a starting point to provide estimates of direct costs and fixed and overhead costs to establish FY 2012 pricing that would increase profit 20% over 2011 from $232,000 to about $275,000 (Figure 34).

Product sales split slightly in favor of product C at 40%, which generated the most profit. Pricing for A and B experienced about 25% discounting according to quote sheets and lost order analysis, while C had maintained price.

In the course of contemplating its 2012 pricing policy and strategy, Padco reviewed the costs of 2011 to evaluate cost plus pricing. Manufacturing overhead and direct labor would remain at about $874,000 and $442,000 for 2012, and so would average factory wages at $20 and direct labor hours worked out at about 22,100 annually (Mfg. OH as a percentage of direct labor was about 198% or about 2 to 1). Management saw

			Products					
Padco 2011 income statement			A		B		C	
($,1000s)			35%		25%		40%	
Sales	$2,456	100%	$860	100%	$614	100%	$982	100%
Materials	614	25%	198	23%	209	34%	207	21%
Direct labor	442	18%	169	20%	104	17%	145	15%
Mfg. OH	874	36%	335	39%	206	34%	287	29%
CGS	$1,930	79%	$702	82%	$520	85%	$640	65%
Gross Profit	$526	21%	$158	18%	$94	15%	$342	35%
Gen. & Adm.	$165	7%						
Operating Profit	$361	15%						
Sales & Marketing								
Commission	$84	3%						
Salaries, other	45	2%						
Total	$129	5%						
Pre-tax profit	$232	9%						

Figure 34. Padco 2011 income statement.

that it would need to allocate about $40 of overhead for each direct labor hour in its products (Figure 35). Additionally, it had been adding a 50% markup to total manufacturing cost for office and selling overhead and for profit.

Figure 36 shows the products' 2011 performance for unit volume, average selling price after discounts, direct material and labor costs, and estimated manufacturing overhead and markups. Allocated manufacturing overhead, which amounted to 198% of direct lepra, accounted for between 40% and 48% of total product cost. Markup to cover general, administrative, and selling expenses, added another 50% to cost. Cost plus resulted in 2011 unit selling prices of $337, $635, and $342. In total, allocated manufacturing overhead and SG&A markup added between 250% and 290% to the products' direct cost.

Padco wanted a costing and pricing alternative to cost plus that could help it make routine quick decisions about price discounts. While giving up some margin in 2011 had not significantly hurt profitability, it wanted a way quickly to determine if trading margin for volume would help attain its 2012 profit target of $275,000.

According to lost order analysis and sales reports, 2011 cost plus prices for A and B exceeded market prices by over 20%, which reflected

2011 Mfg. overhead allocation	
Mfg. OH	$874,000
Direct Labor	442,080
Avg. Wage	$20
Dir. Labor Hrs.	22,104
Mfg. OH/Hr.	$40
Mfg. OH % DL	198%

Figure 35. Padco Mfg. OH allocation.

2011 Product performance summary						
	A		**B**		**C**	
Volume	3,126		1,289		2,808	
Avg. Unit SP	$275	100%	$500	100%	$350	100%
Dir. Matl.	63	23%	170	34%	74	21%
Dir. Labor	54	20%	85	17%	52	15%
OH Allocation	107	39%	168	34%	102	29%
Tot. Mfg. Cost	$225	82%	$423	85%	$228	65%
50% Markup SGA and Profit	112		212		114	
Cost Plus SP	$337		$635		$342	
$ Over Market	$62		$135		($8)	
% Over Market	22%		27%		−2%	

Figure 36. Padco 2011 product performance summary.

the price discount experience of the two products (Figure 36). C's cost plus price matched or fell below market by a very small amount. This led management to conclude that A and B were more susceptible to discounting than C and conducted "what if" scenarios on different prices to estimate the impact on volume and margin.

It used 2011 average selling prices as the basis for changing prices between −10% and +10%, and estimated corresponding increases or decreases in volume between −5% and +25%, assuming discounted prices would increase sales and that higher prices would reduce sales (Table 42).

In taking this approach, Padco reformulated the question, "What can be done to increase sales volume?" to "How can pricing be used to increase profit?"

Table 42. Padco's CVP Analysis for 2012 Pricing Policy

Scenarios		Selling price		Volume		Target cost-volume-profit range		2012 Projections			
		% Change from 2011	Avg. selling price	% Change from 2011	Unit volume	Sales ($1,000)	% of total sales	Cm%	CM$ ($1,000)	Pre-tax profit ($1,000)	Pre-tax profit %
		A	B	C	D	E	F	G	H	I	J
1	A	0%	275	0%	3,126	$860	35%	54%	$468		
	B	0%	500	0%	1,228	614	25%	44%	271		
	C	0%	350	0%	2,808	983	40%	61%	601		
	Company Total				7,162	$2,456	100%	55%	$1,339	$232	9%
2	A	–10%	248	20%	3,751	$928	35%	50%	$461		
	B	–10%	450	20%	1,474	663	25%	38%	255		
	C	–10%	315	20%	3,370	1,061	40%	57%	607		
	Company Total				8,594	$2,653	100%	50%	$1,323	$215	8%
3	A	–5%	261	10%	3,439	$898	35%	52%	$468		
	B	–5%	475	10%	1,351	642	25%	41%	266		
	C	–5%	333	10%	3,089	1,027	40%	59%	609		
	Company Total				7,878	$2,567	100%	52%	$1,343	$235	9%

4	A	5%	289	−5%	2,970	$858	35%	56%	$484		
	B	5%	525	−5%	1,167	612	25%	47%	285		
	C	5%	368	−5%	2,668	980	40%	63%	616		
	Company Total				6,804	$2,450	100%	57%	$1,385	$278	11%
5	A	10%	303	−15%	2,657	$804	35%	58%	$468		
	B	10%	550	−15%	1,044	574	25%	49%	280		
	C	10%	385	−15%	2,387	919	40%	64%	592		
	Company Total				6,088	$2,297	100%	58%	$1,340	$233	10%
6	A	10%	303	−20%	2,501	$756	35%	58%	$441		
	B	10%	550	−20%	982	540	25%	49%	263		
	C	10%	385	−20%	2,246	865	40%	64%	557		
	Company Total				5,730	$2,162	100%	58%	$1,261	$154	7%
7	A	−10%	248	25%	3,908	$967	35%	50%	$480		
	B	−10%	450	25%	1,535	691	25%	38%	266		
	C	−10%	315	25%	3,510	1,106	40%	57%	632		
	Company Total				8,953	$2,764	100%	50%	$1,378	$270	10%

The company's summary of six "what if" calculations show the ranges of price and volume for A, B, and C, assuming its manufacturing and SG&A overhead costs would not significantly change in 2012 is shown in Table 42.

Analysis of Table 42

Scenario 1 restates 2011 prices and unit volumes to be able to evaluate scenarios 2–7.

In Scenarios 2–7
    Col. A shows the percent increase/decrease from 2011 Avg. selling prices.
    Col. B shows the resulting 2012 selling prices.
    Col. C shows the percent increase/decrease from 2011 unit volumes.
    Col. D shows the resulting 2012 unit volumes.
    Cols. E to J show the projected results on 2010 sales, contribution margin, and pre-tax profit.

Scenario 1 is no change in selling price or volume.

Scenario 2 lowered selling prices by 10% and increased volume by 20%, showing a pre-tax profit of $215,000, less than in 2011. Trading higher volume for lower price (and contribution margin) did not increase profit.

Scenario 3 lowered selling prices only by 5%, show a small estimated increase in volume of 5%, but produced a pre-tax profit almost equal to 2011.

Scenario 4 increased prices by 5% and estimated a volume decrease of 5%, but showed a projected pre-tax profit near the firm's 2012 target of $275,000. Management realized that unit selling price affected profitability more than volume; fewer units in this scenario (6,804) produced more margin than more units in *Scenario 3* (7,878).

Scenario 5 continued with higher prices and lower volume, but pre-tax profit fell. Although contribution margin percent slightly increased, contribution margin dollars decreased due to lower volume.

In *Scenario 6*, the company wanted to test the impact of a 20% volume decrease with a 10% price increase. Management concluded that combination diminished profit too much and that a 15% volume decrease was all it could accept in a trade between price, margin, and volume.

After *Scenario 2* confirmed that trading lower price (and contribution margin $) for higher volume reduced profit, the company was curious to see how much volume would be needed to reach its 2012 profit target of $275,000 if it reduced prices 10%. *Scenario 7* showed that a 25% volume increase would be needed, leading management to conclude that the situation would cause serious production problems and bottlenecks. *Scenario 4*, even with a small price increase but about a third less volume and generating about the same profit, was a better alternative.

Padco found the contribution format approach to costing and pricing easier to use than having to work through overhead allocations and that by using only price and volume variations it could quickly determine the impact those two variables would have on profit. It concluded that cost plus pricing, while providing a sound basis for covering overhead and profit, had resulted in prices higher than market and with contribution pricing it could revise them down and still operate profitably. Pricing for 2012 would be set at the average unit prices experienced in 2011 and that discounting between 5% and 10% could be accepted—if offset by compensating volume increases. Discounts of 20–25% experienced in 2011 were too deep to make up with volume.

The firm's 2012 pricing policy (Figure 37) and strategy sets forth prices based on 2011 average pricing, which it considered "market" after having to take discounts in 2011 and evaluating market and customer feedback from lost order and sales reports.

Base prices are quoted at 5% percent over market, but will allow 5–10% discounting with compensating volume increases of at least 5–10%.

Product C, whose cost plus price approximates market and did not experience much discounting in 2011, will not be discounted unless accompanied by a commensurate volume increase.

Two factors enabled Padco to decide confidently to accept discounting and include it in its pricing policy and strategy:

1. operating above breakeven and
2. good contribution margins—above 25% to 30%.

2012 Pricing policy & strategy			
	A	B	C
Cost Plus Prices	$337	$635	$342
Market Price @ 2011 Average	$275	$500	$350
SP @ 5% Above Market	$289	$525	$368
Direct Material	63	170	74
Direct Labor	54	85	52
CM $	$171	$245	$224
CM %	59%	47%	61%
SP @ 5% Discount From Market	$261	$475	$333
CM $	144	220	207
CM %	55%	46%	62%
(Volume increase 5% to 10%)			
SP @ 10% Discount From Market	$248	$450	N/A
CM $	130	195	
CM %	53%	43%	
(Volume increase 5% to 10%)			

Figure 37. Padco's 2012 pricing policy.

Chapter 2 explained that profit is not realized until sales revenue exceeds total costs—total variable and fixed costs. Companies with low-margin products that cannot support price discounts will take longer to reach breakeven and profitability than with more profitable products. Discounting low-margin products extends the time and volume needed to break even and be profitable. Although higher sales volume is the solution to breakeven, attempting to increase volume by discounting low-margin products is counterproductive. Companies operating above breakeven already have covered direct and fixed costs so any additional sales—even discounted—will add to profit as long as net revenue exceeds direct costs—as long as contribution margin is positive.

Job shops and machine companies calculate their shop rates similar to product companies' cost plus method. They divide manufacturing overhead by the estimated number of direct labor hours to be worked,

Mfg. OH @ $1,139,000

30 direct labor employees

50 weeks/yr. @ 37.5 hours/week

56,250 estimate DL hours/year

$$\frac{\$1,139,000}{56,250} = \$20.00 \text{ OH per direct labor hour}$$

Direct labor hourly wage	$20
Mfg. OH per direct labor hour	20
Burdened factory labor	$40
50% markup for SG&A + profit	20
Fully-burdened shop rate	$60

Figure 38. Sample shop rate for job shops and machine companies.

add the average hourly factory wage, and add markup for SG&A at about 50% to get the shop rate per hour to charge for services. Figure 38 shows a $60 shop rate composed of average hourly factory wage at $20, manufacturing OH per direct labor hour also at $20, and $20 markup for SG&A at 50% of burdened factory labor.

The owner of BuzzCo Machining, Inc. told me that customers and prospects balked when he quoted his shop rate, saying they did not want to pay that much: They obviously had some idea about job shops and machine companies markup and pricing practices. After compiling several hundred work orders, I calculated BuzzCo's average contribution margin at 48%, with the low at −40% and the high at 83%. Since a 48% contribution margin provides a good spread between direct costs and selling price, BuzzCo's pricing contained sufficient cushion to discount price in the event he got into a competitive situation and wanted the work.

I described the contribution format method of costing and pricing and showed him the following examples comparing cost plus and contribution costing and pricing.

His typical cost plus pricing, shown in Figure 39, produced a price of $147.50. The second example using the contribution format showed the $147.50 produced a 56% contribution margin—notably higher than BuzzCo's 48% average contribution margin.

I suggested he use both pricing methods. First, use cost plus to derive a price he knows will cover manufacturing OH, SG&A markup, and profit. Second, use contribution pricing to determine the amount of discount he

Typical job quote @ cost plus		
Direct material	$25.00	17%
Plus 10% markup	2.50	2%
Total material cost	$27.50	19%
DL @ 2 hrs @ shop rate $60	120.00	81%
Total job cost and price	$147.50	100%
Contribution Format @ 56% CM		
DL @ 2 hrs. factory wage	$40.00	27%
Direct material @ cost	25.00	17%
Total direct cost	$65.00	44%
Contribution margin	$82.50	56%
Total job cost and price	$147.50	100%
Contribution Format @ 45% CM		
DL @ 2 hrs. factory wage	$40.00	34%
Direct material @ cost	25.00	21%
Total direct cost	$65.00	55%
Contribution margin	$53.00	45%
Total job cost and price	$118.00	100%

Figure 39. BuzzCo's job quoting.

could accept if he had to lower price to get the work. If market price for this job was 20% below his $147.50 quote (see the following calculation example at 45% target margin), he could quickly calculate the contribution margin of meeting this price: He could lower price and be assured of maintaining a margin close to his 48% average.

The calculation for this uses total direct cost and target contribution margin percent as follows:

$147.50 − 20% discount = $118.00 reduced SP

$118.00 − $65 direct cost = $53.00 contribution margin

$53.00 ÷ $118.00 = 45% contribution margin

or

$$\frac{\text{Total direct cost}}{1-\text{target margin}\%} = \frac{\$65.00}{1-45\%} = \frac{\$65.00}{55\%} = \$118.00$$

The combined approach allowed BuzzCo's to avoid having to quote his shop rate and to quickly calculate a job's margin if he had to lower price to get it. It also led to establishing a pricing policy and framework for evaluating the business' performance on a monthly basis using just three factors: sales volume, contribution margin, and fixed costs—the three primary factors involved in the contribution format.

BuzzCo's 2011 income statement in Figure 40 shows sales at $2.7 million, contribution margin at 48%, and fixed costs at $1.2 million (Mfg. OH and SG&A). BuzzCo's owner wanted to grow the business and thought 10% sales growth would be achievable, based on past quote production, hit rate, and average sales per work order.

He had been winning over 500 quotes annually, about 50% of total submitted, and averaged about $5,400 per won bid. Growing sales about 10% to $3,000,000 would require about 550 successful quotes ($3,000,000 ÷ $5,400), about 50 more than 2011. (*Note: This is another example of using quote analysis to inform a sales forecast.*)

Using the contribution format, he calculated that a 10% sales increase to $3,000,000 would more than double the pre-tax profit from $89,280 to over $220,000 due to the firm's good contribution margin and cost structure—the combination of variable and fixed cost—which he did not expect to materially change. Just by increasing sales at the same contribution margin of 48% and maintaining overhead costs BuzzCo could add $133,800 to its bottom line, increasing pre-tax profit from 3% to 7% (Figure 41).

BuzzCo's growth plan called for a monthly review of three basic items:

Financial format			Contribution format		
Sales	$2,720,682	100%	Sales	$2,720,682	100%
Direct material	515,678	19%			
Direct labor	901,723	33%	Direct material	515,678	19%
Mfg. OH	1,139,000	42%	Direct labor	901,723	33%
CGS	$2,556,402	94%	Total Direct Cost	$1,417,401	52%
Gross Profit	$164,280	6%	Contribution Margin	$1,303,281	48%
Selling, Gen. & Adm.	75,000	3%	Fixed Costs	1,214,000	45%
Pre-tax Profit	$89,280	3%	Pre-tax Profit	$89,281	3%

Figure 40. BuzzCo's 2011 income statement.

Financial format			Contribution format		
Sales	$3,000,000	100%	Sales	$3,000,000	110%
Direct material	568,620	19%			
Direct labor	994,298	33%	Direct material	568,620	19%
Mfg. OH	1,139,000	38%	Direct labor	994,298	33%
CGS	$2,701,918	90%	Total Direct Cost	$1,562,918	52%
Gross Profit	$298,082	11%	Contribution Margin	$1,437,082	48%
Selling, Gen. & Adm.	75,000	3%	Fixed Costs	1,214,000	40%
Pre-tax Profit	$223,082	7%	Pre-tax Profit	$223,082	7%

Figure 41. BuzzCo's projected 2012 income statement.

1. Monitoring quote production and sales volume. BuzzCo needed to make sure the sales team was on target to add 50 quotes and to maintain its 50% hit rate at an average of $5,400 per quote won.

2. Managing contribution margin. The work order analysis showed a wide range of contribution margin, from −40% to 83%, but averaging about 48%. BuzzCo's owner felt he could use contribution pricing selectively to discount prices to promote volume, but would decline jobs with less than 40% contribution margin unless there was compensating volume. For example, in Figure 42, should a customer or a prospect want a 15% discount off BuzzCo's quoted $25 price containing a 48% contribution margin, reducing the price to $21.25, BuzzCo could negotiate for more volume to maintain the $480 margin. In this example, 58 units at the lower price would maintain BuzzCo's minimum 40% target margin at $478.50 for the job. If the customer could not accommodate higher volume at this lower price BuzzCo would need to decide to "hold'm or fold'm."

   Accepting the 15% discount would reduce margin to $330, which would work toward the sales volume target but diminish profit. This is a frequent situation for job shops and machine companies where contribution pricing can facilitate the decision to accept or decline a job. It is a classic example of trading volume for margin and of how to reach a "reasoned" decision based on CVP analysis.

3. Controlling fixed costs. BuzzCo's owner did not expect to have to increase fixed costs during 2012 and believed he could limit overhead costs to about $1,000 per month.

Target pricing		Reduced margin @ 15% discount	Equivalent volume @ 15% discount
Unit SP	$25.00	$21.25	$21.25
Material	4.75	4.75	4.75
Labor	8.25	8.25	8.25
Unit cost	$13.00	$13.00	$13.00
Volume	40	40	58
Revenue	$1,000.00	$850.00	$1,232.50
Total cost	520.00	520.00	754.00
Contribution margin	$480.00	$330.00	$478.50
CM %	48%	39%	39%

Figure 42. BuzzCo's target margin pricing.

Incremental—or Marginal Pricing—and Break-even Sales

CVP analysis shows the effect on profit by discounting price in return for more volume to make up for lost contribution margin dollars. Incremental, or marginal, pricing (incremental pricing, marginal pricing, and contribution margin pricing are interchangeable terms) also involves lowering price to get the sale, but takes break-even sales into account.

Knowing your company's break-even point and when it is reached can allow management to consider creative pricing strategies and to take on business that otherwise might not seem desirable. Figure 43 illustrates a 9-month Y-T-D (year to date) situation where Ben Hill Manufacturing, Inc., a men's contract trouser manufacturer, is approaching breakeven and has posted a Y-T-D 7% pre-tax margin of $436,470 nine months into the fiscal year.

Annual overhead runs about $2,000,000 with monthly overhead about $166,667 ($2,000,000 ÷ 12). Break-even sales, based on historical 30% contribution margin, are about $6,666,667. Although 3 months of booked sales remain, the firm has additional production capacity and is considering taking on $500,000 in less profitable business from Sears and J.C. Penney at 20% contribution margin. The company owner calculated that year-end sales without the less profitable business would produce a $776,470 profit, but with the incremental business it could increase profits from $100,000 to $876,470.

Incremental pricing offers flexibility to pricing policy that calls for meeting target margins and covering overhead. In this example, Ben Hill's

9 Month sales Y-T-D			Booked sales remaining 3 months @ 30% cm		Incremental sales remaining 3 months @ 20% cm	
Sales	$6,454,900	100%	$2,800,000	100%	$500,000	100%
Material	3,227,450	50%				
Labor	1,290,980	20%				
Contribution Margin	1,936,470	30%	840,000	30%	$100,000	20%
Overhead	1,500,000		500,000		0	
Pre-tax Profit	$436,470	7%	$340,000	12%	$100,000	

	12 Month Income Statement w/o Incremental Sales		12 Month Income Statement with Incremental Sales		Difference	
Sales	$9,254,900	100%	$9,754,900	100%	$500,000	
Contribution Margin	2,776,470	30%	2,876,470	29%	100,000	
Overhead	2,000,000	22%	2,000,000	21%	0	
Pre-tax Profit	$776,470	8%	$876,470	9%	$100,000	

Figure 43. Ben Hill's incremental pricing.

owner wanted to evaluate the impact on profit of producing and selling more volume but at a lower margin.

The company was able to consider this pricing strategy because:

1. It knew its break-even sales level and when it would reach it,
2. It knew direct costs,
3. It had available production capacity, and
4. The additional work would not require any increase in overhead.

Ben Hill's owner had been contracting with Sears and J.C. Penny and knew they were also sourcing from Mexican factories but needed domestic suppliers to balance out production levels, and would give him work even if he were slightly above Mexican pricing.

He typically used cost plus pricing, which involves multiplying direct unit cost by a factor of 2.5 to 3.0 to cover overhead and profit. As shown in the following example (Figure 44), when the 2.5 or 3.0 factor was applied to his average $4 per unit cost for direct material and direct labor, cost plus pricing resulted in a much higher selling price than contribution margin or incremental (marginal) pricing.

Unit Cost/Price	
Material + 10%	$3.00
Labor	1.00
Total unit cost	$4.00
Cost plus pricing	
SP @ Factor 2.5	$10.00
SP @ Factor 3.0	$12.00
Contribution margin	
SP @ CM 20%	$5.00
	$4.00/(1 – 20%)

Figure 44. Ben Hill unit cost.

His marginal pricing resulted in a $5 selling price considerably below the $10–12 range he expected domestic competitors to quote using cost plus. Thus, he knew he could negotiate a profitable price between $5 and $10 to$12, a considerable price advantage, and maintain contribution margin close to the company's 30% average: He calculated that with the $500,000 additional business his company contribution margin at year end would be 29% with an additional $100,000 profit (see Figure 43).

While incremental pricing and discounting both involve a reduction in selling price to gain business, there are differences in the timing and situations in which they are used. As noted previously, Ben Hill was able to use incremental pricing because it knew it was approaching break-even sales, production capacity was available, and no additional fixed cost or overhead would be incurred.

1. When a firm is operating at or above breakeven, any additional (incremental) sale will add to profit as long as the selling price exceeds direct costs—contribution margin is greater than zero.
2. Production capacity must be available otherwise the firm would need to acquire additional production equipment, thus incurring investment or fixed cost, which would absorb profit and nullify the business case for taking on the incremental sale.
3. If taking on the incremental business requires any additional fixed cost or overhead (additional production capacity and administrative, for example), the incremental contribution margin dollars must exceed the fixed and overhead costs to realize a profit.

Incremental pricing should be contingent on the presence of these three conditions whereas price discounting does not require them. The Padco and BuzzCo examples of price discounting illustrated trading margin for volume to maintain contribution margin without regard to breakeven. Trading margin for volume to maintain profit levels is okay, but it might not put the firm in the black if those sales and contribution margin do not help the company exceed fixed costs to attain breakeven.

Product Mix and Sales Mix Affect Profit

There have been several examples showing how customers, volume, and low-margin versus high-margin products and services affect profit and margin.

- Customers affect profit and margin by the amount of indirect costs they require or the volume of sales they generate for the company.
- Higher volume increases profit and margin as long as contribution margin is positive.
- High-profit products and services will increase profit faster than low-profit products and services.

A corollary to the last point is that *a greater proportion* of higher-profit products and services among total sales will increase profit. This first example of Padco's 2010 income statement, Figure 45, has Product A at 35% of sales, B at 25%, and C at 40%, producing a 54% contribution margin, a $232,000 pre-tax profit, and 9% margin.

In Figure 46 Product B's decrease to 14% of sales together with commensurate increases in A and C sales percentages raises contribution margin to 55% and pre-tax margin to 11%.

Figure 47 shows Product B, the least profitable at 43% contribution margin, increasing its proportion of sales to 45%, resulting in a decrease in company contribution margin to 51%, and pre-tax margin reduced to 7%. Thus, increasing the proportion of low-margin products relative to higher-margin products lowers overall company profit and margin. Note in all three examples that total sales did not change from $2,456,000; only the composition of the sales mix changed.

	($,1000s)		A		B		C	
			35%		25%		40%	
Sales	$2,456	100%	$860	100%	$614	100%	$982	100%
Materials	614	25%	198	23%	209	34%	207	21%
Direct labor	442	18%	181	20%	115	17%	145	15%
Commission	84	3%	25	3%	30	5%	29	3%
Total Direct Cost	$1,140	46%	404	47%	354	58%	382	39%
Contribution Margin	$1,316	54%	$456	53%	$260	42%	$601	61%
Mfg. OH	$874							
Gen. & Adm.	165							
Salaries, other	45							
Total Fixed Costs	$1,084	44%						
Pre-tax Profit	$232	9%						

Figure 45. Padco sales mix #1.

	($,1000s)		A		B		C	
			43%		14%		43%	
Sales	$2,456	100%	$1,056	100%	$344	100%	$1,056	100%
Materials	583	25%	243	23%	117	34%	223	21%
Direct labor	446	18%	220	20%	69	17%	156	15%
Commission	79	3%	31	3%	17	5%	31	3%
Total Direct Cost	$1,107	45%	494	47%	203	59%	410	39%
Contribution Margin	$1,349	55%	$562	53%	$141	41%	$646	61%
Mfg. OH	$874							
Gen. & Adm.	165							
Salaries, other	45							
Total Fixed Costs	$1,084	44%						
Pre-tax Profit	$265	11%						

Figure 46. Padco sales mix #2.

The principle holds true even when total sales increase: Profit and margin increase faster when higher-profit products' sales increase relative to lower-profit products. The following two examples show a 20% increase in Padco's sales—the first by increasing only C's sales, the most profitable, and the second only B's sales, the least profitable. In Figure 48, total sales increase to $2,947,000 from $2,456,000 by increasing C's sales to $1,474,000 producing an 18% pre-tax margin.

($,1000s)			A		B		C	
			20%		45%		35%	
Sales	$2,456	100%	$491	100%	$1,105	100%	$860	100%
Materials	670	25%	113	23%	376	34%	181	21%
Direct labor	435	18%	109	20%	199	17%	127	15%
Commission	94	4%	14	3%	54	5%	25	3%
Total Direct Cost	$1,199	49%	236	48%	629	57%	334	39%
Contribution Margin	$1,257	51%	$255	52%	$477	43%	$526	61%
Mfg. OH	$874							
Gen. & Adm.	165							
Salaries, other	45							
Total Fixed Costs	$1,084	44%						
Pre-tax Profit	$173	7%						

Figure 47. Padco sales mix #3.

($,1000s)			A		B		C	
			29%		21%		50%	
Sales	$2,947	100%	$855	100%	$619	100%	$1,474	100%
Materials	718	25%	197	23%	210	34%	311	21%
Direct labor	515	18%	180	20%	116	17%	218	15%
Commission	99	3%	25	3%	30	5%	43	3%
Total Direct Cost	$1,331	45%	402	47%	357	58%	572	39%
Contribution Margin	$1,616	55%	$453	53%	$262	42%	$901	61%
Mfg. OH	$874							
Gen. & Adm.	165							
Salaries, other	45							
Total Fixed Costs	$1,084	37%						
Pre-tax Profit	$532	18%						

Figure 48. Padco sales mix #4.

In Figure 49, total sales increase 20% but by increasing only B's sales to $1,120,000; pre-tax margin decreased to 15%. Thus, increasing more of C produced a better result than B because C is inherently more profitable than B.

As the two previous examples show, selling more profitable products relative to less profitable products increases profit and margin. Maximizing

	($,1000s)		A		B		C	
			29%		38%		33%	
Sales	$2,947	100%	$855	100%	$1,120	100%	$973	100%
Materials	783	25%	197	23%	381	34%	205	21%
Direct labor	526	18%	180	20%	201	17%	144	15%
Commission	108	4%	25	3%	55	5%	29	3%
Total Direct Cost	$1,416	48%	402	47%	637	57%	378	39%
Contribution Margin	$1,531	52%	$453	53%	$483	43%	$595	61%
Mfg. OH	$874							
Gen. & Adm.	165							
Salaries, other	45							
Total Fixed Costs	$1,084	37%						
Pre-tax Profit	$447	15%						

Figure 49. Padco sales mix #5.

profitable products in the sales mix is an ideal situation, but most companies find it difficult to do.

- Product direct costs and margins often are unknown, thus
  making it difficult to determine profitability across products
  and product lines.
- Because most SMMs do not conduct market research and
  do not know the number and location of prospective new
  customers, they cannot know where to sell more profitable
  products.
- Many companies cannot make an "apples-to-apples"
  comparison to competitors' products and therefore cannot
  develop strategies to increase market share of their products
  by overcoming competitors' actions.

These conditions make it difficult for product management and sales
management to design and execute a sales mix to maximize profit.
However, even by preparing a preliminary sales forecast and sales
mix using estimates of costs and margins at the product level, a company will have taken an initial step toward strengthening product

management and positioning itself to increase profit. Doing so will set the stage for setting target margins at both the company level and product level.

Target Margins

About half the number of firms in the questionnaire reported having target margins but only about 25% said products and services met their margins, due to various reasons:

- Price discounting
- Pricing high as a cautionary measure because of not knowing costs and margins
- Not knowing competitor or market prices
- Not having competitive advantage, but rather "me too" products and services.

These reasons point to the uncertainty about setting prices and target margins and underscore the book's premise that SMMs typically operate without knowledge about their costs and margins, customers, markets, and competition. Fortunately, since costing and pricing are not exact sciences, there are practicable measures SMMs can use to cope with costing and pricing vagaries and yet pursue target margins and target pricing.

Padco and BuzzCo Machining both arrived at target margins after finding it difficult to maintain their quoted prices. Both sought an alternative to cost plus pricing that would allow them to assess margin for volume trade-offs while keeping an eye on fiscal profit targets, which led to flexible pricing policies that accommodated discounting within specified ranges as long as offsetting volume occurred. While each took a slightly different path to establishing target margins, their approaches involved the following items:

Changing their income statements to the contribution margin and segmented formats and determining:

1. Company-level and product-level profitability using contribution margin company cost structure of variable costs and fixed costs

(BuzzCo saw that a 10% increase in sales would double pre-tax profit).

2. Target or ceiling price: the price intended to achieve company's fiscal profit goals.

3. Market price: the prevailing price or price ranges determined by customer feedback, lost order analysis, requested discounts, and other market and competitor research and intelligence.

4. Floor price: the minimum acceptable price based on cost and margin analysis both at the company and product levels.

Ben Hill's owner used incremental pricing to justify taking on less profitable business while maintaining pre-tax margin. The incremental business he accepted increased both pre-tax margin percentage from 8% to 9% and added $100,000 to the bottom line. A key factor in his analysis and decision was that he knew the company was approaching break-even sales.

The following examples illustrate the three firms' target ceiling prices, market prices, and floor prices.

In Figure 50, Padco used its cost plus-derived prices as target ceiling prices assuming they would be optimal. It used 2011 average selling prices as substitutes for market pricing, which were consistent with feedback from its sales force about competitors' prices. Floor pricing was based on its pricing policy, which stipulated a maximum 10% discount from 2011 market pricing if commensurate volume accompanied the discount. Accordingly, it would not accept prices for A and B below $248 and $450, respectively. Product C would not be discounted.

BuzzCo's owner used his shop rate to set target ceiling pricing as long as the market would go along with it. However, he knew customers and

Padco	Prod A	Prod B	Prod C
Target/Ceiling Price @ Cost Plus	$337	$635	$342
2012 Market Price @ 2011 Avg.	$275	$500	$350
Floor Price @ 10% Discount From 2011 Market Price	$248	$450	N/A

Figure 50. Padco 2012 target pricing.

market forces would want discounts. Nevertheless, he expected that as long as he could maintain an average 48% contribution margin, which he felt reflected market pricing, and average monthly sales annualized to $3,000,000, he could meet his $223,000 fiscal profit projection. Although he would not accept jobs containing less than 40% contribution margin he would take on small unit volume jobs at this margin if machining capacity existed since they would have a negligible effect on total profit. Overall, he would not take jobs below 40% contribution margin if the average company contribution margin started to fall below 48%. (Figure 51)

Ben Hill's owner knew the apparel industry measured its unit direct costs for labor and material down to the penny, consistently used cost plus pricing, and that stiff domestic and import competition kept pricing low: There was no point in establishing separate target ceiling and market prices. He concentrated on total sales volume and 30% average contribution margin rather than unit pricing and used incremental pricing to evaulate lower-margin orders when he was approaching breakeven. (Figure 52)

BenHill and BuzzCo are similar in that both companies produce products for other companies, both could employ discounting, and both could employ incremental pricing. Ben Hill, however, approaching break-even sales with additional production capacity, chose incremental

BuzzCo

Target/Ceiling Price @ $60 Shop Rate	Owner would quote to see if market would accept his rate.
Market Price @ Average 48% CM	Owner used avg. 48% CM as indicator of market price.
Floor Price	Decline jobs less than 40% CM.

Figure 51. BuzzCo target pricing.

Ben Hill

Target/Ceiling Price @ Cost Plus with Factor Range of 2.5 to 3.0 of Direct Cost	Similar industry pricing based on cost plus.
Market Price	
Floor Price	30% average CM for company, invoking marginal pricing when advantageous.

Figure 52. Ben Hill target pricing.

marginal pricing after analyzing the impact on margin and dollar profit and saw that the incremental revenue would only slightly reduce CM to 29% but maintain pre-tax profit in the 8–9% range.

It should be apparent that setting target margins cannot be done in a vacuum—that certain conditions and circumstances should exist to improve chances for their success.

- Reformatting the income statement to contribution margin format facilitates understanding the company's cost structure (proportion of variable and fixed costs to total costs) enabling it to forecast the impact on profit due to changes in price and volume. It is also critical in determining the company's break-even sales, which is important to know in the case where the firm is or has been operating at a loss due to insufficient volume. (Discounting can be counterproductive when oper-ating below breakeven.) Hence, the first step in setting target margins begins at the company level; not the product level. Set company-level fiscal profit targets first, then establish product target margin ranges commensurate with company cost structure and contribution margin that will produce the desired bottom line results.
- Knowing or having some understanding of market and competitor pricing strengthens confidence in deciding whether to take or decline a discount.
- Knowing product direct costs is critical for determining product contribution margin and for devising discount ranges (if discounting becomes part of the firm's pricing strategy).
- Sales mix can significantly affect profits and profitability, as Padco's examples of its CVP analysis, Table 42, and resulting 2012 pricing policy illustrated.

Not meeting target margins is a red flag indicator that products and ser-vices are not competitively priced. Akin to the canary in the mineshaft with respect to low and high hit rates, this early-warning indicator could result from the following conditions:

- Not knowing direct costs
- Not knowing market or competitor prices
- Products and services not sufficiently differentiated from competition or lacking competitive advantage.

Up to this point for simplicity, illustrations and examples assumed a generic product. However, products differ in many ways and the nature of the difference has profound implications for product management that affect costing and pricing, strategies by which the product is marketed and sold, type of customer and customer mix, and the selling cycle and sales distribution channel.

Strategic Implications of Simple versus Complex Products

Table 43 illustrates some of the differences and the strategic implications confronting product management. It characterizes products along a spectrum from simple to complex. The product categories (Standard Product or Components, Assemblies, Custom, Engineered) are generalities suggesting differences in number of parts, design, production requirements, and so forth, and the examples (paints, varnishes, lift truck parts, pre-fab, robot controlled) are intended to typify—not specify—various products in each category.

Unit Price and Size—Since costs increase as products gain complexity in materials, labor, and support and overhead (design, engineering, and research, for example) price also increases, which influences the type and size of customer. Simpler products generally require less material, sub-parts, and components; whereas complex products require more material, attachments, sub-assemblies, design, testing, and so on, that increase their size. Higher-priced products suggest specialized applications and narrower markets with particular needs. Simpler products and commodities are lower priced and therefore have broader market appeal with generalized needs.

Table 43. Simple versus Complex Products

Simple versus complex products			
Simple	←	**Product type** →	**Complex**
Standard Product and\or Sub-Components	Standard Assemblies	Custom	Engineered Systems
paints, varnishes, enamels	portable machine tools	chemical formulations	computerized palletizing machines
nuts, bolts, fasteners, washers, stamped parts	lift truck attachment	forward-looking infra-red radar and laser	robot-controlled manipulator
business accessories, printing, envelopes	shelving parts, utility racks, metal furniture	architectural wood/metal work	transportation, earth-moving equipment
forging/castings, disposable hand tools	small firearms, wire harnesses	pre-fab building frames	loading arms, swivel joints, pumps, compressors
Strategic implications of product type			
low	Unit Price		high
small	Size		large
short	Sales Cycle		long
quick—owner, purchasing dept.	Decision-Making		prolonged, committee
N/A or few	Quotations/RFQs		complex, many
inside sales, reps, internet	Sales Channel		company-employed, professional, executive
small	Commissions		high

Sales Cycle and Decision Making—While selling cycle and decision making are not 100% correlated, there certainly is a strong positive relationship, and both are affected by price. Decisions to purchase less-costly simpler products require less deliberation, often by business office or plant personnel, and hinge mostly on price. Complex products involve considerable negotiations about specifications, performance, delivery schedules, training, installation, technical support, replacement parts, warranties, in-plant or field demonstrations, and involve multiple personnel (production and operations, purchasing, sales and marketing, accounting, and finance) in the decision. Since the costs to promote and sell simpler products are much lesser than higher-end products, companies producing and selling the latter must have considerable working capital to support the longer selling and decision-making cycles.

Quotations and RFQs—Because simpler products typically sell at lower prices it is uncommon to use quotes and RFQs unless very high quantities over a long period are involved. Where quotes and RFQs are used they are most likely brief or automated incurring little expense to prepare. Complex products, however, usually involve detailed and expensive quotes and RFQs, and depending on the number of prospects, customers, competitors, and industry hit rate (if low), can have many outstanding at any given time.

Sales Channel and Commissions—Companies producing and selling simpler products generally do not require highly trained, and in some cases, sophisticated executive sales forces. Rather, inside sales personnel, reps, and the Internet can provide sales coverage and customer support to handle purchase orders and routine sales orders, which require little if any sales commission and keep sales transaction costs down. Complex products, however, require the sales force to possess extensive knowledge of product specifications, technical and performance data, specialized customer needs and requirements, financing, leasing, and legal issues, honed consultative selling skills, and in some cases postgraduate education. Accordingly, the sales, marketing, and promotional costs and commissions associated with selling complex products are very high. Given this high expense, companies that produce and sell complex products must know their markets and focus on qualified prospects and MVCs to avoid wasting valuable sales, marketing, and promotional working capital on less promising opportunities.

The type of product can tremendously affect the sales, marketing, promotional, and financial aspects that confront SMMs when developing strategies to grow, whether with existing products and customers or new.

This is one of the reasons that growth strategies must be tailored to the company and its situation and why generic strategies often fail.

Summary

One of product management's key duties is to manage the winners and losers in the product line from a profitability, competitive, and marketability perspective and decide which can support the company's growth or if new products are needed to attain its overall growth goals.

Questionnaire findings show three principal areas of product management that SMMs need to strengthen to be able to develop effective growth strategies:

1. Costs, margins, and pricing.
2. Marketing research and competitor intelligence (covered in Chapter 8).
3. Sales forecasting and sales reporting at the product level (covered in Chapter 10).

There are steps that companies can take to get a handle on product profitability (even if estimates are used), using contribution format and the segmented income statement. This format shows products' relative contribution to sales and to profit and sets the stage for in-depth product analysis and evaluation. Product sales and profit data presented in the segmented income statement format simplify looking at individual products' contribution to company sales and profit by showing the sales mix—the relative percentage each product contributes to sales volume and profit. It also proves helpful in assessing alternatives to cost plus pricing, such as incremental (marginal) pricing, and in establishing pricing policies with regard to the timing, guidelines, and limitations of discounting.

Examples of target margins comprised three elements—ceiling price, market price, and floor price—and demonstrated how incremental pricing provides flexibility, under certain circumstances, to trade price for volume without jeopardizing company's profit goals.

The fundamental criterion for assessing a product's future should be the profit it generates. Graph 9 depicts the major strategic question regarding the P in C-P-M™, "Can existing products support company growth objectives? If not, will it need new products to support its growth objectives?"

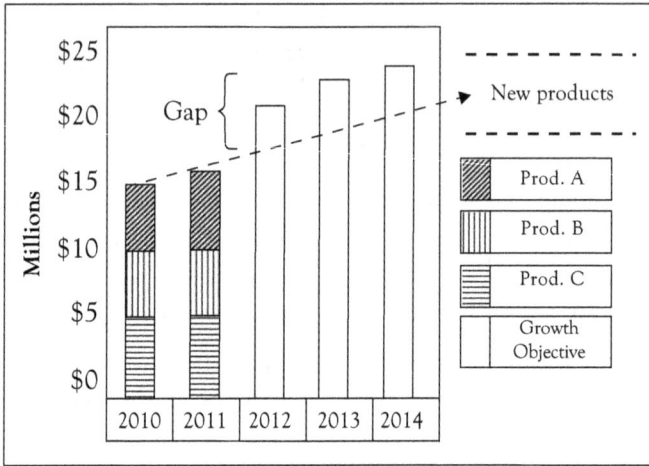

Graph 9. High-level strategic question about products.

CHAPTER 7

New Product Development

Much has been written about new product development (NPD) and how to improve the process to do it faster, cheaper, and with better results. This chapter is not about how to improve SMMs product development but rather focuses on the business case—the strategic rationale for pursuing new product development as a growth strategy, whether the company is positioned for NPD, and whether a prospective new product is the "right" one for the company. It presents steps that SMMs can take to avoid common mistakes that increase development costs, delay new products' getting to market, and that defeat their efforts to develop new products. It is more about the business case and strategic justification ("why") for new product development (and early detection and avoidance of potential failures) than about "how." As the following material will show, much of the reason for new product failure stems, again, from SMMs' lack of understanding of their markets and their competitors.

Six Out of Seven New Products Fail

Remarkably, with all the assistance given to SMMs' product development efforts from both the public and private sectors, the success rate of new products is low. About one out of seven new products is considered successful, which is approximately a 15% success rate. This includes all categories of new products—consumer, industrial, B2B, line extensions and modifications, new firm, industry, and world—truly innovative and breakthrough new products and technologies. Of course, the success rate for the former categories is much higher than for the truly innovative categories that involve considerably more investment and risk. But, on average, the success rate is about 15%.

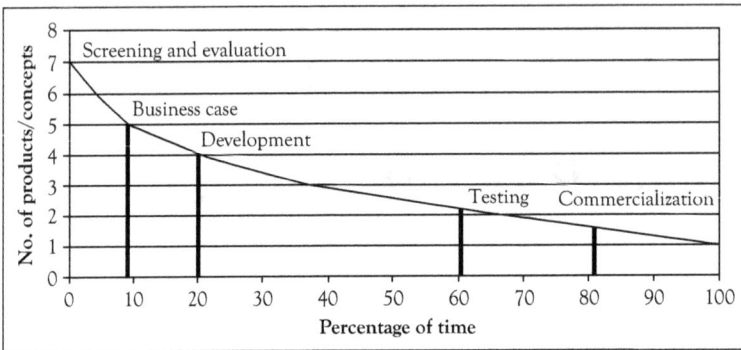

Graph 10. Attrition rate of new products.

Source: Cooper, Robert G., (2011). *Winning at new products: creating value through innovation* (4th ed., Fig. 1.5, p. 14). New York, NY: Basic Books. With permission by Robert G. Cooper.

Dr. Robert Cooper, an expert in product development and co-founder of the Product Development Institute in Ontario, Canada, author of several books on new product development, including *Winning at New Products:Creating Value Through Innovation* (4th ed., 2011 Basic Books), presented three graphs at a Georgia Tech conference on new product development.

The first shows the attrition rate of new products. For every seven new ideas that enter the NPD process, about four enter development, 1.5 are launched, and only one succeeds. He shows the products progressing through five delineated stages until one successful product exits the process. In his product development process, Stage-Gate®, products must meet specific objective evaluation criteria, defined as gates, in order to progress to the succeeding stage. The purpose of evaluation criteria, which are stringent yet can be tailored to the company, is to identify and eliminate potential failures before the company expends considerable resources.

The second and third graphs, Graphs 11 and 12 show the reasons cited for new products' failure and deficiencies in the processes companies use to develop new products. Both show that issues pertaining to markets and customers account for most of the failure, not product and technical issues, such as design and prototyping, and production processes. This is not surprising in light of SMMs' responses to the questionnaire: Since

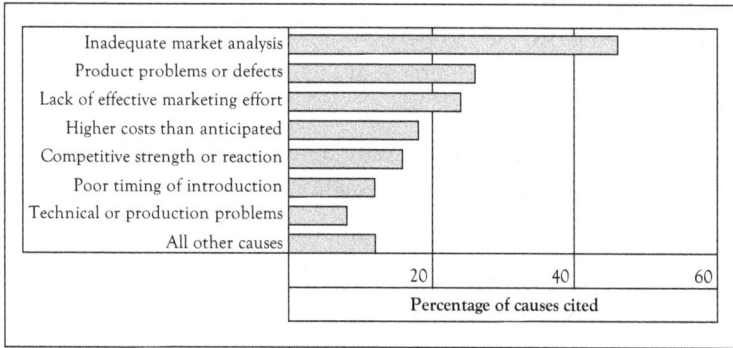

Graph 11. Causes of new product failure.

Source: Cooper, Robert G., (2001). *Winning at new products: accelerating the process from idea to launch* (3rd ed., Fig. 2.1, p. 25). New York, NY: Basic Books. With permission by Robert G. Cooper.

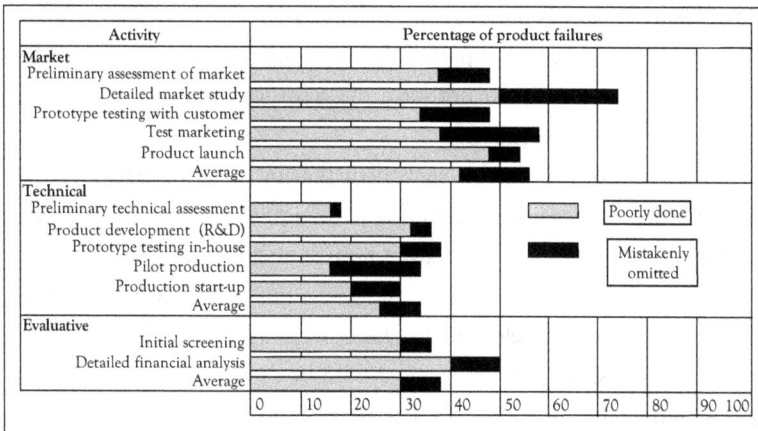

Graph 12. Deficiencies in the new product process.

Source: Cooper, Robert G., (2011). *Winning at new products: creating value through innovation* (4th ed., Fig. 1.5, p. 14). New York, NY: Basic Books. With permission by Robert G. Cooper.

most have insufficient insight into markets and competitors and have never conducted marketing research, it is likely they would not be able to execute effectively in these areas when pursuing NPD.

Georgia Tech frequently received calls from individuals and companies asking for help with new product development. Individuals mostly asked us to help find manufacturers that would help build their new product or prototype it, prepare materials sourcing and bill of materials, CAD designs, and so forth—the *technical* activities. (The most famous request asked for help with the development of a flying tractor that could fly from crop to crop.) Companies, by contrast, generally wanted us to help them find customers since they had already developed a product—the horse was out of the barn. A commonality with individuals and the companies was the absence of a clearly defined problem or need, the solution, basis of differentiation from existing products or solutions, the target customer or market—the *customer and marketing* activities.

Many consultants and service providers, with all best intentions, think they have good solutions to help SMMs successfully develop new products. They base their solutions, which involve improving the product development process, on laudable, very successful, expensive, and notable models—such as those of sophisticated and complex systems characteristic of General Motors and Toyota. In Chapter 1, I point out that solutions appropriate to Type 4 companies do not work with smaller Types 1–3 companies that plainly do not have the resources and culture to adopt such systems and procedures.

There is also considerable sentiment that by applying lean manufacturing principles (again, the *technical* activities) to product development processes—for example, eliminating non-value-added activities from the design, prototyping, production, and so forth—SMMs would improve their new product development. The questionnaire and Cooper's findings, however, show that emphasis should be directed instead to investigating and analyzing marketing, customers, and competitive issues—the factors most commonly overlooked or poorly executed. As Graphs 11 and 12 show technical activities are not the predominant cause of new product failures. Nevertheless, in spite of all the good intentions to help SMMs improve their NPD efforts, focusing on technical activities might speed up the development and launch of the *wrong* product.

The Babe's "Swing and a Miss" and NPD

Babe Ruth's batting record mirrors the success rate for new products. Yes, he hit 714 home runs, but when you look at his other batting statistics you see in Figure 53 that his HR success rate was also only about 15%. He did much better just getting on base with hits and base-on-balls, BB.

G	AB	R	H	HR	RBI	BB	SO	Avg.	OBP	SLG
2,503	8,398	2,174	2,874	714	2,217	2,062	1,330	.342	.472	.690

Figure 53. Babe Ruth's batting record.

Babe struck out 1,330 times, which amounts to 3,990 swings (assuming 3 swings and not accounting for foul tips and called strikes). Add his 714 home run swings and you get a total of 4,704 swings to hit 714 home runs, or one home run per 6.5 at bats (4,704 ÷ 714). Adding non-HR base hits, foul balls, and HRs after the first or second swing of course would increase the number of swings and reduce the percentage.

$$714 \text{ home runs} \div 4,704 \text{ at bats} = 15\%$$
$$1 \text{ home run per } 6.5 \text{ at bats} = 15\%$$

His percentage getting on base was much better. He got on base 2,160 times with non-HR hits (2,874 hits minus 714 home runs) and 2,062 times with BB, totaling 4,222 times on base, showing he got on base 50% of the time, exclusive of his home runs.

$$(2,160 + 2,062) \div 8,398 \text{ at bats} = 50\%$$

He did much better getting into scoring position by just getting on base than by trying to hit the ball out of the park. Similarly, SMMs would do better in NPD by focusing on the "basics"—making sure the product is the "right" one (waiting for the right pitch) than by going for the home run.

Getting the Nest Ready for the Eggs—Making Sure the Product Is the "Right" One

By "basics" I am referring to generally accepted good business practices the questionnaire addressed, such as knowing about costs and margins, having and using information about customers, gaining insights into markets, and about competitors. Most SMMs do not have sufficient insight into these areas and it is this lack of good information that is fundamentally problematic for SMMs in their pursuit of growth strategies—not their technical processes—particularly regarding new product development.

To improve the chances for success there are three areas that should be looked at early in SMMs' development of new products—"to get the nest ready for the eggs."

- The type of new product.
- The company's "readiness."
- The presence of and adherence to effective business practices.

1. **The type of new product.** There are three general types of new products, each with very distinct strategic and risk implications:

   - Product modifications, line extensions, cost reductions.
   - Replacement or substitute product.
   - New to the industry, world, truly innovative, breakthrough, disruptive.

   Product modifications, line extensions, and replacement or substitute projects pose much less risk than innovative, breakthrough projects and involve simpler strategic issues. Generally, Types 1–2 companies are better suited for product modifications, line extensions, or replacement products because NPD is a resource-intensive strategy and many smaller firms' balance sheets, personnel, and NPD experience are insufficient to take on the risks, high cost, and uncertainties of innovative, breakthrough projects.

   SMMs must thoroughly evaluate these implications early in C-P-M^{TM} and financial analyses where growth strategies call for NPD. It will help them quickly assess the amount of risk, degree of difficulty, and investment that might be involved in NPD.

   Figure 54 illustrates the risks and strategic implications of the three types of new products.

   Product modifications and line extensions are the easiest to pursue particularly if the firm has done a good job with C-P-M^{TM} analysis, lost order analysis, and getting customer feedback. Lost

Three types of new products			
Type	Risk/ Commitment	Market	Selling Implications
Product Modification/Line Extension	Low = selling a variation of a known product Little market and competitor research	Existing customers and markets	Same sales force and channels Some training Modest investment in advertising and promotion
Replacement or Substitute Products (new to firm but similar to competing products)	Low to moderate, but high risk of "me too" products Market and competitor research necessary (competitor matrix and user benefits)	Existing and/or new customers and markets Profiles of target customer and prospect list Lead generation to support selling effort	May need different sales force and channels New product training Budget for advertising and promotion, collateral materials Market penetration pricing?
Leading Edge, New to the World, Disruptive (new to both firm and markets)	Very high with major investment in R&D High failure rate— spectacular returns EXTENSIVE market and competitor research Field and market testing	New customers and markets Profiles of target customer and prospect list Lead generation to support selling effort	New sales force and channels Comprehensive training—technical, features, and benefits Budget for advertising and promotion, collateral materials Targeted/ specialized pricing

Figure 54. Three types of new products.

order analysis and customer satisfaction feedback should have provided some insight into potential improvements to existing products and services that could inform this strategy. Changes to the sales organization probably would not be needed, since existing customers are the target market. Some sales training, however, might be needed to promote the benefits of the product's improvements.

Replacement or substitute products (new to the firm)
require more caution because unless the new product offers distinct improvements in quality, performance, price, and so on, over competitors' products they will fall into the "me too" category—simply knock-offs of competitor products. Although new to the firm, they already might be or are already in competitors' product lines. Unfortunately, since most manufacturers know little about their competitors and cannot make an apples-to-apples comparison between competing products, most new products in this category wind up being "me too" products. While they can generate nominal increases in sales and margin, in the end, they do not result in sustainable growth or improved competitive advantage. Avoiding the "me too" syndrome requires some investment in market and competitor research.

If the SMM intends the new product for new markets or customers, it will need to develop target profiles, using SIC/NAICS codes to qualify prospective new customers, and provide leads for the sales force. These data also can inform the sales forecast, territory plan, and sales call prioritization.

Sales force training or a new sales force might be needed, depending on the extent of difference in the new product's features, capabilities and capacities, and applications and departure from the firm's existing customer base and market. The costs to promote, communicate, and advertise to the new target market will increase working capital and must be factored into a sales and marketing budget and into the total cost of the new product. Lastly, competitor investigation should reveal the pricing differentials of the competing products—base prices, features, and add-ons, if applicable—and provide some direction as to the pricing strategy.

Replacement and substitute products carry more risk and investment than do modifications and line extensions. However, the extent of incremental risk and investment really depends on the degree of departure from the firm's existing product lines and customer and market bases. The greater the departure, the greater the risk and investment, and therefore the greater the need for due diligence—crossing t's and dotting the i's.

New-to-the-industry-world, truly innovative, breakthrough, disruptive products involves considerably more risk and investment in research and development, production technologies, sales and marketing resources, working capital, and in due diligence. In most cases, it represents a radical departure from the company's existing *C-P-M*™, and possibly its core business. Accordingly, only companies with strong balance sheets, deep pockets, and a strong and experienced management team are best positioned to pursue this strategy.

According to Cooper, modifications, line extensions, and replacement products account for almost 52% of new products; new-to-the-world and innovative new products account for about 10%. (Figure 55).

Improvements to existing products	26%
Additions to existing product lines	26%
New product lines	20%
Cost reductions	11%
New-to-the-world products	10%
Repositionings	7%

Figure 55. Types of new products.

Source: Cooper, Robert G., (2011). *Winning at new products: creating value through innovation* (4th ed., Fig. 1.6, p. 23). New York, NY: Basic Books. With permission by Robert G. Cooper.

2. **The company's "readiness."** This pertains to a company's financial situation, employees' skills pertaining to financial analysis, marketing acumen, decision-making policies and procedures, and NPD track record. Since NPD is a resource-intensive strategy, readiness involves a holistic look at the business to identify weak areas to correct before committing many resources, for example:

• Does the company have sufficient financial resources and personnel with appropriate experience and knowledge to shepherd a new product from concept to commercialization? Do its financial ratios and trends in sales, profit and profitability, and cash flow indicate a green light? If not, can the firm borrow the needed capital?

- Does ownership and management support NPD? Without senior management's support no new product project will succeed. Good indicators of support are unequivocal commitment of sufficient financial and human resources and adherence to scheduled periodic progress reviews.
- Is ownership and management willing to kill the project if its viability—financial, technological, competitive, and economic—indicates weakness? Legacy projects persist because some owners and senior managers cannot accept objective assessments of "pet" projects that have drained resources and that are unlikely to succeed.
- What is the company's track record with new product development—number of new products developed, winners, losers? A less-than-successful history with NPD, or the absence of one, should indicate a yellow or red flag.

3. **The presence of and adherence to effective business practices.** This derives directly from the questionnaire and includes financial, accounting, and costing, marketing research, and sales and product management areas. As previously noted, most SMMs are not effective in these areas.

Key questions that companies need to ask include, "Are there effective systems and procedures for reporting product and customer sales, costs and margins, and trends; for gaining insights into markets and competitors; and for planning, forecasting, and follow-up?" Specific to a new product project: "Has the company prepared a 'definition of success' for the new product(s)—annual sales volume, target profit, market penetration, for example?" "Has the company developed criteria by which to periodically evaluate the progress and viability of the NPD project such that a go-kill decision can be made?"

It is impossible to specify the optimum amount of control and structure a company needs to pursue NPD. However, at a minimum, sufficient financial resources should exist accompanied by routine regular review of financial performance and detailed cost and sales reporting to evaluate the rate of return on investment in working capital and capital investment.

If a company does not have effective financial and sales reporting, particularly at the product level, it will not be able to monitor and evaluate expenses incurred in developing and launching a new product and will not be able to assess whether the product has achieved the outcomes management intended. The absence of insightful intelligence on target markets and competitors, as Cooper's graphs show, is frequently the cause of new product failures.

It also is critically important for the company to define what the new product is intended to accomplish in terms of sales volume and profit, such as filling a gap in the product offering (see Graph 13), satisfying customers' needs or solving a problem, bringing on new customers, or entering a new market.

A vital good business practice in the context of new product development is the fortitude to kill a project if periodic reviews indicate it will not be successful or attain the desired ROI. Unfortunately, NPD lore offers many examples where companies lack go-kill criteria, resulting in legacy projects that soak up valuable financial and personnel resources.

Fortunately, much of the data, information, and material needed to help a company define success for a new product, establish evaluation criteria, and determine if it is the right one can derive from financial and *C-P-M*™ analyses presented in Chapters 2 through 6.

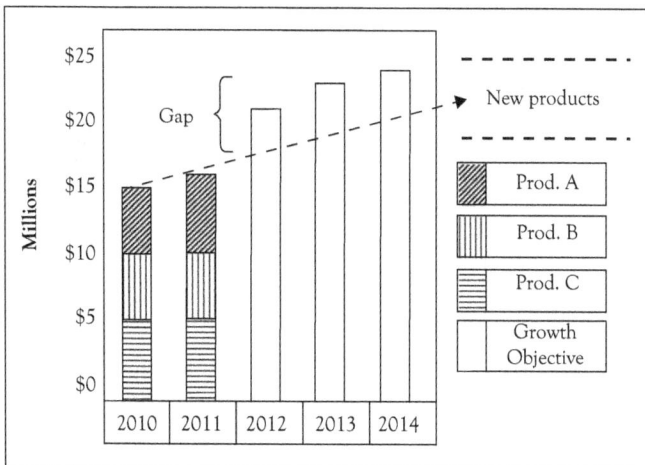

Graph 13. Filling the product gap.

- Financial situation and ratio analyses not only indicate a company's current situation but also inform as to whether a company can afford to pursue NPD as a growth strategy. If a company determines via product and product line performance analysis that existing products cannot support desired growth and that a new product(s) are needed, as the graph illustrates, the gap between growth objective bars and existing products' potential sales represents a revenue target for the new product(s).

Profit and margin targets using the contribution format and company cost structure (Chapter 2), similarly, can be projected as shown in Figure 56. In this case, the firm wants new products to increase sales 20% from $1,000,000 to $1,200,000. Further, it estimates it will need $50,000 in capital investment for new equipment, forecasting a 15% profit increase of $30,000 from $200,000 to $230,000.

Revenue and profit margin targets for the new product(s) are $200,000 in sales ($1,000,000 to $1,200,000), and $30,000 in pre-tax income ($2,000,000 to $230,000) thus providing quantitative criteria by which to evaluate the strategy's progress.

The Ansoff[1] Product-Market-Growth matrix, Figure 57, illustrates the four basic decisions confronting companies when contemplating growth strategies: Grow with existing products to existing customers

Estimate of Profit From Sales Increase				
	Current Sales Volume		Increased Sales	
	Amount	Percent	Amount	Percent
Sales	$1,000,000	100%	$1,200,000	100%
Variable costs	600,000	60%	720,000	60%
Contribution Margin	400,000	40%	480,000	40%
Fixed costs	200,000		250,000	
Pre-tax Income	$200,000	20%	$230,000	19%
Capital investment			$50,000	

Figure 56. Estimating profit increase from sales increase.

Ansoff Product-Market-Growth Matrix		
	Products	
	Existing	New
Existing	❶	❸ Modifications, line extensions, replacements, substitutions, etc.
New	❷	❹ Truly innovative, new to the firm, industry, new to world, break-through, disruptive, etc. Diversification, acquisition, joint venture, etc.

Figure 57. Ansoff product–market–growth matrix.

and markets, grow with existing products to new customers and markets, grow with new products to existing customers and markets, and grow with new products to new customers and markets. Since this chapter deals only with new product(s), strategies pertaining to existing products (Quads 1 and 2) are blank. Chapter 9 discusses in more detail the Ansoff matrix and implications of various growth strategies in each of the four quadrants. In the context of preparing the nest for the eggs, a company needs to decide which type of product(s) is appropriate to pursue—Quad 3 or 4.

The following scenario typifies my experience with SMMs' new product development:

"Management informally discusses various ideas until someone decides to make a prototype and starts the process. The project then progresses for some time and probably experiences several prototype iterations. By that time, unfortunately, the company unknowingly has laid the groundwork for failure since due diligence about customers, markets, selling price, demand, and competition were not completed."

Companies can strengthen their preparation and avoid this pitfall by documenting in writing the problem or the need the idea/new product addresses, how the idea solves the problem or fulfills the need, a description of a potential customer or market (e.g., a manufacturer, utility, transportation, civilian government or military, medical, educational), competing products or competitors (if any), rough estimates of cost to produce, selling price, and volume. Much of this should derive from the *C-P-M*™ analysis and the opportunities management perceived to grow the business stemming from product analysis and gaps in the firm's product line or of competitors.

Figures 58 and 59 show a format for summarizing the aforementioned information for a product line extension or modification in the concept stage. The company produces and sells adhesive products to mills that produce nonwoven products, SIC/NAICS 2297 and 313230, respectively. It intends to promote the line extension to 57 existing customers (identified via customer database, customer profiling, customer satisfaction surveys) and nine prospective customers (totaling 137 locations) now buying from two competitors, Adhesives U.S.A. and Poly-Ceramics, which has been

Generic Product Concept – Page 1
Line Extension, Modification

Briefly describe the product and what it is intended to do or purpose it will serve.		
✓ Line extension, modification	☐ Cost reduction	
☐ Substitute, replacement product/service	☐ New to firm, industry, break-through	

Product enhances bulk unloading/overhead header system for PLC line in existing nonwoven market niche by increasing applications/capacity to 1500 cycles per minute from 1200. Specifications can be custom-tailored to individual customers' needs/requirements.

Define the End User Market

Consumer Market

☐ Home \ residential (durable)	☐ Electronics \ telecommunications \ computers \ entertainment \ etc.	_____
☐ Health \ beauty \ medical	☐ Sports \ athletics \ recreation	_____

Commercial \ Business \ Industrial Markets

☐ Agricultural \ Forestry			☐ Education (non-research)
☐ Mining	☐ Wholesale (non-food)	☐ Transportation \ Warehousing	☐ Education (research)
☐ Utilities	☐ Wholesale (food)	☐ Information	☐ Medical (non-research)
☐ Construction	☐ Retail (non-food)	☐ Finance \ Insurance	☐ Medical (research)
✓ Manufacturing	☐ Retail (food)	☐ Real Estate	☐ Arts \ Entertainment

✓ Other: Core customers in SIC/NAICS 2297/313230 Nonwoven Fabric Mills remain our target market.

Government

	City	State	Federal	☐ Other
Civilian	☐	☐	☐	_____
Military	☐	☐	☐	_____

Competitors and Issues: Adhesives U.S.A. has been trying to increase header capacity for 18 months and is still 12 months away from achieving this. Development of bulk unloading/overhead header system for PLC line, if successful, will result in market entry 6-8 months before Adhesives U.S.A.

Poly-Ceramics, Inc. has already launched new product with advanced header/delivery capacity, but initial field reports indicate considerable technical/service issues. Our features, if successful and timely, create opportunity to take this business from Polytech.

Figure 58. Generic product concept–Page 1.

Source: Cooper, Robert G., (2001). ATOM-SME. Ontario, CAN: Product Development Institute, Inc. Adapted with permission by Robert G. Cooper.

Generic Product Concept – Page 2
Line Extension, Modification

Performance Characteristics \ Specifications

Describe the materials to be used in the construction of the product.

☐ Fabric   ✓ Standard metals   ☐ Other

✓ Plastic   ☐ Exotic metals   _____

☐ Wood   ☐ Basic materials (rock, sand, clay, stone, etc.)   _____

Estimated Market Costs, Pricing, and Margin

Estimate the market potential, unit cost for materials and labor, additional overhead, working capital, and capital investment. Estimate the price end-users would pay for the product\process\service.

Estimated number existing customers: **57 (123 locations)**	Estimated number of new customers: **9 (14 locations)**
Estimated unit material cost/unit: **$2,500 base; $225 modification**	Estimated working capital: **$78,775 material & labor prototype / field testing / promo materials.**
Estimated unit labor cost: **$275 base; $50 modification**	Estimated capital investment: **$15,000 retooling**
Estimated unit selling price to end-user: **$750 increase to base price of $5,000 = $5,750 new SP**	Estimated other investment / outflow: **$228 commission per unit @ 5%.**

Total market sales/margin projection: **137 locations @ $5,750 = $787,750 @ 41% CM**

Anticipated Problems: Financial, Production / Operations, Marketing / Promotional:

No financial problems – current cash flow can support working capital and capital investment. Tooling can be produced in-house and production capacity is available for prototyping; two customers have agreed to in-plant testing of prototypes. Costs for promotional materials, brochures, wed design, price/tech/spec sheets included in working capital.

Describe Sales Force / Channel Implications/Issues:

Existing sales force including reps/distributors will coordinate in-plant testing, training, and tech support during field trials. Will provide feedback on results, recommendations for changes, pricing and post-sale issues. Inside sales, field sales, and reps/distributors will prepare sales call schedules for 57 customers and 9 prospects following successful field testing.

Figure 59. Generic product concept–Page 2.

Source: Cooper, Robert G., (2001). ATOM-SME. Ontario, CAN: Product Development Institute, Inc. Adapted with permission by Robert G. Cooper.

experiencing technical and service issues (discovered from customer satisfaction surveys, lost order analysis, and sales force reports). It believes it can deliver the new product before Poly-Ceramics resolves its design and production issues with its own product, and attain a 6- to 8-month selling and market penetration advantage.

At the concept or ideation stage, a detailed financial analysis is unnecessary: Rather, a back-of-the-envelope summary shown in Figure 60 showing direct material and labor, selling price, expected volume, working capital as a percentage of sales, and estimated capital investment will suffice. A simple payback (not the present value discounted cash flow after-tax payback used for larger, high-risk, capital-intensive investments), although not always needed, will indicate the project's rate of return (a shorter payback means a higher rate of return).

Product modifications and line extensions usually do not involve a lot of investment and risk and therefore might not require a more detailed

| | Preliminary Financial Projection | | |
| | Direct Expenses | | |
Unit SP/Costs	Base Model	Modification	Total
Base model	$5,000		
Modifications		$750	
SP			**$5,750**
Direct Mat.	$2,500	$225	$2,725
Direct Labor	$275	$50	$325
Commission @ 5%			$288
Total Cost			**$3,338**
Contribution Margin			$2,413
CM%			42%
Incremental Units			137
Revenue	(137 × $5,750)		$787,750
Direct Costs	(137 × $3,338)		457,238
CM			**$330,513**
Working Capital @ 10% of Sales			$78,775
Capital Investment			15,000
Total Investment			**$93,775**
Simple Payback Yrs.	(Tot. Invest. ÷ CM)		0.3

Figure 60. Simple payback calculation.

financial analysis. More complex NPD projects involving considerable expense and investment should require detailed financial analyses based on good market data, competitor intelligence, and a sales forecast, and include depreciation and after-tax cash flows to calculate the ROI and NPV (net present value) based on discounted cash flows. In most cases, depending on a company's financial situation, a 2- to 3-year payback is acceptable. However, very complex and costly projects might take more time to payback—the Japanese are noted for their longer-term view on major strategic investments.

Figures 58 and 59 summarize the following:

- Describes the nature of the project: line extension, modification, and so forth.
- The model or product feature affected (header system and flow rate).
- Identifies the market (manufacturing, specifically core customers in SIC/NAICS 2297/313230).
- Gives a competitive reason for making the changes (to exploit competitors' problems and weaknesses with their products—derived from competitor intelligence, sales reports, lost order analysis, and customer satisfaction surveys).
- Estimates selling price and market potential (number of existing and prospective customers—derived from primary and secondary marketing research, sales reports, customer satisfaction surveys, and telemarketing qualification of suspects/prospects).
- Estimates the direct costs for not only on-going material and labor, the cost of the prototype, but also working capital and capital investment (derived from cost reports and cost accounting procedures).
- Potential problems involving finance, production, sales and marketing.
- Describes activities for the sales force and distribution channel.

They also provides quantitative revenue, cost, and margin data by which to objectively evaluate the project:

- Sales to 137 locations @ $5,750/unit totaling $787,750. Provides target sales goals for sales force/distribution channel.
- Unit production and selling cost at $3,338/unit. Provides cost guidelines for assessing production efficiency.
- Contribution margin @ 41%. Provides financial basis for evaluating product performance.

This format also can be used for replacement and substitute products, but with more emphasis on competitive factors that show how the product will provide competitive advantage. Since this type of project deals with a product new to the firm, but likely already in competitors' product lines, it should avoid becoming a "me too" product with a high potential for lackluster results. *C-P-M*™ involving lost order analysis and customer feedback that provide comparisons to competing products and services and reasons why customers buy or don't buy from competitors should play a major role in the decision to pursue this type of new product. Feedback about competitors' selling prices, product performance, durability, quality, warranties, sales coverage, and so forth, from these sources should highlight existing products' weakness relative to competitors and lead to performance features that satisfy customers at least as good as or better than competitors' products.

Leading edge, new-to-the-world products are much different. They generally result in products and services that affect markets in unexpected ways. In many instances, their target market, costs for prototyping and development, direct and selling costs, and selling prices cannot be estimated at the start. Unfortunately, there is no template or format for getting to preliminary market potential, cost-benefit, and so on, other than supposition in the early stages, unless, of course, the new product or technology is being designed for a specific application or solution where the end-user is known.

While the decision to pursue NPD as a growth strategy is important, it is equally important that the product is right for the company at that time, given its readiness to pursue NPD, that it is financially stable, that good business practices are in place and are followed, that a definition of success and evaluation criteria have been established, and that management has the fortitude to kill a potentially unsuccessful project.

To Kill or Not to Kill—Effective Valuation Criteria

The earlier section in this chapter about effective business practices mentioned criteria by which to assess the viability of an NPD project so that a go-kill decision could be made in the event that periodic reviews indicate red flags. Cooper's studies reveal that many companies engaged in NPD either do not have such criteria or fail to act on data that indicate a project will not produce the desired ROI. Graph12 showing deficiencies in NPD processes illustrates this in the Evaluative section—50% of companies either poorly executed financial evaluation or omitted it. The absence of or failure to abide by evaluation criteria is one of the factors contributing to new products' high failure rate, on-going survival of legacy projects, too many new product projects in the pipeline, and delays getting winners to market.

In "*Portfolio Management for New Products: Creating Value Through Innovation*," Cooper[2] presents six quantitative evaluation criteria:

1. Strategic fit and importance
2. Competitive and product advantage
3. Market attractiveness
4. Leverage—core competencies
5. Technical feasibility, and
6. Financial reward versus risk

These criteria were developed from his studies of best business practices of hundreds of companies engaged in new product development. He recommends that companies pursuing NPD adapt some form of these criteria and apply them periodically to determine if their project(s) are meeting or progressing toward the definition of success established in the product concept. He also strongly recommends that if a project fails to measure up to the criteria that a decision must be taken to (a) shore up the weak areas and reassess, (b) delay it for a specified time and reassess, or (c) kill it.

In the absence of good evaluation criteria, weak projects consume scarce resources and potential winners languish and are late to market. It is critically important to SMMs who are engaged in NPD that a definition of success and quantitative evaluation criteria be established at the product concept stage. The lack of evaluation criteria or failure to abide by go-kill decisions characterize the dysfunctional, systemic, organizational, and cultural factors mentioned earlier.

Hydro Engineering Co., Inc., a 100-year-old, 150-employee producer of heavy-duty industrial pumps in a mature global industry, strengthened its product development program by tailoring Cooper's evaluation criteria. It applied them to about 25 projects in its new product pipeline, which included mostly modifications and line extensions, some relatively more advanced opportunities, and two legacy projects. The legacy projects fell by the wayside and one project the development team was excited about also fell out because the criteria exposed fallacies in critical assumptions about market attractiveness and competitive advantage. The team estimated it avoided about $200,000 to $300,000 in development costs. *Remember—the process for developing new products should also involve the elimination of failing or potentially unsuccessful products that do not meet minimum evaluation criteria in order to conserve resources for more promising products.*

Too Few Ideas or New Products in the Pipeline and Pipeline Constipation

Chapter 3 pointed out the importance of keeping the prospect pipeline full to maintain a fresh supply of potential new customers. Similarly, SMMs need a pipeline for new products, periodically refreshed and updated, particularly where new product development is a primary or major growth engine—Q3 and Q4 in the Ansoff matrix. Many companies, though—even those that want just one or two new products—experience difficulty coming up with good ideas for new products. They either do not know where to begin, have some, or too many ideas. Typically, the former stems from a lack of strategic focus and the latter two from not being able to prioritize ideas and opportunities—lack of evaluation criteria.

The *C-P-M*™process, as presented in Chapters 3 through 6, that deals with customer profiling using SIC and NAICS codes results in considerable information that can be used to identify market and competitive opportunities for new products. The dilemma confronting many SMMs is matching those opportunities with ideas for new products. One statistic I heard said 99 ideas are rejected before approving a new product concept for development. Whether or not this statistic is entirely accurate, the point is that many ideas must precede the selection of one product concept for development.

Several company owners and managers have said to me, "We would like to develop a new product but don't have an idea where to start," or

"We've got so many ideas we can't decide which ones to pursue." The former characterizes having no method or process for generating ideas for new products and the latter stems from not having practicable criteria by which to evaluate and prioritize ideas and concepts.

Targeted Innovation Versus the Shotgun Approach (a.k.a. Putting the Cart in Front of the Horse)

There are two approaches to addressing the lack of ideas. One is the shotgun approach and the other is structured, based on C-P-M^{TM} and financial analyses. Shotgun ideation involves brainstorming, recording the ideas, and then having the company come up with some informal methodology (multiple voting techniques and sticky notes, for example), by which to select the ones to pursue. Because C-P-M^{TM} or other strategic framework do not precede the ideation in this scenario, the resulting ideas may or may not align with the business' strategic thrust, core competencies, or even fall within the realm of practicality due to financial or other weaknesses. In the structured approach, C-P-M^{TM} precedes brainstorming— thus, framing the issue and providing strategic guidance.

Hydro Engineering's C-P-M^{TM}, showing that existing products could not get the firm to its sales volume target ($7.5M above current level) within 5 years, adopted the structured approach illustrated by Figure 61, resulting in over 170 ideas. The three-axis x-y-z framework found in Cooper's "*Winning at New Products: Accelerating the Process from Idea to Launch*," which is adaptable and scalable to most SMMs, enabled company employees to focus on generating ideas within its strategic and core arenas. (The firm's sales VP wanted to make sure the structured ideation did not result in ideas for new digital clocks, which were considerably outside the firm's core competency and strategic thrust.)

The box at the center illustrates the firm's existing C-P-M^{TM}, which is shown in detail along the three axes – x axis: **what** (application of the technologies to various industry/market needs); y axis: **who** (customers and markets); and z axis: **how** (technologies germane to pump operation).

The 170 ideas derived mostly from the second and third areas are as follows:

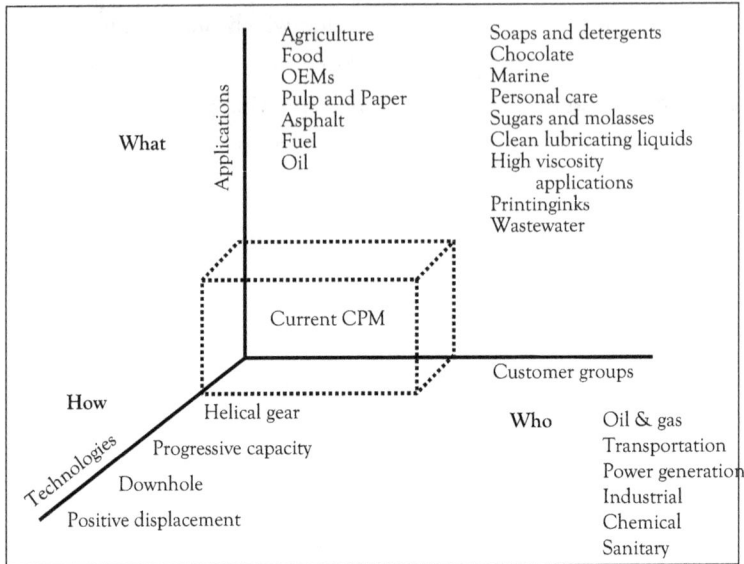

Figure 61. Three dimensions of innovation.

Source: Cooper, Robert G., (1993). *Winning at new products: accelerating the process from idea to launch* (2th ed., Fig. 11.4, p. 307). New York, NY: Basic Books. Adapted with permission by Robert G. Cooper.

1. Developing/acquiring technologies that can be used with existing applications, markets, or customers. (The "how" axis.)
2. Finding/developing new applications within existing technologies that can be sold to existing markets and customers. (The "what" axis.)
3. Finding new markets and customers who can use with existing technologies and applications. (The "who" axis.)

The company tailored Cooper's six evaluation criteria, screened and evaluated the 170 ideas, and prioritized 25 for further study, thus priming its new product pipeline with the objective to generate $7.5M in new revenue. As mentioned earlier, the adoption of quantitative evaluation criteria led to killing legacy projects and avoiding $200,000 to $300,000 in development costs, thus freeing up resources to develop other products.

This structured framework, in contrast to shotgun brainstorming, guides ideation toward products and services that are congruent with a company's readiness and improves the chances that new products are the "right" ones.

Sources of Ideas

SMMs in search of ideas for new products can tap many resources—employees, owners and senior management, sales personnel, R&D (larger companies), customers, suppliers, competitors, and so forth. Studies and anecdotes, however, say that suppliers and customers produce the most successful ideas for new products. (And, of course, there is the old suggestion box.)

A 2004 article in *Product Innovation Management*[3] dealing with 137 new product projects in B2B companies exceeding $50 million in sales found that long-term, high-sales-volume customers add more value to the ideation process for *incrementally* improved products than for truly innovative, new-to-the-company products. Alternatively, a *diverse* mix of influential customers results in "competitively superior products ... for highly *innovative* projects."

This article suggests that SMMs lacking ideas for growth should utilize individuals familiar with their business, for example, employees, long-term customers, and suppliers for product modifications, line extensions, and so forth. The pump company's employees generated ideas for incremental products in its core competencies and strategic thrust. A more diverse mix, such as university professors, industry experts and consultants, inventors, and so forth, might be better for ideas for riskier, more innovative, new-to-the-company growth initiatives.

Fifteen Important Questions

SMMs should ask these 15 questions when contemplating new product development as a growth strategy:

Financial

1. Is the business operating above break-even sales?

   If not, it could be a yellow or a red flag—See Chapter 2 regarding the implications of pursuing growth strategies when sales are below breakeven.

2. Is cash flow sufficient to invest in working capital and capital expenditure to pay for the cost of developing a new product(s)?

NPD is a resource-intensive (financial and personnel) proposition. If cash flow is insufficient, can the firm borrow money or inject more equity to finance the strategy?

3. Is the firm's balance sheet strong enough to support NPD?

If the firm's five basic financial ratios (quick, current, sales-to-working capital, accounts receivable, and debt-to-equity) are outside of minimum acceptable levels, there might be insufficient cash or credit available to pay for NPD. SMMs contemplating new-to-the-industry or world, break-through NPD need very strong balance sheets.

Customers: Needs/Problems/Opportunities

4. Has the firm identified any problems or opportunities within its customer base—particularly with MVCs—that indicate opportunities to develop products or services to (a) grow that business or (b) that can be sold to other existing customers or prospects identified via SIC/NAICS?

Existing customers, especially MVCs, are the low-hanging fruit for sources of ideas and opportunities to develop new products. Lost order analyses and customer satisfaction feedback are good sources for identifying needs, problems, and opportunities.

Product Performance

5. Are there any products that are not meeting sales or margin expectations?

If so, can they be improved by lowering costs or increasing promotional efforts to justify keeping them in the product offering?

6. Has there been a comprehensive strategic review of product performance, sales mix, and product mix that indicates NPD is a justifiable path to growth?

Determining that changes to sales and product mix, or that the product offering in general cannot generate the desire growth, is a good basis for pursuing NPD.

Market and Competitor Knowledge

7. Does the firm know the number and location of prospective customers or prospective existing customers via customer profiles using SIC/NAICS?

   Most SMMs do not conduct market research and experience shows they often develop new products without adequate knowledge of potential new customers—the cart is in front of the horse. Customer profiling based on SIC/NAICS provides a sound basis for locating prospects similar to existing customers (representing the best match for new products), especially where product modifications or line extensions and replacement or substitute products are involved. The number and location of prospective customers (a) informs sales and marketing budgets, sales forecasts, sales call planning, schedules, and prioritization and (b) provides quantitative data by which to evaluate sales force performance with respect to market penetration, sales coverage, sales appointments and presentations, proposals submitted and won, and products sold.

8. Are competitors known and has the firm made an apples-to-apples comparison to competitors' products to quantify relative competitive strengths and weakness?

   Direct comparisons to competitors' products should be a major decisive factor in determining if existing products can support a company's growth targets and for assessing the changes needed to strengthen a product's competitiveness. This latter point includes decisions regarding product modifications and extensions or replacement/substitute products. NPD projects should be postponed where competitors or competing attributes, features, and relative performance factors of the products are unknown or uncertain.

9. Is the new product sufficiently differentiated—even if it is a replacement/substitute product—to convince the customer/prospect to choose it over a competing product?

10. Does the new product solve a problem or offer a distinct advantage or benefit to the customer or prospect such as lowering costs, better quality, faster service, more reliability, easier maintenance, better tech support, and so on?

Questionnaire results and Cooper's graph on Deficiencies in the New Product Development Process (see 'Detailed market study') show that many companies have insufficient insight into competitors and conduct competitive analysis poorly—if at all.

Business Readiness, Basic Systems, and Procedures

11. Does the company have financial and cost reporting to both (a) monitor the direct production costs for prototyping and building production models and (b) evaluate these costs against preliminary estimates and throughout the process to launch? Does the company prepare sales reports down to the product level to evaluate sales performance?

    Cost reports are needed to monitor the investment expended during design, prototyping, production, testing, and launch and to evaluate the product's ROI post-launch. Sales reports are needed for evaluating sales activity and results post-launch. Without these reports, management will not be alerted to problems and will not be able to take remedial action to keep the project on track toward forecasted outcomes.

Management Experience, Track Record with NPD

12. Is management experienced in designing, developing, and launching new products? If not, can the company hire or contract to have this expertise available for guidance from design, through launch, and to post-launch?

Definition of Success, Evaluation Criteria, and Go/Kill Decision Ability

13. Has management determined what it wants the new product to accomplish in terms of growth: increased sales via product extensions, modifications, replacement, substitute, or breakthrough products; extending or filling gaps in the product line; opening or further penetrating new markets; or countering competition? Have cost–benefit analyses, ROI, profit, and cash flow projections been made?

14. Have quantitative criteria been developed for monitoring and evaluating the project from design and concept through launch? For example, budgets for prototyping and production, field testing, market

analysis and launch strategies (sales potential, competitive comparisons, promotional, advertising, and channel strategies, and training)?

15. Has management established criteria by which to make a go-kill decision; for example, when initial costs for prototyping and production exceed estimates, or market and competitor analysis show potential poor performance or customer acceptance, or revenue and margin indicators show financial return below expectations? Does management have the fortitude and experience to make a go-kill decision?

Many new product projects languish or fail because management has neglected to set effective evaluation criteria and is unwilling to kill a potentially poor performing project, leading to delays in getting promising products to market, high development costs, and legacy projects.

> It is just as critical to identify potential failures early via effective evaluation criteria and terminate them, as it is to hit the ball out of the park.

Summary

New product development, despite its popularity and almost universal recognition as a "must do" for companies' long-term survival, is not suitable for all SMMs and should be pursued with preparation and due diligence, given the high failure rate of new products. Past chapters and questionnaire results show that many SMMs do not follow good business practices, such as knowing product costs and margins, conducting marketing research, and monitoring competition, that must precede not only the decision to pursue NPD, but also to inform decisions about which types of new products to develop: modifications, line extensions, replacement, substitute, leading edge, or new to the world. A SMM that does not have these basic business systems, practices, procedures, and policies in place should not consider NPD.

Additionally, once in the process of developing new products, many SMMs fail to implement effective checks and balances to ensure the product is the right one and to evaluate its progress through development to launch. Most of their NPD activities focus on the technical aspects rather than on the marketing and competitive aspects, which often are executed poorly or altogether omitted and are the most frequent reasons for new product failure.

SMMs' attempts to generate ideas for new products often lead to poor selections because they do not establish clear criteria on which to evaluate the ideas. Many new products fail because they do not match the company's core competencies and strategic thrust, financial situation, organizational skills and capabilities, and customers and markets. The adoption of more structured ideation practices, rather than wide-open shotgun ideation, could improve the likelihood that an idea would fit the SMM's definition of success for a new product.

SMMs would improve their chances for success by stepping back and waiting for the right pitch just to get on base (better analysis and due diligence), rather than trying to hit the ball out of the park (shotgun marketing and hasty pursuit of the potentially wrong product).

In this chapter, I have attempted to explain why SMMs should approach new product development cautiously, primarily because most attempts fail; only about 15% of new products succeed. Cooper's studies show most failures result not from technical reasons, such as problematic production processes, and R&D but from factors external to the business, such as insights into market and customer needs and competitors. Questionnaire responses to questions dealing with customers, markets, and competitors mirror the Cooper's findings—SMMs do not cross the t's and dot the i's when it comes to market and competitor insights and knowledge.

This chapter's discussion of NPD dealt with organic new product development—a company designing and producing its own new products—and did not talk about NPD via acquisition or purchase of existing products, technologies, patents, and companies. Whether a company pursues NPD organically or via acquisition, the outcome is the same—it changes or adds to the company's product offering—only the strategy for achieving it changes. The strategic issues and conditions underlying the two approaches to NPD also differ, which are discussed in Chapter 9.

CHAPTER 8

Marketing Research and Competitor Information

General business principles say that a company should have information about its markets and competition when developing a business, sales, marketing, or growth strategy. Yet my experience and SMMs' responses to the questionnaire show that SMMs do not have good data and information about their markets. The following Tables 44, 45, and 46 summarize companies' responses to the questionnaire regarding marketing research and knowledge about their markets.

Job shops, machine companies, and product companies equally—both 61%—have never conducted marketing research, yet most say they can define their market segments. However, as shown in Table 7 in Chapter 1—Actual Market Segment Descriptions, those definitions are too vague to direct sales personnel to new markets and new customers.

A key question asked if the company knew the number of establishments or potential customers in its defined segments. Only 40 (19 + 21) of the 108 (126 – 18) firms answering the question knew some or all establishments or potential customers despite 107 (Table 44) saying they can define their market segments. For purposes of planning and directing sales force activity, knowing the number and location of customers and prospects is critical.

Questions about their knowledge of competitors and about collecting competitive intelligence indicate they lack good empirical data and information. Ninety reported knowing competitors; yet only 20 collected some data. In spite of this, 85 reported their products and services possessed at least some competitive advantage—24 more than the 61 who reported knowing competitor's strengths and weakness (S&W). It is curious they believe they have at least some advantage without knowing or having good data about competitors (see Table 46).

Table 44. SMMs' Marketing Research and Segment Definitions

Market Research	Job shop				Product				Type			Total
	1	2	3	Total	1	2	3	Total	1	2	3	
Within last 5 years	0	5	4	9	0	7	7	14	0	12	11	23
Longer than 5 years	0	0	0	0	0	1	0	1	0	1	0	1
Never	4	19	11	34	2	28	14	44	6	47	25	78
Don't know, not asked, unanswered	8	3	1	12	12	0	0	12	20	3	1	24
Total	12	27	16	55	14	36	21	71	26	63	37	126
Market Segments												
Can define	9	20	14	43	13	32	19	64	22	52	33	107
Can't define	3	7	2	12	1	4	2	7	4	11	19	19
Total	12	27	16	55	14	36	21	71	26	63	52	126

Table 45. Know Number of Establishments

Know No. Establishments	Job shop				Product				Type			Total
	1	2	3	Total	1	2	3	Total	1	2	3	
Don't know, not asked, unanswered	6	0	0	6	12	0	0	12	18	0	0	18
Don't know estab.	6	21	12	39	2	17	10	29	8	38	22	68
Know some	0	4	1	5	0	8	6	14	0	12	7	19
Know establish.	0	2	3	5	0	11	5	16	0	13	8	21
Total	12	27	16	55	14	36	21	71	26	63	37	126

Table 46. SMMs' Knowledge of Competitors

	Job shop				Product				Type			
	1	2	3	Total	1	2	3	Total	1	2	3	Total
Not asked, answered	12	17	0	29	12	14	0	26	24	31	0	55
Do not get info	0	7	15	22	1	10	18	29	1	17	33	51
Conduct informally	0	3	0	3	0	5	2	7	0	8	2	10
Have formal process	0	0	1	1	1	7	1	9	1	7	2	10
Total	12	27	16	55	14	36	21	71	26	63	37	126
Can I.D. competitors	6	13	10	29	9	32	20	61	15	45	30	90
know S&W	2	7	6	15	6	26	14	46	8	33	20	61
Some, certain advantage	5	12	10	27	11	30	17	58	16	42	27	85

Given the discrepancies between:

- no marketing research yet knowing market segments but not the number of establishments and prospects, and
- not collecting competitor data but nevertheless believing competitive advantage exists

most market and competitor information that SMMs use could be anecdotal. Of the 61 firms saying they know competitors' strengths and weaknesses, only 10 collect any data, Table 47.

Table 47. Knowing Competitors' Strengths and Weaknesses

Collect information	Job shop				Product				Type			
	1	2	3	Total	1	2	3	Total	1	2	3	Total
No	0	3	5	8	0	8	11	19	0	11	16	27
Not asked	2	1	0	3	5	6	0	11	7	7	0	14
Informal	0	3	0	3	0	5	2	7	0	8	2	10
Yes	0	0	1	1	1	7	1	9	1	7	2	10
Total	2	7	6	15	6	26	14	46	8	33	20	61

Simplifying Marketing Research and Competitor Intelligence

Most SMMs I have assisted did not employ dedicated marketing specialists or researchers. So when it was time to develop sales, marketing, or growth strategies, insightful market information was absent. (This is why shotgun marketing is so prevalent—it does not require any on-going marketing research and intelligence gathering efforts or insights into markets and competitors.) However, marketing research and competitor intelligence can be simplified and made less expensive. This is done using three sources of data previously presented:

1. Customer analysis and profiling,
2. Lost order analysis, and
3. Customer satisfaction feedback.

Since the cost to compile much of this information already would have been incurred during *C-P-M*™ analyses, any additional effort or refinement of the data for use in strategy development is minimal. Figure 62 shows how the three items, when combined, establish the groundwork for considering preliminary market opportunities and competitive improvements to product and service offerings.

Customer Profiling. Customer profiles, based on SIC codes, and employment size more sharply define the types of businesses that have

Additional value of C-P-M™ analyses		
	Internal use	Marketing research and competitor intelligence
Customer Profiling	Identify winners and losers in the customer mix. Develop account management strategies to strengthen the business relationship and to find ways to make current customers more profitable to sell to.	Develop profiles using SIC codes and employment size for finding new customers like MVCs (most valuable customers) in existing or new markets.
Lost Order Analysis	Reduce the time and cost to prepare a quote. Improve operations to shorten delivery time, improve quality and product performance, modify price if necessary, improve customer service, sales coverage and sales channels, etc.	Identify competitors; their strengths and weaknesses. Improve competitive position and value-proposition: product performance, quality, delivery, customer services, tech support, sales coverage and sales channels, etc. The dollar amount of bids and quotes can be used as a proxy for sales potential without having to conduct marketing research.
Customer Information, Feedback	Learn the competitive factors customers consider important when selecting suppliers. Learn how well the company is performing on these competitive factors. Improve customer satisfaction through continuous improvement.	
Overall strategic objective: To sharpen market definitions, become a target marketer, and strengthen competitive position.		

Figure 62. Customer analysis and profiling, lost order analysis, and customer feedback aiding marketing research and competitor intelligence.

potential for adding customers and increasing sales. This greatly reduces the guesswork involved in deciding what markets to research and overcomes the problems associated with vague and poorly defined market descriptions.

Finding more customers who are similar to existing customers, which is the most common growth strategy, simply calls for finding prospects that match the profiles of existing customers. Chapter 3 mentions 10 projects that used this strategy to identify growth opportunities.

Lost Order Analysis. Lost order feedback is used internally to improve the time and expense of preparing quotes and to make changes in operations, and externally to improve products, pricing, quality, delivery, customer services, sales coverage and channels—all things to improve the firm's competitive situation. But one of the biggest benefits is that the dollar amount of bids prepared is an excellent substitute for estimating the potential to increase sales with minimal cost or conducting marketing research. However, the sum of dollars bid will be much less than the actual market potential because it does not include all bids submitted by competitors for that order or product.

Chapter 4 mentioned Peachstate Construction, a metals fabrication company that submitted about $100 million in quotes but was winning only about 10%. The $100 million was a pretty good estimate of sales potential. A reasonable use of this piece of data for growth planning purposes would be to estimate a target increase in the hit rate, for example, up to 30% from its historical 10% to 13%, which would add $3 million to sales.

Conveyor Specialty, Inc., a producer of palletizing equipment also mentioned in Chapter 4, is another example. Using quotation and lost order analysis and data obtained on competitors, it estimated the sales potential for its palletizing equipment at $116 million but was only participating in $14.3 million and raised its forecast from 70 units to 100 units per year. It used profiles of existing customers to locate prospects for its existing product line, and significantly rearranged its inside and outside sales personnel and sales channels. Inside sales focused on qualifying the prospects and generating leads. Independent reps were converted to exclusive status to increase and gain more influence over sales coverage. All this was accomplished without conducting extensive primary and secondary marketing research.

Customer Feedback. Customer feedback from customer satisfaction surveys provides three dimensions of information—the last one being the most pertinent to competitor intelligence:

- Factors that are important to customers in their selection of suppliers of products and services the firm offers.
- The identification of competitors (some the company might not have known about) and their performance on the factors.

The combination of lost order information and customer survey feedback not only provides critically important information about changes that can improve a company's competitive situation but also identifies competitors and their relative strengths and weaknesses.

All three—customer profiling, lost order analysis, and customer feedback—are done at nominal additional cost, provide huge benefits, and help answer the big market questions:

- "Where are the opportunities?"
- "How big is the market?"
- The biggest "how to" question—"How can we increase sales and grow profitably?"

This approach greatly minimizes the guesswork in market research and in getting intelligence about competition. It places marketing research and competitor intelligence within the realm of affordability and practicality for SMMs.

Low Cost versus High Cost Market Research and Competitor Information—An Incremental and Sequential Approach

Figure 63 illustrates how customer profiling, lost order analysis, and customer feedback can be used with three other types of research and information gathering: prospect qualification, secondary marketing research, and direct contact, also called primary marketing research. The five items shown in the lower cost area are so considered because they either have already been completed via *C-P-M*™ or can be completed at relatively lower cost than direct contact, shown in the higher cost area. They also are appropriate to all types of SMMs while direct contact, which is primary marketing research, entails considerable design, administration, and interpretation costs. Because direct contact costs more, it is better suited to Types 2 and 3 that more likely can afford it.

The incremental and sequential approach builds on *C-P-M*™ (customer analysis and profiling, lost order and quotation analysis, and customer feedback) and progresses to prospect qualification and secondary and primary research, if needed. It uses facts derived from *C-P-M*™ to augment what might be known by management about the firm's potential to grow. In doing so, it improves the quality of decisions about growth strategies.

Prospect qualification, also called "prospecting," calls for contacting prospective businesses to learn if they are candidates for a firm's products and services. The projects I conducted used clients' customer profiles based on SIC/NAICS to select prospects from publicly available

	Incremental and sequential approach to marketing research and competitor intelligence		
	Type 1	Type 2	Type 3
Lower cost	Customer profiling		
	Lost order analysis		
	Customer information, feedback		
	Prospect qualification		
	Publicly available sources of information (secondary marketing research)		
Higher cost		Direct contact with industry specialists, suppliers, competitors, experts and consultants (primary marketing research)	

Figure 63. Incremental and sequential approach to marketing research and competitor intelligence.

marketing databases. It was used primarily to assess the interest or demand for clients' products and services in new target markets or to assess the receptivity of existing customers to clients' ideas for new products and services.

The incremental and sequential approach also takes into account the type and size of the SMM. The five low-cost items shown in the chart are ideally suited for Type 1s who have limited resources. While Type 2s and 3s also can benefit from this approach, they might need direct contact or primary marketing research to determine more accurate market potential and to better define competitive factors and sales channels, particularly if pursuing riskier and more expensive growth strategies, such as new product development. The higher cost of direct contact or marketing research projects derives from having to design, administer face-to-face interviewing in the field or telephone interviews, and analyze a questionnaire that probably uses open-ended and follow-up questions that add considerable administrative cost.

The marginal and sequential approach has been very useful with clients who say they do not know where to begin to research markets, to increase sales, or that they have so many ideas they do not know which to pursue. It is practicable, methodical, and easily understood once customer and product data are compiled, analyzed, and summarized so that owners and top management clearly see the implications of $C\text{-}P\text{-}M^{™}$ analyses and opportunities. The task of prioritizing ideas or growth opportunities involving existing or new products is greatly simplified once product profitability and number of potential customers is known, the dollar value of potential sales (derived from lost order information and prospect qualification), and competitors' relative strengths and weaknesses is documented.

The following seven examples illustrate the use of profiling, prospect qualification, secondary research, and direct contact to estimate market potential and to generate business.

Forashe International, a Type 2 company mentioned in Chapter 3, wanted to open a new market with a new adhesive formulation that did not contain styrene, which the EPA had listed as hazardous. After reviewing three industries known for volatile organic compounds (VOC) and styrene use—fiber fiberglass-reinforced plastic (FRP), pipe coating, and manufactured housing—it chose FRP because of its less costly testing requirements and certificates of performance required by the two other industries and it also had bath ware customers.

Table 48 shows Forashe's estimates of unit and dollar volumes, market penetration, and sales potential for three target market segments after completing the research. The sales manager calculated sales potential by multiplying units × lbs. per unit × the dollar selling price per unit, and roughly estimated Forashe's target penetration of one out of five prospects for steel and gel coat and two out of five for acrylic based on feedback from field trails.

The sales manager was able to segment bath ware by type of product (sink, tub, and shower) and also by process (steel, acrylic, or gel coat), and develop forecast numbers based on units, pounds per unit, and his own costs and pricing. He also produced a list of all prospects in each segment, which enabled him to prioritize product launch and segments and develop a detailed sales call plan, schedule, and budget.

His initial attempts using SIC/NAICS customer profiles to identify prospects in marketing databases was unsuccessful because they did not identify specific styrene users. His searches resulted in thousands of

Table 48. Forashe's Estimate of Market Potential

Enameled steel bath ware					
Segment	Units	Lbs.\ unit	Sales Potential	Target Penetration	Sales Goal
Bath Sink	1,811,862	5	$7,704,943	20%	$1,540,989
Kitchen Sink	511,252	12	5,217,838	20%	1,043,568
Tub	891,669	30	22,750,935	20%	4,550,187
Total			$35,673,716		$7,134,743

Acrylic bath ware					
Segment	Units	Lbs.\ unit	Sales Potential	Target Penetration	Sales Goal
Bath Sink	569,190	10	$4,840,961	40%	$1,936,384
Kitchen Sink	558,642	22	8,517,056	40%	3,406,822
Tub	198,382	45	6,186,543	40%	2,474,617
Shower	97,891	30	2,035,154	40%	814,062
Whirlpool	469,865	85	27,677,398	40%	11,070,959
Wall Surround	98,572	45	3,073,968	40%	1,229,587
Total			$52,331,079		$20,932,432

Gel coat bath ware					
Segment	Units	Lbs.\ unit	Sales Potential	Target Penetration	Sales Goal
Tub	2,450,632	45	$110,280,000	20%	$22,055,688
Shower	651,875	30	19,556,250	20%	3,911,250
Whirlpool	33,677	85	2,862,545	20%	572,509
Wall Surround	887,150	45	39,921,750	20%	7,984,350
Total			$172,620,000		$34,523,797

companies using polystyrene plastics and resins, but not down to the level of FRP product he sought. Fortunately, the EPA (publicly available data and secondary research) had listed 1,400 companies and the amount of styrene they emitted, which provided the exact data he needed. He also referenced industry and trade association publications. After paring down the EPA list, he qualified 22 companies and arranged 13 in-plant demos.

By accessing public information and subsequently directly contacting prospects, he was able to segment the market, prioritize the segments, and develop a launch plan. This is a classic example of combining public information and direct contact to identify and prioritize growth opportunities. The cost for this project, estimated at about $3,000, assuming the sales manager's salary at $75,000 annually and 80 hours for the project, was relatively small because he accomplished it himself without outside assistance. Within 5 years, Forashe developed four key customers that generated about $1 million per year each and accounted for about 25% of its total business.

Chatham HVAC, a Type 2, 20-year-old $6 million company, realizing that its business and local markets had matured, sought to purchase a $600,000 machine to automate sheet metal duct fabrication to reduce costs and to convert competitors to customers with a novel value-added proposition—the delivery of fabricated and preassembled duct to job sites at a price below their current costs for duct plus on-site labor to assemble. It combined both low-cost and high-cost market research to assess the financial and market risks, and directly contacted target customers and their competitors to test the new product concept. It also purchased industry construction reports that forecasted moderate growth in its primary market segments—hospitals, government, military, industrial, and schools and colleges. The firm's financial situation, despite a flat sales trend and low net profits and moderate cash flow, could support capital investment due to good net worth, working capital, and liquidity. Management's insightful knowledge of its markets and competitors, combined with the results of direct surveys and public market reports, led it to decide in favor of the project. This is a textbook example of an SMM doing its *C-P-M*™ and due diligence before launching a new product—it put the horse in front of the cart. Estimated cost of the research, including industry reports, was about $5,500.

Southeast Cut & Saw, Inc., a 60-employee, Type 2, producer of industrial saw blades wanted to expand sales into SIC 2421/NAICS 321912-321113 (Sawmills and Planing Mills), a new market segment for the company. It used a publicly available marketing database to identify and locate sawmill plants, segmented by number of employees, and found almost 300 prospective new customers (a.k.a. "suspects"). It telephone-qualified 130 using inside sales employees, asking about their usage of saw blades, enabling the company to estimate the sales potential in that market segment at $2,650,000 per year (Figure 64). With this information, the firm prepared sales call plans/schedules and prioritized on-site initial visits according to location and plant size. This project cost about

	Estimate of market size—sawmills plant purchases			
Emp. Size	1 to 20	21 to 99	100+	Total
No. of Plants	139	92	61	292
Phone Qualified	80	30	20	130
Avg. Purchases	$5,000	$25,000	$75,000	
Sales Potential by Plant Size	$400,000	$750,000	$1,500,000	
Total Market Potential				$2,650,000

Figure 64. Estimate of sawmill market size using plant purchases.

$4,500, as follows: about 1.75 hours average per qualified prospect to call 292 companies, qualify them, record results, prepare sales plans/schedules, and so forth, at $20 per hour for telephoning wages (1.75 hours × 130 × $20 = $4,550).

Dan's Machine Shop, a 10-employee Type 1 company in metro Atlanta, found over 30 prospects with annual budgets for buying machining services interested in learning more about his machining capabilities. He initially focused on SIC 3400 Metalworking Machinery and Equipment/NAICS 333512 Machine Tool Manufacturing that comprised over 500 Georgia locations, but narrowed his search to metro Atlanta's two area codes at that time, 404 and 770, to reduce the number of suspects to a more reasonable 292, excluding locations with less than 10 employees. He telephone-qualified 34 and learned their annual budgets for contracted machining services ranged between $1,200 and $4,500, and concluded the sales potential for his services were between $276,000 and $1,035,000 (see Figure 65). Considering his sales of $200,000 were just below breakeven, the area's sales potential represented an opportunity to become profitable. This project generated leads he otherwise would not have been able to find, given that he was a machine operator as well as the company's only sales person.

The project's budget of 40 hours ($1,200) limited the number of suspects to call and had to terminate with 71 calls, of which 61 got through to the person in charge of buying contract machine services. Thirty-four said "yes" to getting more information about Dan's Machine Shop or a sales call, a 56% "hit rate" (34 out of 61 contacted).

The average time to generate a qualified lead was 1.2 hours, costing on average about $35 each. Considering the national average cost of a

	Estimate of metro atlanta sales potential plant purchases				
Emp. Size	Under 10	10 to 25	26 to 50	Over 50	Total
Total 3400 in Ga	46	222	130	153	551
No. of Plants (404) and (770)		108	61	61	230
No. of.Locations Called		37	23	11	71
Successful Calls		33	23	5	61
Answering #6 "Yes"		19	13	2	34
Est. Annual Budget ~ Low					$1,200
Est. Annual Budget ~ High					$4,500
Total Market Potential				$276,000 to $1,035,000	

Figure 65. Estimate of machine shop market size using plant purchases.

Project statistics	
Average time to generate a qualified lead	40 hours ÷ 34 leads = 1.2 hours
Average cost per lead	$1,200 ÷ 34 leads = $35
Average cost per FTF sales call	$150–$200

Figure 66. Lead-generation costs and statistics.

face-to-face sales call ranges between $250 and $400, including travel, lodging, and so forth, Dan felt the $35 was a bargain, Figure 66.

VIS, Inc., a Type 2 producer of visual inspection systems to detect the fill capacity of containers in the industrial liquids industry priced between $14,000 and $55,000, wanted to expand into the food preparation industry, targeting these 10 SICs:

- 2032 Canned Specialties
- 2033 Canned Fruits, Vegetables, Preserves, Jams, and Jellies
- 2035 Pickled Fruits and Vegetables, Vegetable Sauces and Seasonings, and Salad Dressings
- 2047 Dog and Cat Food
- 2082 Malt Beverages
- 2085 Distilled and Blended Liquors
- 2086 Bottled and Canned Soft Drinks and Carbonated Waters
- 2091 Canned and Cured Fish and Seafoods
- 2095 Roasted Coffee
- 2099 Food Preparations, Not Elsewhere Classified

The project covered 763 suspected companies in Indiana, Kentucky, Michigan, western New York, Ohio, western Pennsylvania, and West Virginia where it had sales coverage with company sales and commissioned reps. VIS contacted all 763 companies to qualify them in terms of production processes, types of products, and interest of buying the detection systems; 246 qualified—a 32% "hit rate". It sent literature to all 246 and followed up via telephone and on-site demonstrations, producing 38 quotes totaling $840,000. The project's budget included 300 telephone hours (six people on the phones for two weeks) at $15 per hour plus material and postage at actual cost of $858, totaling $5,358. The average cost per quote was $141.

Swiss Solutions, mentioned in Chapter 3, a Type 1 seven-employee start-up making customized rubber rollers for the carpet/textile industry, had been unsuccessful at networking to establish leads in the local community. The owner, who was also the only sales person, believed his custom rollers would work well in the packaging industry and wanted to develop prospects within a 100-mile radius to minimize his travel to promote to prospective packaging customers. After screening over 1,300 packaging-related companies in Georgia, Tennessee, and Alabama that were listed in a marketing database, he selected 200 for qualification due to size, SIC/NAICS, and proximity, and prioritized a schedule for telephoning and qualifying them. Within 3 months, he had called all 200 suspects and set up 28 sales appointments over the following 2 months—a 14% "hit rate." He developed several new customers, one who ordered between $4,000 and $8,000 per month of a new product he helped tailor to the customer's needs, and four others who ordered about $1,000 per month. Budgeted cost to call 200 suspects, qualify them, send literature, and set up appointments = $4,000.

Coastal Industrial Equipment, also mentioned in Chapter 3, a Type 2 firm that produces and sells capital equipment to cut steel tubing up to 4″ diameter, had been operating at or below breakeven after losing about a third of its sales following the 2001 recession and 9/11. It sold both domestically and overseas, but prioritized finding new domestic customers in its established consumer and automotive markets—companies producing tubing for playground items, tables, bicycles, mufflers, struts, and so forth. It commissioned three research projects involving six SIC/NAICS pertaining to steel/iron pipes, tubes, and fabrication and three SIC/NAICS for copper and aluminum, on an assumption that it might consider adapting to nonsteel metals. The professional B2B market researchers called 605 companies and qualified 89 as interested in either a sales call or literature, or both, which is a 15% hit rate typical of this type of marketing research. The projects cost $11,450, on average about $20 per company called, is also typical for this type of project. The project also unexpectedly revealed more than 200 companies its six national reps were unaware of, leading the company to hire a sales manager to improve sales organization, communication, and lead follow-up.

As the examples illustrate, market research can take various forms and paths and can vary in sophistication and expense, depending on a company's needs and budget. Obviously, the more extensive the research, the more costly, as with Chatham HVAC and Coastal Industrial Equipment. Since each company's needs and budget differ, the nature and scope of a marketing research project should be tailored to each situation. In many cases where the SMM simply wants to increase sales with existing products, a qualification or lead-generation project using SIC/NAICS profiles of existing customers fills the need at nominal cost, typically between $3,000 and $5,000, depending on the number of suspects the company wants to qualify. Selling existing products to existing or similar types of customers is the least costly and risky of all growth strategies and easiest to execute.

My experience with this type of project involves selecting about 200 suspects from a database of thousands of establishments that match SIC/NAICS and employment profiles because 200 seems to be the number that most SMMs can manage over a couple months. Any more than 200 overwhelm company personnel's ability to follow-up on leads with appointment setting, mailing literature, and so on. Two hundred suspects, on average, result in about 30 to 40 qualified leads, which is about a 15% to 20% hit rate and corresponds to the results presented earlier. The cost per qualified lead or quote (depending on the size and nature of the project and intended results) varies from around $30 to $50.

Note the use of plant purchases or budgets as a proxy for sales potential by Southeast Cut & Saw and Dan's Machine Shop. While the criteria of SIC/NAICS and size are good initial indicators that a company might be a prospect, plant purchases or budgets get to the heart of the matter quickly.

There are common denominators underlying the success of these projects. None of the companies simply started researching. Rather, they all had either made some assumptions about their target markets or had conducted some review and analysis to better define the nature and scope of the research.

Forashe International initially researched three industries (secondary research) before choosing FRP and further narrowed its focus to bath ware because it had some knowledge of that product area via existing customers. Although customer profiles using SIC/NAICS did not give the sales manger the information he needed to identify specific prospects, his continued research eventually found the EPA data that did. The company's due diligence began with a broad review of prospective industries and eventually narrowed to specific prospects in one segment of one industry. It progressed from a generalized definition of market and industry to one that specifically defined the target customer.

Chatham HVAC realized that although the cost of market research could be high and might show its product concept was not viable, avoiding a $600,000 mistake justified the expense of due diligence and market research. Chatham's GM had already run the preliminary financial cost–benefit analysis based on his direct material and labor costs, had a good handle on the volume needed to justify the purchase, had identified target customers and competitors, but did not know the economic and industry outlooks for his geographical market and whether the target market would be receptive to his idea. He knew his costs, target customers, competitors, and their locations, but lacked critical information; whether the industry and economic outlook and customer acceptance were favorable. Thus, he was able to narrow down the scope of the research effort and knew exactly the types of information missing, which helped him define nature, scope, and budget limitation of the project.

Southeast Cut & Saw's project was simply lead-generation for its sales force to locate new customers that matched existing customer profiles for an existing product familiar to the prospective customers. It had a clear definition of the target customer and promoted a product prospects knew.

Dan's Machine Shop, because of its small size and understanding that it could not service a big geographical area, localized its research to metro Atlanta and limited the SIC/NAIC to Metalworking Machinery and Equipment attempting to become a sub-contractor to larger machining companies. It had a clear definition of the target customer.

VIS, Inc. wanted to expand from industrial liquids to food processing with its existing product line, an example of selling existing product to new customers or markets. Visual inspection technology had improved, particularly VIS's, leading to the assumption it could transition to food processing because it had insights into food processing requirements that its technology could handle. In targeting the 10 SIC/NAICS classifications, it narrowed its research to a market segment for which it had a reasonable basis to assume its products would be known and the technology accepted. It had a clear definition of the target customer and promoted a product the customer knew about.

Swiss Solutions, assumed its customized rollers would work well—better than OEM rollers in operation, durability, and maintenance—in another industry, the packaging industry, which proved correct. Its owner focused on one particular segment of industry that used rollers rather than shot gun marketing his sales and promotional efforts.

Coastal Industrial Equipment, similar to Southeast Cut & Saw, wanted to sell existing product to companies similar to its existing customers through its existing sales channels. It clearly defined its target market and offered a product that prospects could easily understand. The interesting aspect of this project was the 200 prospects of which its six national reps were unaware.

Table 49 summarizes these projects' type of research, cost, and results. As noted earlier, the hit rate is the number of suspects that express interest in the company's products and services, want a follow-up or sales call, or literature as a percentage of the number of suspects actually talked to—voice-mails and call-backs do not count. According to the results

Table 49. Summary of Market Research Costs and Results

Company	Type	Research	Cost	Results	Hit rate
Forashe	2	Both secondary and primary	$3,000	1,400 prospects, detailed market analysis and sales plan, 22 qualified prospects, 13 demos	n/a
Chatham HVAC	2	Both secondary and primary	$5,500	green light for $6M investment	n/a
Southeast Cut & Saw	2	Plant purchases, lead-generation	$4,550	130 qualified prospects, market analysis = $2.3M, sales plans	44%
Dan's Machine Shop	1	Plant purchases, lead-generation	$1,200	34 qualified prospects, market estimate > $276,000	56%
VIS, Inc.	2	Lead-generation	$5,358	38 quotes @ $840,000	32%
Swiss Solutions	1	Lead-generation	$4,000	28 qualified leads; several new customers	14%
Coastal Industrial Equipment	2	Lead-generation (3 projects)	$11,450	89 qualified leads; 200+ companies 6 reps were unaware of	15%

in this table, hit rates vary considerably although typically averaging about 15%—for each 100 suspects about 15 will be interested in the products and services. Factors contributing to higher hit rates include a crisp, clearly defined market description, a product or service description that prospects know or understand easily (Southeast Cut & Saw, Dan's Machine Shop, and VIS, Inc.), and the professionalism conveyed by the person contacting the prospect.

Lead-generation market research is particularly well suited for Type 1 and Type 2 companies because of its low cost, ease of design and administration, generally predictable results, and flexibility. Beyond just asking qualifying questions, lead-generation projects can accommodate questions to get information that might provide better insight into the suspect's candidacy as a prospect, such as plant purchase and budgets, which provide a proxy for sales potential, as in the case of Dan's Machine Shop and Southeast Cut & Saw. This type of research is also good for getting early feedback on NPD projects that involve product extensions or modifications and to test product concepts with prospective new customers.

Lead-generation and prospect qualification also tackle the issue of SMMs not conducting marketing research and not knowing the number and location of prospective customers. The market to be researched, by default, is automatically defined, since this type of research uses customer profiles based on SIC/NAICS and employment size, thus avoiding market descriptions that are vague, poorly defined, or industry descriptions (sellers) rather than market descriptions (buyers).

Secondary research, since it involves publicly available data such as government, trade associations, industry publications, and research reports, is a valuable, low-cost starting point. However, it does not provide the granular detail down to the level of decision maker or buyer and whether a prospective company is in fact interested in the product or service offering and therefore worth pursuing. It does provide good overview information, trends, and insights that might inform an SMM of the overall pros and cons of a given market or industry.

Primary research, for example, focus groups (primarily for consumer products), surveys, field tests, face-to-face or telephone interviews, and observation gets down to the granular level, but usually incurs more expense for project definition, design, administration, and analysis. It is better suited where the amount of investment and risk are high, such as with an NPD project where the product is new to the company, industry, or breakthrough. Chatham HVAC's use of primary research for its $600,000 investment for a new machine comprised extensive telephone surveys of prospective customers and competitors. Because of the higher cost, Type 1 firms might not be able to afford primary research.

Be Patient—Rome wasn't Built in a Day

Marketing research generally does not produce immediate results. Secondary research can provide very good and insightful information, but it is not normally actionable. Primary research does a good job of substantiating secondary research findings, providing additional information and insights into the attractiveness of a market, marketability of a new product, the willingness of target prospects to try or buy a new product or service, and might even identify ready buyers. Lead-generation—or prospecting—ascertains if a prospect is interested, has a budget, but still does not result generally in an immediate sale.

Three factors affect the time between obtaining market information, identifying prospects, and getting the sale: B2B quoting, the sales force, and price. In the case where a company sells via quotations, it must get an invitation to quote from the newly identified prospect, and possibly have to submit several quotes before a sale occurs. Second, selling activities (contacting the prospect, sending literature, following up on the lead and more depending on the nature of the product or service), must happen quickly to reinforce the prospect's interest and to solicit an appointment and invitation to quote to build the relationship. The product or service's price also affects the time between prospect qualification and the sale: the higher the price the longer the time between initial contact and sale.

In addition to the likelihood of not producing immediate actionable results and sales, marketing research might also not produce data and information that companies want or need to know.

It's Okay to Chase Rabbits Down a Dry Hole

Marketing research does not always produce positive or expected results. In some cases, it shows there is no or limited market opportunity or produces data contrary to a company's opinions or beliefs about markets, its competitive situation, or growth potential.

Rooftop Industries, Inc., a Type 3 manufacturer of rooftop HVAC systems introduced in Chapter 4, wanted to find new markets since it had fully penetrated its "bread and butter" education market. Quotation analysis, Table 50, showed that its 84 national reps' 2-year total quote production was 1,021, of which 361 were for schools. Also, only about half the reps had produced quotes. Publicly available information showed there were about 91,000 K-12 schools nationally. Assuming each school represented one building and a 20-year life for an HVAC system, we estimated an annual replacement market of about 4,500 schools—not including new construction. Clearly, reps' quote production and the secondary public information showed (a) the firm's school market was not being fully penetrated (we estimated about a 2.4% market penetration) and (b) that reps' sales coverage was inadequate. Rather than pursue new markets, this firm needed to get its reps to increase quotation production and sales performance to get more penetration of its existing market. Estimated cost for the lost order and preliminary market research, less than $2,500.

Table 50. Rooftop's Two-Year Quote

Two-Year summary of quotes			
Market	No.	Sold	% Won
School	361	109	30%
Government	16	5	31%
Industrial	61	10	16%
Commercial	432	59	14%
Other	80	10	13%
Hospital	71	9	13%
Total	1,021	202	20%

Textile Global, a Type 4 producer of woven and nonwoven synthetic products for industrial and consumer applications, needed to determine if there was a market for a breakthrough nonwoven technology that could combine various synthetic materials into new products with unique performance properties. The company considered it a disruptive new technology whose output could displace existing materials used in multitudes of products. Over 200 potential applications were reviewed, for example:

- Soil sealing systems used in landfills or manure pits,
- Engineered fiber-reinforced composites for use in automotive bodies or boat hulls,
- Inflatable buildings used as emergency structures and temporary shelters,
- Reinforcing wrap to repair aging concrete structures such as bridges, overpasses, and high-rise buildings,
- Soft composite belting used in conveyors, treadmills, and grocery store check-out.

Six were selected as possibly complementing the firm's existing product line without cannibalization. Publicly available information and direct interviewing of competitors, suppliers, and potential customers concluded there were insufficient opportunities to displace existing materials at their prevailing costs, volumes, and performance properties. The company avoided a possible multi-million-dollar "problem" investment. Estimated cost for this direct research, $20,000 to $25,000.

Sports Products, a Type 2 producer of specialty sport ropes, had fully penetrated the climbing market via specialty and big box retailers and Internet sales and wanted to explore industrial applications for its technology-enhanced high-performance ropes. We reviewed public information, contacted industry gurus and specialists, and interviewed petroleum and chemical companies to learn about their purchases of specialty ropes for safety and rescue applications. We found insufficient demand of ropes for these applications and that the market was fragmented (difficult to locate a clear entry point or buying authority). Estimated cost for this research, less than $5,000.

The owner of **BuzzCo**, a 30-employee machine shop mentioned in Chapters 2, 3, and 4, wanting his own product line to expand his business beyond producing parts for other companies, needed help in deciding whether to buy the assets of a company that produced and sold a device that lubricates railroad rails as wheels rolled over them. Internet searches found a large Pennsylvania company that produced and sold a competing device with distribution in Europe and South America and strategic partnerships with lubricant companies. It was obvious he should not pursue this for competitive reasons, but additionally his business was not set up to produce and sell its own product line. It would not have been a strategic fit with his core business and he would have had to develop a sales distribution channel. Estimated cost is about $500 for Internet search and a few telephone calls.

Madsen Pipe, introduced in Chapter 3, a Type 3 producer of large steel pipe used in highway, bridge, and foundation construction thought wind-turbine towers might be a market for its thick-walled pipe. We found abundant government data on wind energy, as it is subject to government regulation, that listed the number of existing and planned towers, locations, engineering and structural data, turbine manufacturers, and economic and legislative issues affecting the industry. We also conducted on-site and telephone interviews of turbine tower manufacturers and suppliers. At the time, vertically integrated global turbine manufacturers were consolidating the industry, thus raising barriers to entry into the supply chain. Through the on-site and telephone interviews we learned that engineering, structural, and liability issues exceeded Madsen's capacities in those areas. Although the research showed no potential for

Madsen to enter the wind energy industry, the firm felt the $3,000 cost for the project allowed its sales and marketing personnel to stay focused on its core business while management continued to explore new market and growth opportunities.

Bulldog Machine & Die, Inc., a Type 2, 25-year old machine company founded on a proprietary hardening process for steel and exotic metals, built a very profitable business replacing OEM high-impact parts for air jet looms. The especially hardened replacement parts significantly outperformed OEM parts—a distinct and unmatchable competitive advantage. As loom technology matured and the equipment migrated to developing countries, Bulldog Machine & Die's business fell and leveled off around breakeven, unable to find niches for its proprietary hardening capabilities.

A different product it made for one customer, however, encouraged Bulldog's owner to look for other customers that might need similar products—components used in high-pressure and destructive environments such as underground shale oil wells. He took on a B2B telemarketing lead-generation project to find new customers, understanding that it would take some time, maybe up to a year since bidding and quoting would be required. However, he was unwilling to allow the B2B telemarketers to describe to prospective customers the unique features of the product he made for his drilling equipment customer, for reasons of confidentiality.

The project narrowed down 18 SIC/NAICS industries to 2 SIC/NAICS *3533/333132 Oil & Gas Field Machinery and Equipment* and *3561/333911 Pumps & Pumping Equipment* in 13 states, targeting 176 companies. After the B2B telemarketers called 128 suspects resulting in 32 (see Figure 67) wanting a follow-up call and / or literature, an 18% hit rate, Bulldog's owner terminated the $3,850 project after contacting a few because his follow-up calls to them were unproductive—they did not know why he was calling. And, because of the confidentiality constraint, he could not articulate a benefit or advantage of the uniqueness of the features he developed for use in high-pressure and destructive drilling environments. He acknowledged not always sending out literature promptly and not always calling within 48 hours of receiving a qualified lead from the telemarketer, which was the prescribed procedure for responding to a qualified lead.

As with all sales and marketing strategies, or any strategy for that matter, midcourse corrections are needed when desired outcomes do not

	TX	11
	IN	4
	IL, OH, OK	3
	AR, FL, GA, KY, LA, SC, TN, VA	1
	Total	32

Figure 67. Bulldog's qualified leads.

materialize. Given his acknowledgment that he did not always follow pre-scribed procedure and that that up to a year could be needed to develop new customers, he might have been a little impatient. Maybe his assump-tion that only two SIC/NAICs focused on drilling and gas was insuf-ficient and his decision to disallow a description of the drilling product limited his chances of attracting customers in those segments. In effect, not promoting the unique features and attributes he imparted to the drill-ing product deprived him of promoting a competitive advantage and dif-ferentiating his machining business. Although discussed at the inception of the project as a possible limitation, he assumed the distance between Georgia (both he and his customer resided there) and the states he tar-geted for gas and oil customers would not be a factor. Possible midcourse corrections could have included:

- Having the telemarketers re-call the leads to remind them of their initial conversation and interest.
- Being more responsive to leads.
- Setting up a second project to focus on the 16 other SIC/NAICS that matched his customer profiles nearer to Georgia—widening the scope to improve his chances of finding customers.
- Being more creative in promoting the attributes and features his proprietary hardening process offered.

These examples show that marketing research does not guarantee the results some SMMs expect or want and possibly indicate why so many do not engage in it—they do not see the value, particularly if they're looking for the "magic key" that points to the ideal customer that has an order ready to place. In many cases, marketing research indicates where opportunities exist or do not exist and that:

1. Additional research is needed to get to the "ideal" customer or market,
2. The products and services are not sufficiently differentiated, have no competitive advantage, or
3. There is no market for the product or service.

In instances 2 and 3 the firm will have spent nominally to learn there is no or limited market for its products or services or that there is no differentiating competitive advantage, thus realizing there is no point in continuing to market and promote its products and services as they are. This is why the incremental and sequential approach benefits SMMs. It calls for making a small initial investment (or larger in the case of Chatham HVAC and Textile Global where the product development cost is high) to test assumptions and to decide if the results justify further research. There is a benefit to knowing the markets and customers not to pursue (and products not to develop in the case of NPD) and whether products and services are sufficiently differentiated or possess competitive advantage.

While discussing the pros, cons, and cost-per-lead of lead-generation, one owner commented that spending a couple of thousand dollars to know which companies not to call on was cheaper and more effective than having his sales force driving up and down I-85 (the corridor between Atlanta and Greensboro, SC) knocking on doors looking for business. He saw the benefit of knowing whom not to call on and knowing who to call on so that he could better direct and manage his selling efforts. This is the essence of operating for profit and target marketing.

Market Share of What?

Owners and managers have asked if I could tell them their market share. I say I can if they tell me the market(s) or segments they're in.

Expectedly, their answers resemble the vague descriptions given in the questionnaire, such as automotive, die-casting, growers, roll and web business, consumer electronics, and so on. Similarly, a company might define its markets according to the industries identified by its trade association; particularly in job shop and machining businesses. For example, BuzzCo's owner asked if I could tell him his market share, defining his markets as aerospace, defense, transportation, automotive, appliance, business machines, electronics, agricultural implements, ordnance, and environmental listed in his trade association's annual report. After preparing a customer profile from his customer base, we found that his 53 customers represented 10 major SIC/NAICS industries and 32 SIC/NAICS subcategories—quite a wide swath of types of companies. Job shops and machine companies are quintessential shotgun marketers because they do not differentiate and serve many types of businesses, as BuzzCo's customer analysis showed.

After asking to define their markets and getting their answers, I follow up with, "If I told you your market share, what would you do with that information?" Suppose, just using aerospace as an example, which is composed of about 1,300 companies with $170 billion in sales, and BuzzCo's average sales of about $3 million, I told him his market share was 0.0018% in aerospace. What if I told him, based on 1,300 aerospace companies, his two aerospace customers represent a 0.1538% market share? What if the establishments in the 32 SIC/NAICS categories totaled to 12,348 companies, giving his 53 customers a 0.4292% market share? Since many SMMs cannot define their markets and likely are shot gunners, the concept of market share, while interesting, does not offer much strategic or actionable value, particularly when even gross estimates indicate share in fractions of a percent.

I suggest to SMMs that rather than dwell on market share, they define their markets, determine the number of establishments (including existing customers) in those markets, and measure their success in terms of increasing sales to existing customers and adding new ones in those target markets. Chapter 3 describes BuzzCo targeting three SICs because secondary marketing research reported them as growing: 3400 Fabricated Metal Products, 3600 Electrical and Electronic Equipment, and 3700 Transportation Equipment. Lead-generation and qualification produced 143 leads within 100 miles out of 1,639 establishments in those three SIC codes that matched his SIC/NAICS and employment size profiles. One hundred forty-three target companies are more meaningful—and actionable—than a decimal percentage market share. His sales and marketing goal of converting 143 prospects to customers is more meaningful and actionable than saying he wants to increase his market share 10%.

There are two factors that make it difficult—if not pointless—to determine market share for small industrial B2B companies. Particularly in the case of job shops and machine companies: Their products are not discrete end-products, but rather are subparts for other products or parts of equipment that make other products. In other situations, industrial B2B products are consumed in the production process. Consequently, most industrial B2B products cannot be counted and recorded as in the case of automobiles, refrigerators, lawn mowers, and consumer products in general. Lastly, since most SMMs are privately owned and do not publish their unit production and sales, there is no practical way to know their output by which to determine market share.

Market share for consumer products, conversely, is ubiquitous because trade journal literature regularly publishes consumer product sales across extensive product markets, for example, automotive, food and grocery, beverage, clothing, pharmaceuticals, cosmetic, cleaning, and toiletries. Fortunately, the details in these journals break down these various markets' unit volume and sales into clearly defined segments, for example, SUVs, trucks, pet food, alcohol and soft drinks, women's, men's, and kids clothing. Therefore, the *M* in *C-P-M*™ is easily determined for consumer products.

Figure 68 summarizes the earlier examples illustrating techniques for estimating *M* for B2B companies. The total dollar value of quotations is an estimate of sales potential and the dollar value of lost orders serves as an estimate of additional business should the company decide to pursue that lost business. Lost orders also identify establishments that know about the company but might not be awarding it business; companies can increase "market share" (if that is how they want to gauge growth) simply by increasing their hit rates. Lead-generation and prospecting identifies

Ascertaining sales or market potential			
Company	Quotation/lost order analysis	Lead-gen/ prospecting	Plant purchases/ budgets
Swiss Solutions		✓	
Conveyor Specialty	✓	✓	
Peachstate Construction	✓		
Rooftop HVAC	✓		
Metro Plastics	✓		
BuzzCo	✓	✓	
Southeast Cut & Saw		✓	✓
Dan's Machine Shop		✓	✓
Coastal Industrial Equipment		✓	
VIS, Inc.		✓	

Figure 68. Summary of techniques to estimate market potential.

prospective new customers, and by extrapolating average sales order or selling price and estimating penetration rates (as did Forashe in the FRP example) a company can estimate sales potential. Plant purchases and budgets allow reasonable estimates of sales potential at the plant level and, when totaled for all prospects, give an estimate of sales potential for the group.

In spite of not having the luxury of publicized unit volume and sales data to determine market share, industrial B2B companies do have other means by which to determine the *M* in *C-P-M*™. Secondary marketing research, while providing general information about an industry or SIC/NAIC category that SMMs can use to make preliminary assumptions about attractiveness, is not actionable to the point of identifying specific market segments or prospective new customers. More targeted measures such as primary (direct) research and lead-generation narrow down the general findings of secondary research and lead to quantifiable estimates of market and sales potential. And for companies that use quotes and bids to generate sales, the total amount of quotes submitted serves as proxy for market potential.

However, even though a company has researched and quantified its target markets, knows who to call on, and the sales force is prepared and presents the firm's product and service offering, competition still stands in the way of getting the order.

The Competitor Matrix—an Easy Way to Make Sense of Competitor Information

Since most SMMs are family-owned and -operated, there is little public information about them other than their websites, brochures, and other sales literature. Websites often describe a firm's product line, applications, technologies, equipment capacities, markets served, specialized services and capabilities, and so on. But that does not provide insight into the company's ability to attract and keep customers, how its products and services stack up against other companies' products, services, pricing, delivery, quality and warranties, and reputation. Nevertheless, websites are a good starting point for "low-hanging fruit" competitor information when developing growth strategies that include making products and services more competitive to gain customers. Fortunately, there are other sources of good information about competitors.

Quotation and lost order analysis and customer satisfaction surveys, already discussed, are two very good ways to learn about competition. Companies that have used these two methods not only have learned how their products and services stack up to competition, but also often discover unknown competitors. When data from quotation and lost orders, customer surveys, intelligence collected from sales and field activities, Internet searches, and websites have been accumulated, it needs to be organized so that management can make sense of it to create insights into how to better compete.

The competitor matrix is an easy framework for doing this and has proven to be a simple and inexpensive tool by which to organize information about competitors. It is simply an electronic spreadsheet listing competitors and competitive factors, one along the columns and the other down the rows. I call it a "numbers hotel" because the cells represent empty rooms that need to be filled: A worksheet with five competitors and six competitive factors will have 30 cells that must be filled in. If a company has conducted quotation and lost order analysis and a *3-fer* customer satisfaction survey, it will have identified its competitors and the factors that are important to customers when choosing suppliers. I tell clients to fill in as many cells for which they have information and the remaining empty cells then point out the remaining areas that must be further researched. This limits the quantity and type of competitive information needed to see the competitive landscape and avoids miscellaneous data that might or might not be germane or useful.

Figure 69 shows a generic competitor matrix that lists five companies beginning with the company that is conducting the project and four competitors.

Generic competitor matrix—product A						
	Competitive factors					
Competitors	Price	Quality	Perfomance	Delivery time	Sales coverage	Overall reputation
Company						
Competitor 1						
Competitor 2						
Competitor 3						
Competitor 4						

Figure 69. Sample generic competitor matrix.

In this example, four competitors are known or have been identified in quotation or lost order analysis or in customer satisfaction surveys. Similarly, competitive factors are known or have been derived from lost order analysis and or customer satisfaction surveys (the six shown are generic for example purposes). Cells then are populated with available data and information. The remaining empty cells specify where the company must obtain missing information, through a specifically designed marketing research or competitor intelligence project. Note the matrix illustrates only Product A. If the scope of the competitive analysis includes multiple products, product lines or services, multiple matrices might be needed. It can be used for competitive comparisons in the case of existing products as well as potential new products.

- Identifying potential competitors. Quotation and lost order analysis, customer feedback, and the use of product SIC codes are good sources by which to identify potential competitors for existing products, possible product modifications, line extensions, replacement, or substitute products in the case of NPD. Direct competitors likely will be known, but often it is unknown competitors that cause unexpected friction after a product launch. In most cases, whether an existing or new product, an SIC/NAICS code can be used to identify companies that produce similar products, thus providing a good idea of all potential competitors.

- Listing competitive factors. The example listed typical competitive factors, such as price, quality, and delivery, but as the two following examples show, many other factors might be involved. Lost order analysis and the *3-fer* customer satisfaction survey are two good sources for identifying the actual factors and criteria customers use to select suppliers.

Coastal Industrial Equipment (metal tubing cutting equipment) created a matrix, Table 51, to see if a modification-line extension would fill a void in competitors' product lines. It compiled five competitor models' features, specs, capacities, prices, footprint, and more, totaling 33 competitive factors, shortened to eight factors for this example. Note that the information in rows and columns can be inverted: competitive factors in rows (since there were too many to put in columns) and competitors in columns.

It abandoned the project because the information showed their modification-line extension lacked sufficient differentiation to permit a

Table 51. Coastal Industrial Equipment's Competitor Matrix

Competitor matrix				
Factors	Company	Competitor 1	Competitor 2	Competitor 3
Price	$30,000	$37,000	$47,000	$35,000
Floor Space	20 Sq. Ft.	Depends on machine	Machine is 6 to 8 ft square, and the bundle unloader is 30 ft long	25 Sq. Meters
Cycle Time	4 sec (full hitch)	Operator Control	Operator Control/ up to 60 parts / minute	Length Control
Cutting Method	Dual Blade	Dual Blade	Dual Blade	Disc Blade
Power Source	Hydraulic/Air	None	Hydraulic	Electric/Air
Processor	AB Micrologic	None	Allen Bradley PLC	PLC
Operator Panel	Panelview	None	Touchscreen	Touch Screen Operator Interface
Feed Control	Servo	N/A	Optional	Air Cylinder

competitive advantage, which was a red flag, and avoided adding another headstone to the new product development cemetery of failed ideas and products—not to mention saving money on product development and marketing costs. Chapter 7 pointed out the importance of early detection and avoidance of potential failures.

Conveyor Specialty, producing computerized palletizing equipment, prepared a very detailed competitor matrix, Table 52 based on lost order information, customer satisfaction surveys, websites, and input from the sales force, that showed its total price with add-on features was high. To counter the price differential, management decided to improve replacement parts inventory policy and logistics, strengthen customer service and tech support (a primary competitor was having problems in these areas), increase inside sales and field sales coverage to better promote the performance advantages of its add-on features, which it believed provided value for the price. As with Coastal Industrial Equipment, the number of factors was reduced for example.

The competitor matrix is an excellent addition to the material presented in Chapter 6 to answer the P question in C-P-M™, "Can existing products support company growth objectives?" Chapter 6 used sales, margins, price, and sales mix to evaluate a product's strategic value. But they are indicators of a product's competitiveness and don't necessarily tell why a product's sales might be decreasing or why it can't hold margin. A competitive matrix should be prepared on products that under-perform (according to sales, margins, price, and sales mix metrics) to see if their performance or life cycle can be improved to support growth goals. That is the acid test that could lead to NPD as growth strategy if the product fails the test. The competitor matrix forms the strategic link between product performance and apples-to-apples comparison to competing products: The findings should inform strategic decisions for product management and whether to pursue new product development.

As mentioned earlier, quotation and lost order analysis and *3-fer* customer satisfaction surveys provide excellent data on competitors gleaned directly from market sources. When combined with secondary research and all data complied into a competitor matrix at the company level (see Figure 70), rather than at the product level, a company will have a good picture of its competitive position.

Table 52. Conveyor Specialty's Competitor Matrix

Factor	Company	Competitor A	Competitor B	Competitor C
		Competitor matrix		
Model				
Base price	$99,950	$108,000	$100,397	$90,000
Machine specifications				
Speed	33 CPM—10C	35 CPM—10A	35 CPM—10C	40 CPM
Std. load ht. capacity	72"	81"	72"	72"
Max. case size	22" × 16" × 18"	24" × 24" × 25"	24" × 24" × 25"	24" × 24" × 14"
Max. load size	50" × 52" × 72"	54" × 54" × 81"	54" × 54" × 72"	50" × 50" × 72"
Max. load wt	3,000 lbs	3,500 lbs	3,800 lbs	4,200 lbs
Infeed	side		rear	side
Motors	Demag\US Motor\Baldor		SEW	All Demag
Gear boxes	Cone\Electra		SEW	
Apron\striper plate	single plate	bi-parting	bi-parting std	bi-parting std
Layer guides—AB503	std	std	std	std
Brake\meter belt	$10,000	std	std	std
Lift & separate dispenser	$11,000	lift & separate	std	dispenser w\o dogs
Close center rolls	$1,560	std	3 1\8" center std	std
Allen Bradley 550 (keypad)	$1,800	touch screen	touch screen	std
Discharge conveyor—5'0"	optional—gravity	optional—gravity	std	optional—gravity
Interface to 18" wrapper	optional	optional	std	optional
Total	$124,310	$112,000	$100,307	$90,000

Generic competitor matrix—company						
	Competitive factors					
Competitors	Price	Quality	Perfomance	Delivery time	Sales coverage	Overall reputation
Company						
Competitor 1						
Competitor 2						
Competitor 3						
Competitor 4						

Figure 70. Generic competitor matrix–company.

Job shops and machine companies can also use the competitor matrix, but rather than products they would list machines, capacities, capabilities, services, such as wire EDM, CNC, CAD-CAM, precision grinding, welding, fabrication, heat treating, and so on. Almost all machine company websites promote quick delivery at competitive prices, ISO certifications, just-in-time capabilities, and engineering and design services, and list the industries served, such as aerospace, defense, transportation, automotive, appliance, business machines, electronics, agricultural implements, ordnance, environmental, construction equipment, and nuclear. In some instances, they specialize, such as making vacuum or rubber molds, injection molding, die casting, thermoforming or aluminum extrusions, using lasers to cut or to etch or weld, surface finishing, or rapid prototyping.

Years ago, I asked a machine company client about his specialty; he replied that he could do any and all jobs. Given the depth and breadth of the machining capabilities and capacities listed previously, it is difficult today to imagine that any given machine company could not do most or any job. What then are the factors that differentiate one machine company from another if they can all do any and all jobs, provide precise quality, and deliver on time? A job shop or a machine company's competitor matrix must include more than technical specifications—it must determine the factors that differentiate it from the rest of the herd. Quotation analysis and the *3-fer* customer satisfaction survey can provide that insight.

Cost and price always will be major factors, particularly as customers off-shore machining and fabrication to lower their costs, thus forcing job shops and machining companies to lower margins, which is now a permanent competitive state, unfortunately. Job shops and machine companies will need to look beyond cost, price, and technical capabilities to find a competitive edge, even a slight one for which customers will be willing to pay. The generic competitor matrix shown in Figure 70 is a good format for comparing competitors to your company.

Indirect Competitors—the Silent Killers

Competition to this point dealt with direct competitors—companies that make identical or similar products, such as conveyor rollers, steel pipe, saw blades, vision inspection systems—that are designed and built to perform some specific action, solve a problem, lower cost, last longer, or provide better quality. There are other products and technologies, however, that perform similarly but might solve a problem differently or use a different technology.

Forashe International developed an adhesive it felt could be used in manufactured housing to join wood parts, such as studs and rafters rather than using nails, hammers, or nail guns. Paslode, Dewalt, Makita, Neiko, and Bostitch, who make nail guns, would not have been aware of Forashe's product although it would have performed the same function—joining two wood parts. Conveyor belts and conveyor rollers are different products with different performance specs, features, and attributes, but generally do the same thing—move items from A to B. Steel pipe provides structural support and moves slurry, gases, powders, and liquids, but so do pipes made from cement, rubber, ceramics, fiberglass, brass, and copper.

Indirect competitors reside below the radar screen and may not be considered as factors affecting a product's performance and evaluation during the **P** question. However, in the course of looking at a product's strategic value and competitiveness via a competitor matrix, indirect competitors should be taken into account. Good questions to ask that might reveal indirect competitors:

- What is the problem our product solves?
- How is the problem now being addressed or solved?
- How much expense is the customer experiencing now to solve or address the problem or situation? Can the problem be solved cheaper without our product? Be made faster, better?

- What are alternative solutions to the problem other than our product?
- Who are the companies that make or offer products and services that could solve the same problem, at whatever cost?

SMMs looking to develop growth strategies and deciding the *P* question have several tools available to answer it: sales, cost, and margin analyses, sales mix, and now the competitor matrix. By combining all relevant information in the matrix and identifying direct and indirect competitors, SMMs will not only have solid relevant data about *P*, but also reliable— and possibly previously unknown—information about competition.

The USP—Unique Selling Proposition

Businesses have been told about their unique selling proposition—their USP—in the context of promoting, messaging, and selling their products and services. Invented in the 1940s by Rosser Reeves to explain successful outcomes of consumer products advertising campaigns, the term now is almost ubiquitously used to refer to any aspect of a product or service to differentiate it from competitors. The techniques I've come across to help ascertain the USP resemble the company meetings described in Chapter 1 to develop growth goals and objectives using anecdote, supposition, navel-gazing, and sticky notes. Typical questions asked of employees to divine the company's USP:

1. What does the company do or sell?
2. How does it do business?
3. Who are the customers?
4. What do the customers want?
5. What is the biggest benefit from doing business with the company?

As previously explained, most SMMs do not have empirical information on competitors by which to declare how their products and services differ, which is the essential purpose of articulating a USP. It begs the question, "If SMMs do not have effective insight into their competitive situation, how can developing a USP just from anecdote or supposition provide meaningful direction on how to promote and differentiate the firm's products and services?"

Fortunately, *C-P-M*™ provides answers to much of what is asked or implied in these questions. Product and customer analyses certainly answer the first and third questions. The *3-fer* customer satisfaction survey discloses factors important to customers in their selection of the company for products and services, and the relative ranking of performance by the company and its competitors sheds light on questions 4 and 5. While *C-P-M*™ does not specifically inform the answer to question #2, employees should be able to articulate how the firm solicits and develops customers, and through customer satisfaction feedback assess its efforts at customer service and tech support to keep customers happy, satisfied, and retained.

SMMs wanting to develop their USP should conduct *C-P-M*™, including quotation and lost order analysis and the *3-fer* customer satisfaction survey, and compile the findings in a competitor matrix. Then it will have empirical data to inform the USP and be better positioned to accurately promote and communicate why their company, products, and services are better.

Choosing and Prioritizing Markets

The steps SMMs should use to choose and prioritize markets are similar to the process presented in Chapter 3 for prioritizing customers. BuzzCo and Forashe reviewed various markets and industries and after estimating their attractiveness (growth projections, trends, number of potential customers, and estimates of sales potential) narrowed down the possibilities to a few market segments they concluded represented the best opportunities for growth.

BuzzCo reviewed 10 major SIC industries its customers represented and chose to target companies in SIC 3400, 3600, and 3700 based on the margins it had generated with its A customers. It further broke down those three industries to six segments 3494, 3621, 3675, 3644, 3639, and 3728 and identified 1,790 establishments that matched its distance and employment size search criteria. Lead-generation and prospecting, estimates of plant purchases and budgets identified 231 companies to target and prioritize. Its research progressed from the general to the specific.

Forashe carried out a similar process involving three industries: pipe coating SIC 3479/NAICS 325510, manufactured housing NAICS 236115 (no comparable SIC), and fiberglass-reinforced plastic products SIC 3086, 3089 and NAICS 326191 to identify target companies for its new formulation that did not contain styrene. Forashe's research on the requirements to introduce chemical products into the pipe coating and manufactured housing industries showed that testing and certification requirements were costlier and more time consuming than FRP, which eliminated them from consideration. In FRP's favor also was that Forashe already had customers in that industry. Having chosen FRP, Forashe's sales manager narrowed his research to businesses making products similar to its existing bath ware customers, and aided by EPA's documents, divided this market into three target segments: steel bath ware, acrylic bath ware, and gel coat bath ware.

The industry/market hierarchy (Figure 71) illustrates the process of refining research from industry down to a target market, defined by knowing the number and location of prospective buyers. Secondary marketing research is the common tool for starting at the top industry/market levels to determine whether they might be good matches for the company's products and services and core competencies. Primary research and lead-generation and prospecting provide the granular detail for determining sales potential and the final facts needed eventually to choose and prioritize market alternatives. Note that the two research categories overlap because there is no discrete delineation when secondary research ends and primary begins; it all depends on the situation.

Competitive factors are just as important as market factors of size, sales, and profit potential in the decision to target a certain market segment. Although concurrent marketing research and competitor analysis is okay, competitive analysis and evaluation should intensify as the selection of market alternatives narrows. While competitors exist at the industry, market, and segment levels, they most likely will not be easily identified until the company decides to target specific companies where direct competition should occur; at that point, the insight gained from creating a competitor matrix (or matrices where more than one product or service is involved) is critical and can make the difference between success or failure. It is likely SMMs offering multiple products will encounter

Industry/Market Hierarchy	
Industry A group of sellers (e.g. the consumer, healthcare, packaging, transportation, heavy construction, metal fabrication, utilities, etc. industries)—hundreds, maybe thousands of establishments. **Market** A group of buyers—could be an industry subset. (e.g. airlines as a subset of transportation, auto as subset of consumer, hospitals as subset of healthcare, overhead cranes as subset of heavy construction, coal vs. nuclear utilities, etc.).	Secondary marketing research
Market segment Subset of market (e.g. regional vs. national airlines, compact vs. SUV auto, cardiac vs. trauma hospitals, crane vs. excavator) that has been assessed and perceived as having demand for your firm's products and services—based on marketing research and competitor analysis.	Primary marketing research, lead-gen/prospecting
Target market The purposeful selection and prioritization of market segments based upon factors such as size, sales and profit potential, competitive situation, etc. **Niche market** The determination that the firm has a competitive advantage in a target market and can defend its pricing or price premium.	

Figure 71. Industry/market hierarchy.

different competitors in different market segments; therefore, one competitor matrix might be insufficient.

Other Factors to Consider

SMMs should consider social, economic, political and legislative, technological, and global factors when evaluating growth alternatives. Demographic shifts (gender, age, racial and ethnic, and so on) affect the demand for and types of both consumer and industrial products and services, which ripples through supply chains and distribution channels. The men's business suit and tie segments almost disappeared when business attire became casual. Interest rates, inflation, and employment rates affect capital investing and hiring. The 2008–2010 recession curtailed overall economic activity and put growth initiatives on hold. Political and legislative change can benefit or harm industries and markets. The on-again-off-again legislation that allows funding for wind energy influenced Madsen Pipe's decision not to enter that market. Healthcare and tax legislation will affect investing and hiring decisions of businesses. EPA initiatives helped Forashe develop a new formulation without styrene and altered the FRP production process. Technological advances in industrial equipment integrating CAD–CAM and computer-controlling capability have reduced unit labor content and throughput, immensely enhanced quality, and expanded the types of materials that can be processed. BuzzCo's cost structure shifted from labor-cost-intensive to material-cost-intensive as customers' products comprised materials that were more exotic, thus affecting both his customer and product mixes. Bulldog Machine & Die's replacement business of OEM loom products declined as loom technology advances migrated older looms to developing countries. Globalization disrupts supply chains causing factories to move from country to country to lower costs.

There is much more to marketing research than just looking at a given industry, market, segment, and so forth. Good marketing research—particularly secondary marketing research—incorporates these high-level factors. Secondary marketing research can be particularly valuable when used at the start of a project to get an idea of the overall attractiveness of an industry or market a company is contemplating, such as growth trends and forecasts, size, major companies, suppliers, competitive and global issues. It often identifies factors that indicate the industry or market is not suitable, thus allowing the firm to eliminate it early in the process at a minimal cost and look elsewhere for growth opportunities.

Various sources for researching social, economic, political/legislative, technological, and global factors include:

- National Bureau of Economic Research
- Statistical Abstract of the United States
- Various publications of the U.S. Department of Commerce
  - Survey of Business
  - County Business Patterns
  - Survey of Manufacturers

- ○ U.S. Industrial Outlook
- ○ Bureau of the Census
- Survey of Buying Power
- Social Indicators Research
- World Bank Atlas
- Federal Register
- Applied Science and Technology
- Federal Reserve Bulletin
- Monthly Labor Review
- Monthly Catalog of Government Publications
- American Manufacturers Association
- The Economic Statistics Database
- Industry Financial Ratios reports
- University research and reports
- Trade journals and industrial reports
- U.S. Patent Office
- Moody's, Dunn & Bradstreet, Standard and Poor's.

A generic shortlist of questions for researching and evaluating industries, markets, and segments includes but is not limited to:

- Overall growth and trend of the industry or market and the implications of the factors listed earlier. Are the indications favorable? Can unfavorable items be overcome in time to enter the market successfully?
- Whether the number and location of existing and prospective customers in the segment or target market are known. Have preliminary sales or market potential estimates been made? Are there enough prospects to support the company's growth goals? If not, have alternative market segments been identified and prioritized?
- Whether direct and indirect competitors identified? Have the factors upon which customers decide to select a supplier of the product or service been identified and competitive comparisons made? Is there evidence or compelling reason to believe competitive advantage exists?

Summary

SMMs can simplify marketing research and get useful information on competitors by building on the data and information already created through customer analysis, customer profiles, quotation and lost order analysis, and from surveying customers using the *3-fer*. These analyses lay the ground work by identifying prospective customers via SIC/NAICS codes based on customer profiles of MVCs, by identifying competitors and their relative strengths and weakness based on feedback from customers and lost order analysis, and by providing an estimate of market potential indicated by lost order analysis. They simplify finding the number and location of prospective customers, indicating what to do to change products and services to make them more competitive, and make easier the task of estimating the sales, growth potential, and prioritization of markets. The incremental and sequential approach to market research and competitor intelligence keeps research costs affordable by starting with lower cost research and progressing to more costly primary research if needed, particularly where growth involves more risk and investment, such as new product development.

This ground work also allows a company to narrow the scope of secondary or primary marketing research since it already has identified via SIC/NAICS codes the markets and industries that correspond to profitable and valuable customers in its customer base—finding more customers like existing ones is the easiest and least expensive way to increase sales. Rather than pursue a broad-based effort to research markets for growth potential, a company can be specific on the parameters of the search and thus avoid unnecessary research—and in some cases it might find that spending some research dollars early in the process eliminates markets or industries previously thought to have growth potential. It's okay to chase rabbits down a dry hole.

The competitor matrix organizes data and information from quotation and lost order analysis, customer satisfaction surveys, publicly available sources and from field activities. It is useful at the product level to identify specific factors, features, benefits, pricing, and so forth that will make a product more competitive or induce a decision to cull the product from the offering. Similarly, it sheds light on the competitiveness and marketability of new products, such as modifications and line extensions and can provide the information to support a go-kill decision.

Marketing research and competitor intelligence, using internally generated data and secondary and primary research tailored to SMMs' resources and budgets, simplifies getting answers to the big *M* questions in *C-P-M*™:

- "Where are the opportunities?"
- "How big is the market?" and
- "What changes in products and services, pricing, selling, and promotional strategies are needed to increase sales?"

CHAPTER 9

Crafting Goals, Objectives, and Strategies from the Bottom Up

Previous chapters have discussed the *C-P-M*™ process and explained how to analyze and evaluate the firm's financial situation, quotations and lost orders, customers, products, and markets for the purpose of answering the *C-P-M*™ question, "Given our customers, products, and markets, what should we do with the business?" At this stage in the strategy development process a company would have compiled a lot of data and information and now has to apply it to chart out a course of action intended to produce the desired growth.

Making Sense of It All

I call this the "gestalt" of strategy—trying to make sense of all the data and information and come up with a unified, coherent plan to achieve the desired growth. Strategy development should be about gaining insights— and you cannot get it without data, analysis, and information about *C-P-M*™. I equate developing strategy from the various and disparate data to that of people describing what they see in the Rorschach inkblot.[1] There is considerable subjectivity in interpreting both the inkblot and the data and information from *C-P-M*™. But while interpretation of the inkblot is based on an individual's emotions and experiences, the data and information derived from *C-P-M*™ is based on facts that should reduce guesswork in its interpretation.

The book's introduction made the point that strategy is built on insights gained from good analysis, which is the purpose of *C-P-M*™, and therefore it must precede strategy development. Good *C-P-M*™

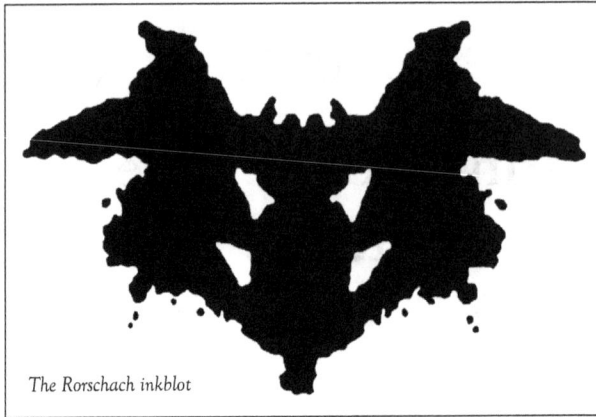

The Rorschach inkblot

analysis eliminates—or at least reduces—the subjectivity, anecdote, and supposition that otherwise would occur without some factual basis for deciding how to allocate company resources as an outcome of strategy development.

A strategic planning facilitator described his approach to helping SMMs develop growth strategy—which turned out to be the example presented in Chapter 2 about the 2-day off-site meeting that resulted in numerous sticky notes and lofty goals and objectives. I asked if he ever challenged the accuracy or amount of data his clients presented during his strategy planning engagements. He did not because he wanted to avoid "paralysis by analysis." It was clear that he did not know what data were relevant in the pursuit of growth strategy development, and probably did not have the capacity to help a firm interpret all the issues that can arise from looking at financial statements, costs, margins, customer and product sales and profit history, and marketing and competitor intelligence. SMMs need help cutting through all the issues and the disparate and incomplete data to be able to focus on the essential factors that will provide sustainable and profitable long-term growth—to be able to "make sense of it all." *C-P-M*™ is intended to simplify the process by having SMMs determine the viability of customers, products, and markets, identifying the winners and losers, and decide how to change, develop, and manage them for the most profitable outcome.

The Industrial Marketing Pyramid

Collins' industrial marketing pyramid (Figure 72) demonstrates the "bottom up" approach to strategy development, using insights about customers, products, and markets. It illustrates that when essential information about costs and margins, customers, products, markets, and competition are available, you can start to consider what to do with the business. It contrasts with the popular approach to strategy development, described in Chapter 1, where management and key employees convene off-site for 2 days, start at the top with desired outcomes, goals, and objectives, and conclude with lofty and vague strategies about how the firm will achieve the outcomes. Those outcomes and strategies are rarely supported by analysis and quantitative data pertaining to customers, products, markets, and competitors and the marketplace. This is why so many growth plans fail and why manufacturers engage in shotgun marketing: There is a lack of good solid data, analysis, and insight upon which to build strategy.

The "bottom up" approach starts with *C-P-M*™—analyses of customer and product sales and profit history, the firm's financial situation, market research and trends, competitor intelligence derived from lost order analysis and customer feedback, and other items particular to the firm's business. All of this precedes any consideration or development of goals, objectives, and strategies. It is intended to identify problems and constraints that could hinder efforts to grow the business and to stimulate thinking about possibilities and solutions to problems and constraints.

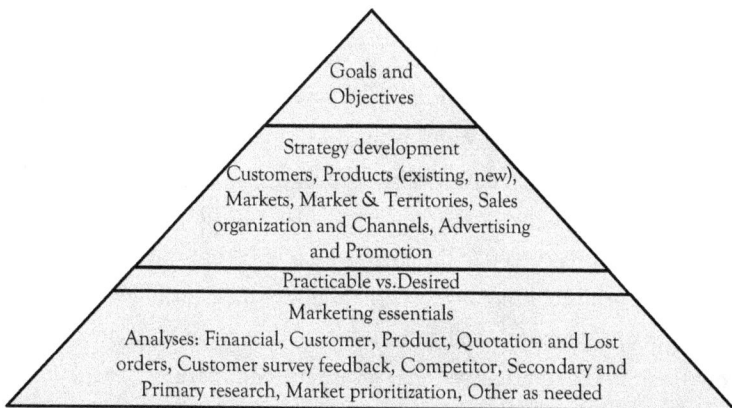

Figure 72. Industrial marketing pyramid.

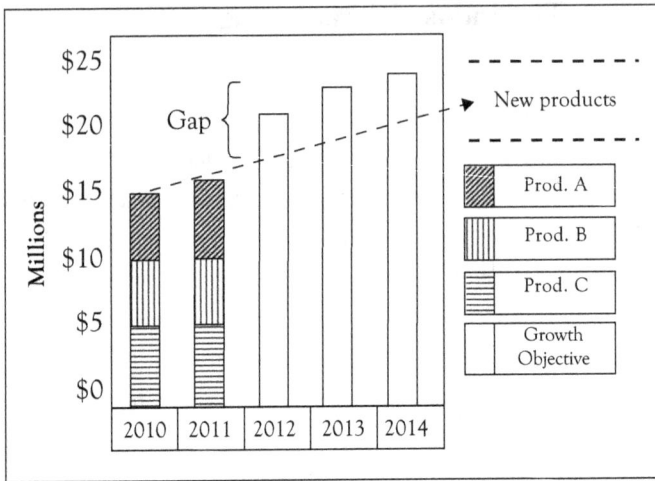

Graph 14. Product analysis to test growth.

For example, Graph 14 shows historical product and total company sales and provides valuable initial and preliminary insight into whether existing products can support management's growth goals. If the answer is no, then management will need to begin to consider how to resolve the gap between projected growth and desired growth.

Products A, B, and C sales are shown in each bar and represent total company sales for 2010–2011. The solid white bars indicate management's desired growth through 2014. The arrow represents the firm's projected sales growth of about 6% annually and at that rate will attain about $18–20 million in sales by 2014. However, if the firm wants to attain $22–$25 million by 2014 it will need to grow at about 10% annually from 2010. The fundamental strategic question is: "Given the firm's product sales history and what is known from the other analyses, can existing customers, products, and markets get the firm to 10% annual growth for the next four years?" This is the point where management needs to consider the insights gained from the financial, customer, and product sales and margin analyses to identify problems and constraints that would need to be addressed to be able to hit the 10% growth rate. If current customers, products, and markets cannot do the job, what are the alternatives? Management must reconcile all of these data before deciding two fundamental strategic questions:

- "What do we want to accomplish?"
- "How do we do it?"

What to Accomplish—Practicable versus Desirable

"What do we want to accomplish?" This is the basic *C-P-M*™question: "Given our current customers, products, and markets, what should we do with the business?" The answer, presumably, is to increase sales and grow, but there remains the matter of deciding how much to grow (5%, 10%, more?), with or without existing or new customers and products, and which markets to target. Goals and objectives, shown at the top of Collins' pyramid, derive from considering the combination of customers, products, and markets that best fit company's resources. For example, deciding to grow 20% would be unreasonable if the firm cannot afford it. Other examples that could hinder a 20% growth objective:

- Existing products lack competitive advantage and therefore cannot counter competitive pressure to achieve 20% growth.
- The firm's current markets might be maturing or in decline.
- Major customers are in trouble, therefore, limiting sales growth.

While growing 20% might be desirable, growing 5% might be more practicable and doable.

When a firm determines that current customers, products, or markets cannot produce desired growth, rigorous analysis and due diligence should follow to find suitable alternatives. This is when alternative growth strategies must be analyzed and evaluated and the firm must focus on what is "practicable" (what can be done given the constraints and uncertainties about the proposed course of actions) versus what is "desired" (what management would really like to do with the business). Shotgun marketers act in stark contrast to this analytical and methodical approach to growing their businesses: There is no reconciliation between "practicable" and "desirable"—it's all the latter.

The practicable versus desired scenario should be framed by constraints, problems, and issues that *C-P-M*™ and financial analyses reveal.

If the firm is facing cash flow and working capital problems, operational and production inefficiencies, sales force problems, and formidable competition, it might not be able to grow at a desired rate and must settle for less. At the end of the day, "practical" versus "desired" must be reconciled so that growth goals and objectives (the top of the pyramid) are not unrealistic and wind up outpacing the company's overall ability to grow.

How to Do It—Four Basic Choices

"How do we accomplish it?" This question pertains to strategy—the "how to" aspect—and gets to the heart of the matter. Collins' pyramid illustrates that after the essential analyses have been completed, management is ready to evaluate and choose the most viable customer, product, and market combinations. There are four basic choices to grow a business according to the Ansoff growth matrix, shown before in Chapter 7 (Figure 73). Simply, it breaks choices for growth down to two basic elements—products and markets (or customers).

1. Selling more of existing products and services to existing customers and markets; the easiest, most affordable, and least risky choice. Quad 1.
2. Selling existing products and services to new customers or markets; the next easiest, affordable, and least risky choice. Quad 2.
3. Selling new products and services to existing customers or markets; a more difficult, more costly and risky choice. Quad 3.
4. Selling new products and services to new customers or markets; the most difficult, most costly, and most risky choice. Quad 4.

Ansoff product-market-growth matrix			
		Products	
		Existing	New
Markets	Existing	❶	❸
	New	❷	❹

Figure 73. Four basic choices for growth–Ansoff matrix.

Q1 (top left) and Q2 (bottom left) focus on existing customers and markets and are the most practicable for Types 1 and 2 manufacturers, given the findings of the questionnaire about costs, margins, customers, markets, and competitors. Types 1 and 2 companies might not have the data and finances to effectively pursue Q3 and Q4 strategies that involve new products. Types 3 and 4 companies, however, generally have more resources, employ specialists to oversee finance and accounting, product management, marketing and sales management, and are better capitalized to generate and act on market and competitor intelligence. Overall, they are much better positioned to take on the investment and risk of Q3 and Q4. *Note: These are generalizations and there always are exceptions.*

Types 1 and 2 firms desiring to grow and who have conducted *C-P-M*™ analyses can execute Q1 and Q2 strategies with minimal cost and risk. Once customer profiles have been developed, progressing to the next step is easy; it is simply a matter of finding prospective businesses that match the SIC/NAICS code and employment sizes of MVCs by using lead-generating and prospecting. There is little if any changes to the organization itself or to the composition of the sales force—inside and outside sales personnel or reps. Sales coverage (the number of personnel needed to contact and promote to the target market) is the only item that could be impacted since more coverage will be needed to contact more prospective customers.

Q2 represents the second easiest and less risky growth choice—taking existing products to new customers or markets. Again, the use of SIC/NAICS codes simplifies the steps for finding new markets. The SIC codes in Table 53 represent the markets a company serves. Should it consider moving into other SIC codes (new industry or market), all it needs to do is to select SIC codes it thinks might contain opportunities for its products and services. Conversely, if it knows of a prospective new company outside of its current market and wants to locate similar businesses, finding that company's SIC/NAICS code and searching the database for businesses that match the SIC/NAICS code will produce a list of prospects.

An example of a Q2 strategy would be a company making a latex bonding formula for backing on bathroom rugs (the application for its existing

Table 53. Sample of End-User Customer Profiles

Basic end-user customer profile					
Cust.	Sales	Margin	SIC code	Description	Size
A	105,000	40%	3625	Relays & Industrial Controls	50
B	150,000	47%	3728	Aircraft Parts & Equipment, NEC	150
C	95,000	56%	3443	Fabricated Plate Work	25
D	300,000	41%	2821	Plastics, Materials & Nonvulcanizable Elastomers	25
E	100,000	0%	3679	Electronic Components, NEC	250
F	250,000	51%	3411	Metal Cans	175
Total	$1,000,000				

market = Q1, SIC: 227305 - Mfg Bathroom Rugs) finding customers who use latex on the backs of their mailing labels (application for different market = Q2: SIC Code 267202 - Adhesive Papers, Labels, Or Tapes).

Q3 deals with new product development (generally modifications, line extensions, substitute products) and Q4 deals with innovative, breakthrough products, and diversification into completely new industries, markets, vertical and horizontal integration, mergers, or acquisitions (Figure 74). *Note: There is a middle ground between Q3 and Q4 where product modification, line extensions, and replacement products are targeted to new markets.* Q3 and Q4, for most SMMs, are very challenging and an argument could be made that Types 1, 2, and some Type 3 firms should pursue Q4 very judiciously because of the tremendous investment required and the inherent risk. Cooper's findings presented in Chapter 7 show that the failure rate of new products is high—about 70–90%—for a number of reasons but mostly because due diligence about customers, markets, and competitors is either done poorly or not at all.

At Georgia Tech, we had a 30-company advisory board made up of manufacturers that were representative of Georgia industry—across SIC/NAICS codes and size—Types 1 to 3. Their responses to the question, "What do you consider as innovation in the context of new product development?" were almost unanimous in favor of Q3 because they said Q4 was too expensive and risky. They preferred incremental product development.

Ansoff product-market-growth matrix		
	Products	
	Existing	New
Existing	❶	❸ *Modifications, line extensions, replacements, substitutions, etc.*
New	❷	❹ *Truly innovative, new to the firm, industry, new to world, break-through, disruptive, etc.* *Diversification, acquisition, joint venture, etc.*

Figure 74. Growth strategies using new products–Ansoff matrix.

If a company decides to grow via Q3 or Q4 it is imperative to have the essential information on hand—especially about markets and segments, prospective new customers, and competition. The reason for this is to reduce uncertainty and risk and to craft growth strategies that make sense—that are aligned with the company's assets, resources, core competencies, and market and competitive situations—and that are practicable and have a good chance of success. Q3 and Q4 require additions to R&D, working capital and investment, possibly more employees with specialized skills and experience, and certainly changes to the sales organization—training on new products, more sales coverage (more personnel), increased sales and marketing expenses for manuals, advertising and promotion, brochures, and so on.

Forashe International, Chatham HVAC, and Global Textile described in the previous chapter contemplated Q3 and Q4 initiatives. Forashe developed a new product for Q3 and Q4. While Q4 generally poses high risk, its situation was less risky because it knew its direct costs, R&D investment was manageable, it was financially stable, and it had done an excellent job of market, competitor, and prospective customer analysis. Finding or developing a distributor or rep sales channel to execute the strategy involved the most uncertainty, but did not carry a lot of risk.

Chatham HVAC's Q3 choice to offer a new product and service via the automated cutting and forming machine to an existing mature market involved moderate risk. Its balance sheet could support the $600,000 investment (low debt, strong working capital, and steady cash flow from operations) and it knew target customers and competitors. Its knowledge of and familiarity with the local and regional market and its competitors offset some risk. Direct interviewing of competitors showed they had sufficient interest in using Chatham HVAC's product, and industry and trade publications showed favorable growth trends in the industry as well as Chatham HVAC's market segments.

Global Textile's consideration of a disruptive new technology priced at $5 million for new markets (Q4) involved considerable risk—high capital investment and unknown demand and price structure. Fortunately, the $25,000 it spent on marketing research helped it avoid a $5 million mistake.

All three companies conducted market and competitor research and financial analysis before committing to their proposed growth initiatives. Two found sufficient upside potential to justify implementation and one abandoned the project because it could not find sufficient potential to displace existing materials at a competitive price in products outside its own markets.

Progressing from Strategy Selection—Q1, Q2, Q3, and Q4—to Goals, Objectives, and Strategies

I have found confusion about the difference between goals, objectives, and strategies. While there is no consensus on the definitions for the three terms, for purposes of the book, I use the following:

Goals are qualitative statements of intent. "We want to grow the business by increasing sales." Goals should be simple enough to express in conversational language so that anyone can understand what management intends or wants to do with the business.

Objectives are quantitative, specific, measurable, and temporal. "We want to grow sales 15% annually for the next 5 years." They add specificity to goals and provide incrementally more detail and insight than goals about what management intends to do.

Goals and objectives describe "*what*" the firm intends to do—the "strategic thrust."

Strategies describe *"how"* the firm intends to achieve its goals and objectives. "We will increase sales 15% annually for the next 5 years by adding 5 new customers, each capable of generating $100,000 in annual sales." Strategies should add the flesh to the bones of goals and objectives and should also address the problems and constraints that must be dealt with. Questionnaire findings show that most firms say they have strategies but have not communicated them to the overall organization. This is because they have (a) not conducted sufficient analyses to be able to detail them out and (b) because they likely do not differentiate between goals, objectives, and strategies.

This distinction suggests a hierarchy and is consistent with Collins' pyramid, which shows *C-P-M*™ analyses representing the building blocks, leading up to the development of strategies and outcomes—goals and objectives. It builds strategy from the bottom up—from the essential analyses up to goals, objectives, and strategies.

C-P-M™ analyses establish "baselines"—data points showing the firm's historical performance by which to measure progress in attaining goals and objectives. I establish baselines during the practicable versus desired stage to help management decide the outcomes they seek. As an example, if sales had been increasing at 5–6% annually management can establish a sales baseline of 6% as the point from which to measure efforts to increase sales to 10% if a 10% annual growth over the next three years is decided. The "10% annually by 2013" then becomes an objective—quantitative, specific, measurable, and temporal—and supports the goal to grow the business.

Goals, objectives, and strategies for Q1 will be straight forward. For example, the goal will be to sell more of existing product to existing customers; a qualitative "what" statement. The objective could be to increase sales 5% a year for the next two years. A quantitative "what" statement to better define the goal, could be to specify the A, B, C customers who would be targeted. The strategy could be to increase FTF sales calls with A and B customers and assign inside sales the task of increased promotional efforts via telephone, direct mail, or other media; the "how" statement.

Goals, objectives, and strategies for Q2–Q4 will be more detailed since they involve adding customers, entering new markets, and developing new products. A Q2 goal could be to increase sales by adding customers or entering new markets. The objective could be to add 5 new customers with sales potential of $100,000 each over the next two years, or to add 5 new customers in SIC 2821 Plastics, Materials & Nonvulcanizable Elastomers with sales potential of $100,000 each over the next two years. The strategy(s) could be to add company-employed sales positions, increase inside sales support to generate qualified leads, and develop new collateral materials to support promotional efforts. Q3–Q4 strategies could have similarly stated goals and objectives, but different strategies, for example, with the addition of "developing two new products capable of generating $75,000 in sales within 30 months."

The greater the number of products, customers, and prospects involved, the more complex the development of strategies. Q1 strategies, being relatively straightforward and affecting mostly only the sales force and working capital for an expanded sales and market budget, have less impact on the total organization than do Q2–Q4 strategies. Therefore, SMMs need a more robust methodology for documenting, organizing, and communicating Q2–Q4 goals, objectives, and strategies that go beyond just sales and profit. They also need to address the impact on operations, manufacturing, sales force and sales channels, competitive position, and the capabilities of the organization and work force to support and execute the strategies.

Five Strategic Areas to Address

Chapter 1 mentions the holistic nature of *C-P-M*™ and its implications for strategy development. Figure 75 illustrates the connection of goals, objectives, and strategies to five key strategic areas. It connects goals and

		Five strategic areas				
		Sales	Profit \ profitability	Productivity	Competitive position	Organization and employee development
What	Goals					
	Objectives					
How	Strategies					

Figure 75. Five strategic areas.

objectives to strategy, facilitates communicating what the business wants to do, and makes it easy for all employees to understand what the growth plan intends to accomplish, when and how it intends to do it, and what their role (responsibilities) in helping the firm achieve its goals and objectives and in strategy implementation will entail. It gets everyone in the same boat rowing in the same direction.

The following hypothetical scenario typifies the conditions confronting many manufacturing companies and exemplifies the application of goals, objectives, and strategies across the five areas. See Table 76.

ABC, Inc., a 7-year-old, 50-employee company, conducted *C-P-M*™ and financial analyses that resulted in the following. Sales had been growing 5–6% for the past 4 years up to $4 million; profitability, cash flow, and working capital were OK; its markets were considered to be growing 5–10% and competition was not considered to be unbeatable—there were some reports of the competitor having product quality issues, missed deliveries, and poor tech support and customer service, but its prices were tough to beat (customer satisfaction surveys indicated this). ABC, Inc. believed its products were competitively viable but needed some TLC (tender loving care) from product management (as indicated from lost order analysis). The sales force was understaffed and inexperienced due to turnover and there was no marketing function. Its customer base was stable, but too much business was concentrated in a few long-term customers.

ABC, Inc.'s owners and managers wanted to expand the business but were uncertain about its opportunities. They did some marketing research, confirmed an average market growth of 8% after refining the definitions of their two market segments, and learned there were a considerable number of companies in these segments of which they had been unaware. Data resulting from lost order analysis and preliminary contact with these prospective companies indicated a market of about $40 million (400 companies @ $10,000 unit price @ 10 units per year).

The company's growth plan, Figure 76, illustrates how goals and objectives can be associated across the five strategic areas of the business, and broken down into strategies. It calls for increasing sales 15% annually for 5 years and increasing profit to 12% pre-tax by 2015.

Sales or revenue. Most companies use sales revenue as the major item by which to describe their growth targets but they infrequently provide

Five Strategic Areas 2010-2015

	Sales \ Revenue	Profit \ Profitability	Productivity	Competitive Position	Organization and Employee Development
Goals	1 Grow the business in existing markets with new customers and some new product development.	4 Increase pre-tax margin and overall profitability of product line.	7 Become highly efficient with all internal and external shareholders and associated transactions.	10 Strengthen competitive position relative to top 2 competitors and win more business in direct competition situations.	13 Add employees in manufacturing, sales and marketing.
Objectives	2 Increase sales 15% annually for 5 years.	5 Pre-tax margin @ 12% by FY-ending 2013. Reduce CGS and SGA by $100,000 by 2012 Reduce Prod. A material cost by 15%.	8 Attain 97% on-time shipment by 2012. Reduce through-put time down to 13 days. Reduce purchasing, accounting, order entry, invoicing, etc. transactions costs by 20% by 2012.	11 Generate 50 qualified leads per year; 100 quotes submitted; 25 percent hit rate by 2013.	14 Hire 3 mfg. with CAD, design, eng. BS degrees; inside sales and outside sales by 2011 – TBD.

What

	3	6	9	12	15
	Adopt lean manufacturing, install new computer\ software for CAD, order-entry\ status. Improve technical support and replacement parts inventory.				Train incumbent mfg. employees in coding and programming; detailed job descriptions for mfg., inside\outside sales to support hiring.
Strategies	Add 5 new customers to generate $100,000 each per year.	Hire materials consultant to locate new sourcing for Prod. A material.	Conduct in-house cost\ benefit analyses of all paper and electronic tranactions: internal intra-company, vendors, suppliers, customers, etc.	Evaluate product line; modifications and line extensions to counter competition.	Provide new sales personnel with prospecting, presentation, communications, and closing techniques.
	Increase sales coverage in medical and agriculture market segments.				
How	Develop or license new products.	Conduct competitive analysis of Prod. A to determine viability of price increase.			Hire contract employees short-term.

Figure 76. ABC, Inc.'s five strategic areas 2010–2015.

sufficient detail that describes how they are going to achieve it. According to questionnaire findings, most companies set sales revenue goals on the company level but do not break down sales by customer, product, sales channels, or markets: The Sales/Revenue area allows the breakdown of sales revenue goals into objectives and strategies, thus providing the reader a clear picture of what the firm desires to do and how it intends to do it. *This can be done on one page.* The information signals to the sales department that growth will come from existing markets by adding new customers, increasing sales coverage to do so, and by developing or licensing new products. The sales manager will eventually need to detail out how he intends to execute the strategies.

Profitability. Earlier I mentioned that growth should be profitable, so along with targets for sales revenue a company should also focus on its bottom line, which is affected by the profitability of the products and services it sells (the sales mix) as well as the efficiency of its operations.

The matrix illustrates the company's goal to increase profit by optimizing its sales mix, by reducing cost of goods sold and SG&A, and by reducing the material cost for Prod A, which has only a 10% margin. See cells 4, 5, and 6.

The reduction of manufacturing and operating costs is a common strategy to improve profits, but in the context of growth strategies the profitability of sales mix must also be considered. The company intends to do this by investigating new materials for Product A to increase yield and by possibly raising its selling price. This will require manufacturing and sales to collaborate on materials sourcing and sales will need to assess Product A's competitive strength to justify and sustain a price increase.

Profitability initiatives can also include developing account management strategies, described in Chapter 3, to improve the margins associated with selling to certain customers or groups of customers or into certain markets. Selling costs are the S component of SGA (Selling, General, and Administrative costs on the income statement). The bases for determining this, of course, result from the *C-P-M*™ analyses that evidence lower-than-desired margins from certain customers. Margins derive not just from labor and materials, but also from activities associated with selling to customers, the product and sales mix, and costs of promotional and advertising activities, customer service costs, and so on, any of which could comprise account management strategies and have a favorable impact on profit.

Note also that the strategy to improve profits extends across Profitability, Productivity, and Competitive Position (cells 6, 9 and 12). This exemplifies the holistic approach to developing strategy—that a growth plan impacts more than one part of the organization.

Productivity. This area addresses better utilization of assets; plant and operations, office, or human resources. It is a function of inputs relative to outputs—becoming more efficient. Typically, manufacturing and production operations dominate the Productivity area, but holistically it should also include sales and marketing, accounting and finance, customer service, quotation management, technical support, parts replacement, and so on. Success in this area will contribute to goals and objectives under Profit and Profitability.

Competitive Position. To be able to articulate strategies intended to improve its competitive position, a company must know something about its competitors. While most companies can name direct competitors, they really do not have information by which to make direct competitive comparisons on a product-by-product or service basis.

This is why most growth plans either omit or gloss over competitive issues, and why many fail to reach desired outcomes. Strategies should address how the firm intends to deal with problems, constraints, barriers—particularly those pertaining to direct competitors.

Quotation and lost order analysis, customer feedback, and publicly available sources of information are three ways to learn about and assess competitors' strengths and weaknesses. Other sources include feedback from sales force, tech support and customer service, and intelligence acquired at trade shows. With data and information from these sources, a company will be able to list specific actions (strategies) that can or should favorably affect its competitiveness.

Examples of measurable specific actions to improve competitive position include increasing quote production and hit rates, increasing sales coverage, reducing customer complaints and quality, delivery, and service problems, increasing replacement parts inventory, generating or increasing qualified leads, and of course, changes to products, product lines, product performance, and pricing (cell 12). Note that actions (strategies) can, again, span more than one strategic area, for example, "97% on-time shipment" and "Adopt lean manufacturing" both can or should favorably impact competitive position. Cells 8 and 11 span Productivity and Competitive Position and cells 6, 9, and 12 span Profitability, Productivity, and Competitive Position. Presumably, sales will increase 15% by adding five new customers if these strategies are successfully executed.

Organization and Employee Development. Many growth plans fail to achieve their intended results because they do not connect company-level goals and objectives to individual employees. Plans that call for growing faster than the company has been accustomed to usually require changes to its organizational structure as well as to the skill-set, knowledge, and expertise of employees; less aggressive plans (Q1, for example) may not require significant organizational and employee changes. Organizational development and employee development should be addressed last in the plan because the preceding areas will (or should) determine how the company is to operate and be managed and who will be responsible for making things happen. New functions and departments might be needed, existing ones might be shut down or changed, additional employees might be needed, and existing ones might need retraining. The example indicates additional permanent and contract employees in manufacturing, marketing, and sales who will need training.

Figure 77 illustrates the company-level perspective but, in practice, each department or functional area should be broken down into its own parts and have its own growth plan that dovetails with the company's. This is where strategies must address critical problems, constraints, and barriers confronting the path to goal and objective attainment.

The "Quad Sheet"—A Simple Way to Monitor, Manage, and Evaluate Strategy Implementation

The quad sheet, another Collins' creation, connects all the data, information, and decisions resulting from a strategy development so that employees

ABC, Inc.'s sales and marketing area "Growth plan"	
Major Problems\Obstacles\Constraints	Measurable Objectives
1. Big-customer concentration, have identified several good opportunities for new customers, but don't have the sales resources to develop them. 2. Costs to promote to and develop new customers (sales and marketing costs) is too high. 3. Quotation system is cumbersome and can't get needed data easily; cost per quote is too high. 4. Sales force too few and inexperienced due to turnover. 5. Insufficient number of prospective new customers and selling opportunities.	1. Increase sales @ 15% annually. 2. Add 5 new customers by 2013 with potential for $100,000 in orders per year. Constrained in short-term by sales force personnel limitations. 3. Generate 50 qualified leads per year; 100 quotes annually; attain 25% hit rate by 2013; minimum 3 FTF selling meetings per week per sales person. 4. Reduce adm. quote costs $25,000. 5. Add 1 new product for medical segment by 2013 with potential sales first 12 months $50,000; $100,000 annually thereafter. 6. Attain Prod. A sales = 60% of sales by 2011.
To Do	Tasks\Assignment\Timeline
1. Add full-time inside sales and outside sales (company-employed and\or reps–TBD) by 2012 to generate leads and to provide sales coverage. 2. Purchase quote module for existing accounting system to streamline data acquisition, analysis and to reduce costs. 3. Focus on commercializing existing ideas for new products, either organic or via licensing. Implement project management system for NPD. 4. Implement quarterly and annual sales performance evaluations and sales\product management practices. 5. Provide telephone speaking training for inside sales positions; prospecting, presentation, and closing training for outside sales\reps. 6. Develop plan to reposition Prod. A in medical and geo-satellite markets. 7. Develop screening criteria for RFQs less than $2,500. 8. Develop a new product development strategy.	1. Rhonda recruit, interview, hire inside sales positions next 6 weeks to focus on lead-generation, customer service and tech support. 2. John arrange addition of quote system in 3 months and recommendations for RFQ screening criteria in 2 weeks. 3. Jim develop project management system for NPD and have ready in 4 weeks. Populate with ideas from customers. 4. Rhonda prepare inside\outside sales job descriptions based upon sales coverage requirements, territories, number of existing and potential new customers, and quote follow-up responsibilities. Due in 1 month. To be used in sales performance evaluations. 5. John prepare options for improving sales forecasting and sales reporting by product, customer, and market, including sales and profit\profitability. 6. Rhonda arrange training for new hires to be complete by FY end 2013. 7. Jim develop promotional materials, pricing strategies, and training sessions to support repositioning of Prod. A.

Figure 77. ABC, Inc.'s quad sheet.

understand how their jobs fit into the grand scheme. It also gives line, department, or function managers a concise version of the company plan relative to their areas of responsibility. Like Collins' four types of manufacturers, the quad sheet is simple in concept and application. It breaks down company-level goals, objectives, and strategies into individual employee "to do" lists and timelines.

Figure 77 illustrates the quad sheet for ABC, Inc.'s Sales and Marketing area, broken down from company-level goals, objectives, and strategies.

The upper left quad recaps the major strategic issues and problems pinpointed during the C-P-M™, financial, and other analyses. The upper right quad breaks down the objectives listed in the company-level plan specific to the sales and marketing area. The bottom left quad lists some of the major actions that need to be taken to attain the objectives. The bottom right quad assigns individual responsibility and timelines for implementing the To-Do list. Items in the company-level plan are reflected in the bottom right quad—it demonstrates that growth plans' goals, objectives, and strategies must be broken down to the employee level.

The Sales and Marketing quad sheet contains data and information on which job descriptions and individual job duties and assignments can be developed or modified to support the company's strategies. Note that the Tasks/Assignment/Timeline quad includes quantitative metrics by which objectively to evaluate the assigned employee's performance, a feature generally missing in many companies' HR performance evaluation procedures. By adopting the quad sheet and assigning quantitative metrics to employees, a company can associate employee performance to its strategic thrust and provide a clear path for meaningful job performance and employee development. The Sales and Marketing line manager also has a clearly defined job plan tied to the firm's growth plan, a system for assigning strategic importance to individuals, and a basis for creating periodic performance reviews. Keep in mind that the goals and objectives derive from management's C-P-M™ and financial analyses, its interpretation of those findings, and its evaluations of alternative Q growth initiatives.

Figure 78 illustrates the relationship and flow of analysis from problem identification, through strategy development, to quantifiable outcomes. The first column lists typical problems, issues, problems that C-P-M™

Finding problem, constraint, issue, opportunity	Data source	Objective	Strategy
Business is concentrated in too few customers.	Financial and customer sales/ profitability analyses.	Increase sales 15% annually via five new customers.	Expand customer base in existing markets by increasing sales coverage.
Insufficient growth potential in new product pipeline and inexperienced sales force.	Quotation and lost order analysis.	Increase resources to generate leads and to monitor, manage, and follow up on quotes.	Increase sales force and product line offering. Update quotation system.
Product line not competitive in medical segment.	Marketing research, competitor analysis, customer feedback.	Add new product by 2012 with $100,000 potential annual sales.	Find new market segments and expand product line.

Figure 78. From problem analysis to strategy to objectives.

and financial analyses reveal. The second column identifies the associated analysis. The third column shows the objectives—quantifiable, specific, and measurable—by which the company will monitor and evaluate its progress in implementing the strategy. The last column lists a strategy that could result from evaluating various courses of action to address the problem, or issue.

The firm's growth plan can be clearly summarized as follows:

"We want to expand the business in medical and agricultural market segments (the firm's existing market segments with existing products— a Q1 strategy) with sales increases of 15% annually by optimizing product mix, product development (a Q3 strategy), strengthening our competitive position, streamlining operations, and improving work force skills in manufacturing and sales."

Note that the type of new product is not specified (modification, line extension, substitute, breakthrough) only that a new product or products are needed. Since new product development is resource-intensive (time, money, materials, and personnel) the firm will study alternatives for the type of product, including licensing existing products or technologies.

I have seen planning efforts result in over two dozen goals and objectives that could not be implemented due to confusion, vagueness, and contradiction. Management could not prioritize or assign responsibility; there simply were too many goals, objectives, and strategies. Good analyses before strategy development will clarify the major issues, constraints to growth, and opportunities and options for growing. Fewer goals, objectives, and strategies—clearly defined and articulated—based on sound analysis and interpretation afford a better chance for success.

C-P-M™ Analysis can lead to Unexpected Outcomes

As with marketing research, C-P-M™ analysis does not guarantee expected outcomes. It will not always lead to obvious choices and sometimes will take management on an unexpected route before reaching decisions not contemplated at the start of the project.

Madsen Pipe, Inc., a Type 3 producer of large steel pipe used in highway, bridge, and foundation construction, initially wanted to know if there was a market for thicker-walled pipe. But in the course of planning the marketing research project, its General Manager asked for an overview of operations. Its C-P-M™ analysis involved plants in five states, multiple welding mills, variations in pipe length, wall thickness, diameter, customers, and markets. An overview of the pipe industry, including competitors, showed it was operating at about 50% capacity, which mirrored C-P-M™ findings of the firm's own mills and plants, and industry growth was projected at less than GNP (gross net product) growth. The industry also was extremely fragmented. C-P-M™ analysis led management to shut down a low-performing and problematic plant, move orders to the remaining four plants, adopt Lean manufacturing to reduce set up times, defects and excess inventory, and install productivity devices to speed up welding output. The firm was okay financially, but barely attaining the 12% ROI target set by its parent company.

While the C-P-M™ and market research did not result directly in identifying growth opportunities for thicker-walled pipe, it did result in short-term improvements in ROI due to lower work-in-process and finished goods inventory and working capital—and positioned it for future growth. Unbeknownst to many at the time (2004 and 2005), China's voracious demand for steel would increase US steel price from $350 per ton to $750, which the firm passed onto customers. The operational improvements combined with the price increase raised the firm's ROI fourfold.

C-P-M™ in this example was conducted as part of a strategic overview stemming from the general manager's belief there was a market for thicker-walled pipe than the firm was then producing. While the research did not substantiate this market at the time of the study, C-P-M™ analysis did generate significant insight into the firm's operational inefficiencies that led to a major restructuring and streamlining. The firm has since confirmed the thicker-wall market, built a new plant, and entered the market with increasing success.

C-P-M™ analysis might not identify immediate growth opportunities but nevertheless can lead to unexpected outcomes that would not have been anticipated if C-P-M™ had not been done in the first place. For example, discovering low-profit customers or products that heretofore had been considered star performers should lead to turnaround strategies in customer management and new customer development, product management, and new product development.

The Chicken or the Egg?

So, what comes first; goals and objectives or CPM™? The top-down, sticky note community says goals and objectives should be developed before answering the C-P-M™ question, "Given our customers, products, and markets, what should we do with the business?" It seems counterintuitive to decide what the company should do (goals and objectives) before determining the status and implications of problems, constraints, trends, and opportunities confronting the business' customers, products, and markets—the ingredients that will need changing to affect the desired outcomes. What is the value of determining goals and objectives before specifying the degree to which customers, products, and markets are capable (or not) of supporting those goals? The top-down community advocates looking into issues and problems and dealing with them during the implementation of lofty and vague strategies rather than identifying issues, problems, and constraints first and then developing strategies to reduce, eliminate, or circumvent them.

The top-down approach results in pursuing "desirable" rather than "practicable" because major issues, problems, and constraints have not been identified and quantified beforehand. Effective objectives cannot be established without first quantifying issues, problems, and constraints; and effective strategies cannot be developed without knowing the specifics of what is to be accomplished. It's all about gaining insights and using them to build growth plans from the bottom up.

Summary

The "what" and "how" of deciding among alternatives to grow is daunting to many SMMs because they either have not attempted it, do not have the proficiency to properly do it, or have not been successful doing it. Admittedly, there is considerable data and information to gather, process, analyze, and interpret—and then decisions must be made about "what to do" and "how to proceed." This chapter presents a methodology to simplify this process and to avoid the vagaries and confusion that frequently result from less systematic approaches to growth strategy.

The hierarchy of goals, objectives, and strategies—and their definitions—clarifies these terms and offers a framework for breaking down company-level growth initiatives into discrete and manageable action steps and illustrates the holistic nature of growth planning—that management cannot just focus solely on sales and marketing activities—it must also address operational and organizational areas, too.

The quad sheet presented a simple and flexible device that breaks down company-level initiatives to department or functional areas and can be used by line managers to assign responsibility to individual employees to support the company-level goals and objectives. It effectively connects individuals to the company's grand strategy.

Follow-up and evaluation has been a major weakness in manufacturers' pursuit and implementation of growth plans, mainly because the plans themselves have lacked sufficient detail and quantitative milestones by which gauge progress.

Up to this point, chapters dealt with the discovery and planning parts of strategy development. The next chapter deals with forecasting, budgeting, and implementation.

CHAPTER 10

Sales Management

SMMs can do the best analyses, conduct the most insightful marketing research and learn as much as possible about competition, make all the necessary changes to products and services, and design the best strategies. But unless the sales organization is well organized, effectively aligned with the company's core competencies and its strategic thrust, and directed and managed, the company will not achieve its growth goals and objectives; sales and marketing strategies will flounder.

Previous chapters dealt with obtaining, analyzing, and interpreting customer and product data, evaluating problems, constraints, and issues involving growth, deciding whether or not to grow—and if so—what strategies present the best options. At the end of the day, after all the analysis, planning, and strategy development, the sales force is charged with implementing the strategies and generating the sales. However, whether they are shotgun marketers or proficient planners, many SMMs are not happy with sales performance or coverage.

Evaluating Sales Performance

Before asking companies to evaluate sales performance, the questionnaire asked about factors considered important to successful selling (Figure 79), whether inside sales or outside sales. Because of the diversity of company types—product companies, job shops and machine companies, and size—there was considerable variance in the responses. The top six items (making sales calls, responding to inquiries, gathering competitive information, following up on lost orders, gathering pre-sales information, and promoting to prospects and customers) were checked the most as Average Importance to Critical, in effect, indicating priorities for sales activities and a proxy for job descriptions for the sales force.

	Not Important	Somewhat Important	Average Importance	Very Important	Critical
Make sales calls (fact-to-face for outside sales; telephone for inside sales)	☐	☐	☐	☐	☐
Respond to inquiries	☐	☐	☐	☐	☐
Gather competitive information	☐	☐	☐	☐	☐
Follow-up\report on lost orders	☐	☐	☐	☐	☐
Gather pre-sales information	☐	☐	☐	☐	☐
Promote to prospects\customers	☐	☐	☐	☐	☐
Write proposals\quotations	☐	☐	☐	☐	☐
Deliver proposals\quotations	☐	☐	☐	☐	☐
Install products or systems	☐	☐	☐	☐	☐
Assure timely and accurate delivery	☐	☐	☐	☐	☐
Do maintenance/service in the field	☐	☐	☐	☐	☐
Provide technical customer support	☐	☐	☐	☐	☐
Report sales and quote status\results	☐	☐	☐	☐	☐
Determine customer credit worthiness	☐	☐	☐	☐	☐
Accept customer returns	☐	☐	☐	☐	☐
Train customers	☐	☐	☐	☐	☐

Figure 79. Factors important to successful selling.

The following three examples (Tables 54, 55, and 56) summarize questionnaire findings for inside sales, outside company sales, and reps for both sales performance and sales coverage.

The questionnaire described the inside sales function generally as taking orders either via telephone or in person at the factory, and distinguished it from industrial telemarketing, which was defined "as a planned effort to initiate and maintain customer contact, solicit new and repeat sales, introduce new products and services, and in general conduct a sales effort using the telephone." Most of the 126 companies reported using inside sales and half of them felt performance was acceptable. However, my own personal experience with clients indicates that inside sales duties and responsibilities are vaguely defined, infrequently evaluated, and often combined with other office and administrative duties and customer service. It's not surprising then that only half of the 105 companies using inside sales rated performance as satisfactory—given the poorly defined duties and responsibilities and vague expectations.

In my experience where inside sales positions were specifically established to support outside sales initiatives their duties and responsibilities were clearly defined, which laid the groundwork for more objective performance appraisals. In those cases, inside sales activities more closely resembled proactive industrial telemarketing to generate sales rather than

Table 54. Judging Inside Sales Performance

	Job shop				Product				Type			
	1	2	3	Total	1	2	3	Total	1	2	3	Total
Good\satisfactory	4	11	5	20	3	20	12	35	24	31	17	55
Poor\unsatisfactory	2	6	3	11	2	2	2	6	4	8	5	17
Don't know, not asked, not answered	5	4	6	15	6	7	5	18	11	11	11	33
Total	11	21	14	46	11	29	19	59	39	50	33	105

Table 55. Judging Outside Sales Performance

	Job shop				Product				Type			
	1	2	3	Total	1	2	3	Total	1	2	3	Total
Use Company Outside Sales	4	18	12	34	4	18	15	37	8	36	27	71
Don't judge performance, not asked, not answered	1	8	2	11	2	5	1	8	3	13	3	19
Do judge performance	3	10	10	23	2	13	14	29	5	23	24	52
Good performance	0	5	7	12	1	9	6	16	1	14	13	28
Poor performance	3	5	2	10	1	4	7	12	4	9	9	22
Unsure	0	0	1	1	0	0	0	0	0	0	1	1

Table 56. Sales Forecasting to the Person Level

	Job shop				Product				Type			
	1	2	3	Total	1	2	3	Total	1	2	3	Total
Prepare sales forecast	3	15	13	31	3	24	17	44	6	39	30	75
Compare forecast to actual	0	4	10	14	1	5	14	20	1	9	24	34
Forecast to sales person level	1	5	7	13	0	8	3	11	1	13	10	24
Prepare sales report	8	22	15	45	10	32	28	70	18	54	43	115
Report to sales person level	1	12	10	23	3	19	15	37	4	31	25	60

order-taking. Effective sales and marketing plans and strategies should use more inside sales, which typically is less expensive than outside sales and reps, to absorb as many administrative and nonselling duties as possible from outside sales and reps so that they maximize time in front of prospects and customers.

Company outside sales performance (Table 55) did not fare much better. Twenty-eight companies out of 52 who judge performance felt it was good. While the questionnaire did not probe the reasons for poor performance a contributing factor could be the lack of direction and expectation given to the sales force by management. Table 56 shows that 75 firms prepare a sales forecast, but only 34 compare forecast to actual and only 24 provide detail down to the sales person level. It is difficult to direct and prioritize sales activities if there is a lack of market knowledge, no forecast of expectations, and no follow up based on forecast to actual performance.

Further, of the 52 companies that judge sales performance, only eight do so monthly, shown in Table 57. Add this to the lack of market knowledge, lack of detailed forecasting to the person level, and of comparing forecast to actual and it is easy to see a disconnect between what management wants the sales force to achieve and actually communicating those goals and objectives. The lack of effective periodic follow up and evaluation compounds the problem.

Recall the research pertaining to new product development in Chapter 7 showing that most new product failures result from a lack of or poorly executed market research and analysis. Couple that with SMMs' lack of adherence to basic forecasting at the product and sales person levels and sales reporting and follow up, and you have almost a perfect storm with respect to growth strategies: Companies not only do not do due diligence in this regard but also do not have the basic business procedures to

Table 57. Frequency of Company Sales Performance Evaluation

	Job shop				Product				Type			
	1	2	3	Total	1	2	3	Total	1	2	3	Total
Firms Evaluating Performance	3	10	10	23	2	13	14	29	5	23	24	52
Annually	0	0	1	1	0	0	0	0	0	0	1	1
Semi-annually	0	5	7	12	0	7	10	17	0	12	17	29
Monthly	0	1	1	2	0	4	2	6	0	5	3	8
Whenever	0	4	1	5	0	2	2	4	0	6	3	9
Not answered, specified	3	0	0	3	2	0	0	2	5	0	0	5

forecast, monitor, and evaluate execution of their strategies. SMMs that want to grow must strengthen these basic business practices to improve their chances for a successful outcome.

Rep performance evaluation (Table 58) did not fare any better than company-employed sales positions. Of the 71 firms using reps, only 14 reported having a system for evaluating their performance, and only 10 of those reported satisfactory performance. Overall, 22 (18 + 4, with and without evaluation systems) of the 71 firms using reps were not happy with their performance. Apparently, the absence of market knowledge,

Table 58. Rep Performance Evaluation

	Job shop				Product				Type			
	1	2	3	Total	1	2	3	Total	1	2	3	Total
No. firms that use reps, distributors, dealers, etc.	6	7	10	23	5	27	16	48	11	34	26	71
Do not have rep evaluation system	3	6	7	16	0	17	10	27	0	23	17	43
Have rep evaluation system	0	1	1	2	0	8	4	12	0	9	5	14
Not asked, answered	3	0	2	5	5	2	2	9	8	2	4	14
No rep evaluation system	3	6	7	16	0	17	10	27		23	17	43
Rep performance good\satisfactory	1	1	4	6	0	7	9	16	0	8	13	22
Not good\ unsatisfactory	1	5	3	9	0	9		9	0	14	3	18
Don't judge, not asked, answered performance question	1	0	0	1	0	1	1	2	0	1	0	3
Have a rep evaluation system	0	1	1	2	0	8	4	12	0	9	5	14
Rep performance good\satisfactory	0	0	1	1	0	5	4	9	0	5	5	10
Not good\ unsatisfactory	0	1	0	1	0	0	3	3	0	1	3	4

detailed forecasting, and lack of periodic evaluation and follow up also applies to rep performance, although reps' situations are / situation is different than company-employed sales. While reps are not employees and cannot be controlled and directed, SMMs still expect them to bring a ready knowledge of the market and selling experience to the table, ready to produce and to provide sales coverage quicker and at less cost than company-employed sales people. Nevertheless, they still are subject to performance expectations.

Evaluating Sales Coverage

Sales coverage is the amount of contact between the sales force and customers and prospects a company needs to promote and sell its products and services. It also is a function of the duties and responsibilities assigned or expected by sales management. Figure 79 in the previous section listed the factors important to successful selling and represents duties and responsibilities sales management could assign, depending on the sales and marketing strategies it chose. For example, if the company uses quotes and bids, then three items pertaining to quotes would be required: writing proposals, delivering them, and following up. The greater the number of duties and responsibilities and the greater the number of customers and prospects, the greater the sales coverage requirements, more bodies are needed, and therefore more cost. Cost is a major factor in determining whether a company chooses to employ, train, and develop its own sales force, use reps, or a combination.

Table 59 shows the number of firms using various combinations of inside sales, outside sales, and reps. The number of sales people, and their composition, a company chooses depends on the number of duties and responsibilities, the number of customers and prospects, and the company's sales and marketing budget. Growth plans that forecast significant sales increases require corresponding increases in working capital and operating cash for sales and marketing expenses. Most firms use only inside sales and reps, apparently because this is the lowest cost arrangement and easiest to assemble; whereas using only outside company sales, the most expensive, is the least used arrangement.

Table 59. Use of Inside, Outside Company Sales, and Reps

	Job shop				Product				Type			
	1	2	3	Total	1	2	3	Total	1	2	3	Total
Use only inside sales and reps	3	7	7	17	4	22	14	40	7	29	21	57
Use inside, outside, and reps	2	3	5	10	1	13	12	26	3	16	17	36
Use only inside \ outside company sales	2	12	4	18	2	3	3	8	4	15	7	26
Use only inside sales	2	4		6	2	5	1	8	4	9	1	14
Use only reps, dealers, distributors	3	0	1	4	0	4	2	6	3	4	3	10
Use only outside company sales	0	2	3	5	1	1		2	1	3	3	7

As with sales performance, SMMs are not entirely satisfied with the sales coverage provided by inside sales, outside company sales, and reps—half of the firms who rated sales coverage rated it poor or unsatisfactory (see Table 60).

Inside sales: 32 of 71 (45%) using inside sales are unhappy (55 of 126 did not answer)

Outside sales: 24 of 47 (51%) using outside sales are unhappy (79 of 126 did not answer)

Reps: 23 of 46 (50%) using reps are unhappy (80 of 126 did not answer)

Good sales performance and effective sales coverage both depend on sales forecasting and market knowledge. Additionally, sales coverage depends on the availability of sufficient cash to pay for payroll, commission, travel, and meals—costs of having sales people promote and sell. If sales forecasting, market knowledge, or cash are absent or deficient, sales performance and sales coverage will not be satisfactory. Sales forecasting should provide goals, objectives, and expectations for the sales force, particularly if forecasted down to the sales person level, and allows a means for evaluating sales performance. When sales management knows of the number and

Table 60. Judging Sales Coverage

Judging company inside sales coverage											
	Job shop				Product				Type			
	1	2	3	Total	1	2	3	Total	1	2	3	Total
Good\satisfactory	3	6	7	16	1	16	6	23	4	22	13	39
Poor\unsatisfactory	3	8	2	13	1	11	7	19	4	19	9	32
Not asked, not answered, or don't know	6	13	7	26	12	9	8	29	18	22	15	55
Total	12	27	16	55	14	36	21	71	26	63	37	126

Judging company outside sales coverage											
	Job shop				Product				Type			
	1	2	3	Total	1	2	3	Total	1	2	3	Total
Good\satisfactory	2	3	4	9	0	7	7	14	2	10	11	23
Poor\unsatisfactory	1	5	3	9	1	8	6	15	2	13	9	24
Not asked, not answered, or don't know	9	19	9	37	13	21	8	42	22	40	17	79
Total	12	27	16	55	14	36	21	71	26	63	37	126

Judging rep coverage											
	Job shop				Product				Type			
	1	2	3	Total	1	2	3	Total	1	2	3	Total
Good\satisfactory	1	1	4	6	1	9	7	17	2	10	11	23
Poor\unsatisfactory	1	5	3	9	0	10	4	14	1	15	7	23
Not asked, not answered, or don't know	10	21	9	40	13	17	10	40	23	38	19	80
Total	12	27	16	55	14	36	21	71	26	63	37	126

location of customers and prospects, it can plan, prioritize, and direct sales activities and subsequently evaluate sales performance based on individuals' execution of sales plans as well as sales production according to the sales forecast. Without working capital to fund sales payroll and related sales, marketing, and promotional expenses, sales coverage will be insufficient to achieve the forecast.

Sales performance and sales coverage therefore are tethered to the sales forecast, sales reporting, market knowledge, and operating cash. Further, since sales performance will falter if sales coverage is insufficient, it is critically important to ensure the best sales coverage the company can afford.

Four very Critical and Strategic Questions

Many SMMs overlook the strategic importance of the composition and configuration of their sales force and sales channel. The issue of sales force and sales channel should be considered as soon as *C-P-M*™ and financial analyses are completed. *C-P-M*™ will show the number and location of customers and prospects, which in turn will give some indication of the sales coverage needed to serve them. Since sales coverage requires working capital, SMMs should consider the following four strategic questions early in the strategy development process after completing *C-P-M*™.

1. How many sales people will be needed to provide sales coverage and to implement the growth strategies?
2. What is the best geographical deployment of the sales force and sales channel to provide needed sales coverage?
3. What composition—factory-employed sales, reps, distributors, inside sales, direct mail, telemarketing, or Internet—is best suited for our type of customer, products and services, and markets?
4. How much will it cost?

SMMs can do everything right to create a growth plan—due diligence, C-P-M™, financial analysis, and strategy development—but the plan will fail if the sales force and sales channel do not possess the right education and experience, communications skills, selling techniques, and product knowledge because it is the sales force and sales channel that is responsible for implementing the plan.

The following hypothetical example of ABC, Inc. illustrates the planning and analysis needed to establish a sales organization configured to the customer, products and services, markets, and to the company's ability to fund it.

1. *How many sales people will be needed to provide sales coverage and to implement the growth strategies?*

    ABC, Inc.'s sales manager (introduced in Chapter 1) grouped 31 existing customers and 68 qualified prospects, which the firm had identified using the lead-generation techniques described in previous chapters, into six territories, totaling 99 businesses on which to build his sales force. In addition to the 68 qualified leads, the firm's marketing research identified 340 other businesses as nonqualified but potential customers that matched its employment size and SIC code profiles, totaling 408 potential new customers. With all this potential, however, the sales manager focused only on his 31 existing and 68 qualified prospects, thus constituting the firm's sales targets priorities (see Figure 80).

    Assuming an outside sales person could make two face-to-face (FTF) sales calls per week and that the firm's 31 existing customers

FTF Sales Calls @ 3 Per Year Needed			No. of bodies needed
Capacity = 2 calls per week; 100 per year			
Existing customers	31	91 F-T-F calls needed per year	1
Qualified prospects	68	204 F-T-F calls needed per year	2
Total	99	295 F-T-F calls needed per year	3

Figure 80. Sales calls per year calculation.

and 68 qualified prospects would need at least three sales calls per year, the sales manager determined that two outside sales people in addition to him could provide the needed sales coverage (99 companies × 3 sales calls = 297 sales calls ÷ 100 sales calls per year per person = 3 people).

He would manage the firm's 31 existing customers, and with the support of a new inside sales position, he would train the two new outside positions and provide them with materials to contact the 68 prospects. The new inside sales person would be responsible for calling on and promoting to the 340 nonqualified suspects and prospects via telephone calls, direct mail, and e-mail.

2. *What is the best geographical deployment of the sales force and sales channel to provide needed sales coverage?*

The sales manager earlier had set up six sales territories: Southeast, Northeast, Midwest, Southwest, West, and Northwest. The resulting territory plan (Figure 81) has the two outside positions evenly split with about 180 qualified and nonqualified prospects. Note that A and B and the sales manager share the Northeast due to the high number of prospects. (Qualified prospects are indicated in parentheses.)

Territory Breakdown				
Total Qualified and Non-Qualified Prospective Customers	Outside Position		Sales Manager	Total
	A	B		
Southeast	48 (8)			48 (8)
Northeast	60 (12)	40 (10)	50 (3)	150 (25)
Midwest	39 (7)	39 (6)		78 (13)
Southwest	30 (5)			30 (5)
West		42 (7)		42 (7)
Northwest		60 (10)		60 (10)
Total Prospects				408 (68)
Existing Customers			31	31
Total	177 (32)	181 (33)	81 (3)	439
Qualified prospects are shown in parentheses ( ).				

Figure 81. ABC, Inc.'s territory plan.

Geography is a major factor in determining sales coverage. High-density territories, such as the Northeast and around Chicago and Indiana, allow for more frequent sales calls because of the shorter distance between customers and prospects than for customers and prospects in Montana, Wyoming, and the Dakotas where windshield time is greater. Consequently, sales call costs could be higher in western expansive territories than for densely populated urban areas. He must now figure out whether to hire and train two company sales people or hire two manufacturers' reps—a major strategic decision.

3. *What composition—factory-employed sales, reps, distributors, inside sales, direct mail, telemarketing, or Internet—is best suited for our type of customer, products and services, and markets?*

The decision to hire and train a sales force or to hire reps depends on several factors, such as the type of product, the geographical distribution and demographics of the customer base, the job description (duties and responsibilities) for the intended sales position, and the amount of money the company has to invest in a sales organization and sales channel. Aside from the number of bodies needed for sales coverage, the composition of the sales organization (inside, outside sales, reps, dealers, and distributors) is very strategic: Ideally, the composition of the sales organization (and its skills, education, and experience) should be tailored to a company's customers, products, and markets.

The education, experience, and communication skill set requirements of sales people may differ depending on whether the customer decision maker is the purchasing agent, plant manager, V.P. of Production, mid-level manager, president, or owner. The size and sophistication of the customer (e.g., Types 1, 2, 3 or 4) is also a factor; the more sophisticated the customer—the more sophisticated should be the sales force.

As noted in Chapter 6, product type (simple versus complex) is a major factor that affects the selling cycle and also the sale force or channel. Complex, highly engineered, and expensive products usually involve extended selling cycles, higher selling costs, and selling to a higher level in customers' organizations than do simple products.

Making sales calls, preparing and submitting quotes, and closing deals typically constitute a sales position's duties and responsibilities. Other duties, such as installation, on-site training, and trouble shooting, determining credit and handling collections and paperwork could also apply. It all depends on the type of product, selling cycle, customer requirements, and so forth.

The ideal set of duties and responsibilities enables the sales force to maximize selling opportunities—being in front of decision makers, quoting, and closing the order. Other selling activities, such as travel, paperwork, installation, trouble shooting, checking order status, and so on, reduce F-T-F selling time, result in a greater workload and in more sales bodies to provide sales coverage, and thus increase the sales and marketing budget and working capital. ABC, Inc.'s sales manager's decision to hire an inside sales person, while adding to the budget, is intended to relieve the outside sales positions of nonselling duties and increase their selling opportunities.

The choice between hiring and training company sales positions or hiring reps is a trade-off between their respective advantages and disadvantages and their cost. Company sales positions generally involve higher costs for salary and commission, training, health and vacation benefits, payroll taxes, and travel, whereas reps work on commission and are paid only when a sale is made. As Table 59 on the composition of sales organizations showed earlier, more firms use reps over company sales positions presumably due to cost.

ABC's sales manager, weighing the advantages and disadvantages and the cost differential between company sales and reps, needed to prepare a sales forecast and sales and marketing budget to see if ABC, Inc. can afford to hire and train its own sales force or hire reps (Figures 82 and 83).

4. *How much will it cost?—the sales and marketing budget.*

In preparing the sales and marketing budget, ABC, Inc.'s sales manager extended his 2012 sales forecast to 2016, showing sales to $6.5 million. But because he needed to decide between company sales positions and reps, he prepared two budgets.

ABC, Inc's Sales & Marketing Budget–Reps					
	2012	2013	2014	2015	2016
Existing Customer Sales	4,000,000	4,340,000	4,636,752	5,193,162	6,027,778
New Customer Forecast	n\a	340,000	363,248	406,838	472,222
Sales	4,000,000	4,680,000	5,000,000	5,600,000	6,500,000
Salaries	25,000	35,000	36,750	38,588	40,517
Commissions @ 10%	–	34,000	36,325	40,684	47,222
Advertising and promotion	10,000	5,000	5,000	5,000	5,000
Travel and lodging	3,000	3,200	3,500	3,750	4,000
Trade show	7,500	2,500	2,500	2,500	2,500
Total	45,500	79,700	84,075	90,521	99,239
Budget % of Sales	1.1%	1.7%	1.7%	1.6%	1.5%

Figure 82. ABC, Inc.'s budget for reps.

ABC, Inc's Sales & Marketing Budget,–Company Sales					
	2012	2013	2014	2015	2016
Existing Customer Sales	4,000,000	4,340,000	4,636,752	5,193,162	6,027,778
New Customer Forecast	n\a	340,000	363,248	406,838	472,222
Sales	4,000,000	4,680,000	5,000,000	5,600,000	6,500,000
Salaries	25,000	125,000	131,250	137,813	144,703
Advertising and promotion	10,000	5,000	5,000	5,000	5,000
Travel and lodging	3,000	8,000	8,400	8,820	9,261
Trade show	7,500	2,500	2,500	2,500	2,500
Total	45,500	140,500	147,150	154,133	161,464
Budget % of Sales	1.1%	3.0%	2.9%	2.8%	2.5%

Figure 83. ABC, Inc.'s budget for company sales.

The first budget (Figure 82) shows reps at 10% commission ($34,000) starting in 2013 when the new sales positions or reps are hired. The salaried inside sales position is already employed in 2012 at $25,000 to generate leads and other support duties. It will increase from $25,000 to $35,000 in 2013 and at 5% annually through 2016.

The budget for two company sales positions (Figure 83) increases salaries by $45,000 for each of the two new sales positions, maintains the salary for the inside position, and increases travel and lodging expenses from $3,000 to $8,000. Note the increase in the budget as a percentage of sales due to company sales positions; they add about 1.3% of sales to the budget compared with reps—from 1.7% to 3.0% of 2013 sales.

The sales manager can now consider the advantages and disadvantages of company sales positions versus reps compared with their respective costs. He decided in favor of company sales positions even though the budget as a percentage of sales is about 1% more than for reps. The nature of the product line, and the fact that ABC, Inc. targets decision makers at the mid-level to executive level, indicated a more educated, trained, and dedicated sales force than he felt he could get with reps.

The sales manager can now articulate his sales plan and selling strategy as follows: "ABC, Inc. will use trained company sales personnel to call on prospective customers in assigned territories at least three times per year. The inside sales position will generate qualified leads, assist in quote preparation and follow-up, provide promotional materials, and conduct routine follow-up with non-qualified prospects."

There is an additional calculation the sales manager could make to ensure that he has the appropriate number of bodies to provide sales coverage: the cost of a sales call which is also useful when assessing the company sales versus rep situation.

Sales call costs impact the sales and marketing budget and are critical when considering company-employed sales positions. For example, ABC, Inc.'s unit price is $10,000 and the sales manager is budgeting two units and three sales calls per initial sale for new customers. Budgeted 2013 Salary and Travel expenses total $133,000 ($125,000 + $8,000) for 295 sales calls (see Figure 80) resulting in an average sales call cost of $450, which is slightly higher than the $300 national average. (Internet searches show sales call costs ranging from $100 to over $400, depending on the nature of the product and demographics of the firm's markets; a range of $250 to

$400 is often cited.) Simple products with short selling cycles sold to customers in high-density industrial markets with short distances between customers and prospects will achieve a higher number of sales calls per day or week and incur lesser costs for sales call. Complex and technical products with long selling cycles sold into geographically dispersed markets will experience fewer sales calls per day or week and incur higher sales calls costs. ABC's sales manager accepts that bringing on and training new positions and targeting new customers requires additional expense and working capital. He expects that over time the new employees will become better at their jobs, thus reducing the costs to bring on new customers.

The calculation for the cost of a sales call is simply total sales expenses associated with an outside sales employee (e.g., salary and commission, payroll taxes, vacation, insurance and benefits, travel, lodging, and communications) divided by the number of sales calls budgeted or made.

Another perspective on the $450 sales cost relates to the sales dollar amount of a single order and the cost to generate a sale. (see Figure 84). The $1,350 budgeted sales call cost for three sales calls represents 7% of the sale of two units at $10,000 each, whereas a rep at 10% commission would be higher—$2,000 versus $1,350. So even if the cost of the sales call exceeds the national average, on a percentage of sales basis, it isn't much different from whether the firm used reps. In this case, using company sales is cheaper than a rep.

Unit SP	$10,000	
2 units per initial order	$20,000	100%
3 sales calls per initial order × $450	$1,350	7%

Figure 84. Sales call cost as a percentage of sales.

Sales call costs are not an issue with reps because they are not employees of the SMM and therefore generally do not incur expenses that show up on the SMM's income statement other than commission. SMMs typically do not monitor reps' travel, and sales call activity and therefore do not have the data by which to calculate sales call costs.

Sales call costs are a good metric for evaluating the effectiveness (converting calls into orders) and efficiency (cost) of outside sales activities. Sales call costs in excess of budget should signal red flags: For example, high sales call costs that do not produce orders could indicate poor targeting of prospects, ineffective selling and closing techniques or both.

Building a Market-Based, Realistic Sales Forecast from C-P-M™, Marketing Research, Sales Coverage, and the Territory Plan

Previous material shows that SMMs' sales forecasting and sales reporting are not routinely prepared and that most of the 75 out of 126 firms who do prepare a sales forecast do so only at the company level and only 24 do so to sales person level: This could contribute to the companies' general unhappiness with sales performance. It's difficult to get the sales force to produce as expected without a forecast to communicate expectations and just as difficult to evaluate its performance without a sales report.

Another aspect of sales forecasting that could reduce its usefulness is the amount of detail and the sources used for input. Table 61 shows only four companies reported comprehensive forecasting on the aggregate company, product or process, customer, sales person, and market. The other 75 companies that prepare a forecast reported forecasting various combinations of total company, product or process, customer, salesperson, market, and so on.

Table 62 shows the various inputs of 21 Type 3 companies into their sales forecasting with sales and key customers used most often; that is just slightly over half of the 37 Type 3 companies surveyed (We assumed Types 1 and 2 would not go to that level of detail and therefore did not ask.) Sales forecasting, ideally, should include the granular detail by sales person, territory, market, product (product line or product category for product management use) or process (for job and machine shops), and build up to total company.

SMMs wanting to increase sales by finding new customers should have some idea of the amount of sales coming from that new business so that it can direct and evaluate sales performance. Fortunately,

Table 61. Detail of Sales Forecast

Detail of forecast	Job shop				Product				Type			
	1	2	3	Total	1	2	3	Total	1	2	3	Total
Total company	2	8	11	21	1	10	12	23	3	18	23	44
Product\process	0	4	1	5	2	15	13	30	2	19	14	35
Customer	2	9	6	17	0	11	6	17	2	20	12	34
Sales person	1	5	7	13	0	8	3	11	1	13	10	24
Market	0	7	2	9	0	6	7	13	0	13	9	22
Company and product\process only	0	2	1	3	0	6	10	16	0	8	11	19
Company and customer only	1	4	5	10	0	4	5	9	1	8	10	19
Company and sales person only	0	3	7	10	0	2	2	4	0	5	9	14
Total company only	1	4	1	6	1	1	2	4	2	5	3	10
Company and market only	0	2	2	4	0	2	4	6	0	4	6	10
Company, product\process, customer, sales person, and market	0	2		2	0	1	1	2	0	3	1	4

Table 62. Sources of Input into Type 3 Forecast

Source of input	Job shop				Product				Type			
	1	2	3	Total	1	2	3	Total	1	2	3	Total
Input from sales			8	8			13	13			21	21
Ask key customers			7	7			9	9			16	16
Input from sales and key customers		Not asked	7	7		Not asked	8	8		Not asked	15	15
Trend analysis			3	3			7	7			10	10
Add target %			3	3			5	5			8	8
Pull out of air			2	2			4	4			6	6
Published data			2	2			2	2			4	4
Modeling software			0	0			3	3			3	3

C-P-M™ analyses of customer data, lead-generation, and prospect data can be used to prepare a detailed sales forecast down to the territory and sales person level.

Tables 63 and 64, using ABC, Inc. again hypothetically, illustrate how that data can be incorporated into a sales forecast. Its 2013 forecast integrates historical customer sales, market research and territory analysis, and sales planning and sales coverage, along with budgetary and financial constraints imposed by the sales and marketing budget, and ties the forecast to the firm's target market, customers, and prospects. Note that this forecast combines a Q1 strategy—existing products to existing customers—and a Q2 strategy—existing products to new customers (markets).

The sales manager combined several aspects of marketing, sales, and product management in preparing the forecast:

- The number of customers and prospects by territory (see previous territory breakdown in Figure 65)
- Customers' purchasing history (customer sales analysis from *C-P-M*™ showed they average 14 units per year)
- Qualifying prospective new customers
- Establishing territories and sales coverage based on geographical distribution of customers and prospects and capacity of sales positions to make F-T-F sales calls
- Estimating market penetration at 25% per year and estimates of initial purchases by prospects at two units.

At unit pricing of $10,000, the estimated total forecast for 68 qualified prospects is $340,000 (estimated market potential at $1,360,000 × estimated 25% penetration first year) and $4,340,000 for the 31 existing customers, totaling $4,680,000. He also prepared a forecast for each sales position, broken down by their territories, which he divided between salesman A and salesman B because they both had portions of the Midwest and Southwest.

ABC, Inc.'s two forecasts, which integrate real market data, will help the sales manager manage his implementation as well as evaluate his progress in attaining his sales goals. Although it took some time and analysis to

Table 63. ABC, Inc.'s Company-Level Sales Forecast

	ABC, Inc. sales forecast						
	2013 Preliminary forecast—Company level						
	Southeast	Northeast	Midwest	Southwest	West	Northwest	Total
	A		A & B		B		
Existing Customers	3	10	5	2	7	4	31
Forecast	$420,000	$1,400,000	$700,000	$280,000	$980,000	$560,000	$4,340,000
Qualified Prospectives	8	25	13	5	7	10	68
Estimated Purchases @ Qualified Prospects @ 2 Units per Year	$160,000	$500,000	$260,000	$100,000	$140,000	$200,000	$1,360,000
Estimated Penetration @ 25%	$40,000	$125,000	$65,000	$25,000	$35,000	$50,000	$340,000
Total	$460,000	$1,525,000	$765,000	$305,000	$1,015,000	$610,000	$4,680,000

Table 64. ABC, Inc.'s Salesman-Level Sales Forecast

		Prospects			
ABC, Inc. sales forecast					
2013 Preliminary forecast–Salesman level					
	Existing customers	Qualified	Non–qualified	Total	Sales
Sales Manager	31			31	$4,340,000
Northeast		3	47	50	15,000
					$4,355,000
Sales A					
Southeast		8	40	48	$40,000
Northeast		12	48	60	60,000
Midwest		7	32	39	35,000
Southwest		5	25	30	25,000
Subtotal		32	145	177	$160,000
Sales B					
Northeast		10	30	40	$50,000
Midwest		6	33	39	30,000
West		7	35	42	35,000
Northwest		10	50	60	50,000
Subtotal		33	148	181	$165,000
Total Prospects		68	340	408	
Existing Customers	31			31	
Total Prospects/ Customers				439	
Sales Dollars	$4,340,000	$340,000			$4,680,000
Sales Units	434	34			468

prepare, previous *C-P-M*™ analyses reduced the time he otherwise would have spent pulling together the various sources for input into the sales forecast. He is now in a very good position objectively to evaluate actual sales force performance to forecast on making sales calls, hitting sales goals— which are $160,000 for A and $165,000 for B—and for monitoring the cost for implementing this strategy to the sales and marketing budget. Overall, he has configured his sales and financial resources to the number and geographical distribution of existing customers and prospects.

Companies facing simpler sales and marketing situations—for example, Type 1 companies and some job shops and machine companies that generally do not produce and sell their own products—could use the format illustrated in Figure 85 just based on existing customers and qualified prospects.

This format assumes also a Q1 strategy with 43 existing customers (shown by customer classification) and a Q2 strategy with 20 prospective new customers determined by marketing research, lead-generation (asking for typical, budgeted, or estimated purchases of the type of product or services being promoted), and prospecting. Further, the 25% market penetration in this and the previous formats are best guesses—saying that management estimates it will get an order from one of four prospects this planning period based on quotation hit rates.

Forecasted sales from existing customers are based on history, estimates, and discussions with the nine MVC, A, and B customers during

Sales Forecast–Type 1 Companies, Job Shops, and Machine Companies						
2013 Preliminary Forecast						
	MVC	**A**	**B**	**C**	**Other**	**Total**
% of Total Sales	15%	12%	6%	24%	43%	100%
Existing Customers	2	2	5	9	25	43
Forecast	$375,000	$300,000	$150,000	$600,000	$1,075,000	$2,500,000

Qualified Prospects						20
Estimated Revenue based on Avg. $7,500 Budget or Plant Purchases						$150,000
Estimated Penetration @ 25%						$37,500
Total	$375,000	$300,000	$150,000	$600,000	$1,075,000	$2,537,500

Figure 85. Simple sales forecast based on customers and prospects.

3-fer surveys. Owners and top management will conduct FTF sales visits on the 9 top customers and the 34 C and other customers will be managed by inside sales via telephone, e-mail, fax, and other lower-cost, non-FTF sales methods since those customers' orders are not regular and therefore less forecastable. However, if reps are used they could still make on-site visits to C and other customers since their travel and FTF costs are not a direct cost to the company. The most significant aspect of this format is / involves the 20 prospects—management will need to make sure that sales activities to call on these companies to solicit requests to quote or bid are carried out, that requests to quote and bid do in fact occur (or find out why not since they are qualified prospects), that requested quotes and bids are promptly submitted, and that lost-order analysis is conducted.

Note that this forecast format does not specify the sales person level because not all companies assign customers to the sales force. In many small companies, owners or top management call on key customers. Since products also are not specified, as with job shops and machine companies, it is easier to manage and report sales by customer—particularly key customer(s).

These sales forecast formats illustrate how the various aspects of *C-P-M*™ can simplify sales forecasting and add value to the process by allowing for a break down to the product, market, and sales person levels. However, if the situation is relatively simple where products, territories, or individual sales positions are not involved, customers are a good basis on which to forecast.

How Are We Doing? Using Sales Reports and Goals and Objectives to Measure and Evaluate Performance in Implementing a Growth Plan

Most companies reported preparing sales reports, with over half reporting sales by a combination of customer, product, and sales person. Ten reported on all five choices: company total, customer, product or process, sales person, and market; and about a third reported only on one—mostly only the company or customer. While sales reporting is a good business practice, its effectiveness increases when compared to actual sales performance, which is only about half of the 75 companies that prepare a forecast, see Table 44 in Chapter 8.

Figure 86 is a sample agenda for reviewing sales performance to forecast. It goes beyond just reviewing sales performance, however. It also incorporates ABC's objectives listed in its growth plan and quad sheet (refer to Figure 77 in Chapter 9), suggesting a more comprehensive review involving sales, production management, and finance. You may recall ABC's plan called for increasing sales from $4,000,000 in 2012 to $6,500,000 in 2016, adding five new customers in 2013 with potential for $100,000 in orders per year (out of 68 qualified prospects and 340 nonqualified), and adding one inside and two outside sales positions to increase sales coverage.

This example listed the people who are to attend the review meeting, the area on which they will report, the topics and content of their report, and the sources of information they will use. The president or owner might only need to report quarterly. The sales manager will report monthly on his efforts pertaining to his sales and marketing quad sheet, and use the objectives (100 quotes annually, attain 25% hit rate, minimum 3 FTF sales calls per week, reduce quote costs $25,000 annually, and so on) to monitor and evaluate his progress in executing strategies. He will also report on and update finished goods inventory. The production and accounting managers similarly have reporting duties and also report on progress in attaining objectives set forth in the growth plan. The point of this formalized agenda is to keep management focused on strategic goals and objectives, and on the progress and problems affecting the execution of the strategies—not just on sales performance as does a sales report.

Helping Reps and Independents Help You

Earlier in this chapter I presented questionnaire findings showing that of 71 firms using reps, 43 did not have a system to evaluate rep performance and that almost a third of the 71 firms were not happy with reps' performance and sales coverage. You might also recall that many SMMs do not conduct marketing research, have not sufficiently defined their markets and segments, and only 27 of 71 knew the number and location of prospective new customers. Only 20 of these firms forecast and report to the person level.

Sample Agenda for Periodic Review Meeting		
Responsibility/Role	Frequency or Period	Report/ Documentation
President/Owner	Quarterly	
Economic reports, major company initiatives, overall company status, etc.		
Sales/Marketing Manager	Monthly	
➢ Growth Plan, Quad review		Discuss actions, progress, problems pertaining to the Growth Plan and Quad sheet for Sales/ Marketing
➢ Actual sales vs. forecasted sales • By product, customer, market, salesman or rep, etc. • Updated forecast ➢ Quote management • No. submitted, won • Lost order analysis ➢ Lead Generation ➢ Sales/Marketing Budget		Compare planned vs. actual using the objectives from Growth Plan • New customer development (5 new @ $100,000 each) • Quote production (100 annually), won vs. lost (attain 25% hit rate) • Lost order analysis and feedback • Leads generated = 50 qualified F-T-F sales calls to make • Dollars budgeted vs. actual ($ and % of sales)
➢ Competitor activities, actions		Reports, feedback from sales force, suppliers, trade shows, etc.
➢ FG inventory status, other	Weekly	Inventory Reports
Production Manager	Weekly	Production, Shipping, Quality Reports Prod A material costs by 15% • Throughput down to 13 days • On-time shipment to 97%
Finance/Accounting Manager	Monthly/ Quarterly	Balance Sheet and Income Statement, A/R and A/P, Cash Flow • Pre-tax margin to 12% • CGS and SGA $100,000 reduction

Figure 86. Sample agenda for periodic review.

It seems intuitive that unless a company can provide reps and inde-pendents with direction, feedback, and support, it will not be happy with their performance. There are a few steps SMMs can take to strengthen the rep and independent relationship to get better results. During his years in the private sector as VP Sales and Marketing and in turnaround situations, Mike Collins put together three guidelines intended to help SMMs with their reps and independents. The first, **Do's and Don'ts of Working With Reps and Independents**, offers common sense ground rules to incorporate into the company–rep rela-tionship, Figure 87.

Collins' **Rep Performance Rating Scale** (Figure 88) addresses two aspects of rep management: determining what you want a rep or inde-pendent to do and having criteria by which to evaluate their performance.

Do's and don'ts of working with independents

Do's

- Provide special compensation for new product ideas and new market development sales calls.
- Provide on-going technical training.
- Include the primary points of sales coverage in the written contract and agree to an annual factory and rep performance evaluation.
- Provide on-going information like new product bulletins, applications reports, and information on sales successes.
- Make sure all factory sales and support people "walk in reps' shoes" by making the difficult market and product development sales calls.
- Give independent reps the same level of respect and support the firm would to its own employees.

Don'ts

- Not paying commissions even when the firm has collected from the customer.
- Fail to provide enough leads to help reps probe market segments for additional sales.
- Expect reps to develop a segment\niche marketing plan for the firm.
- Fail to return phone calls, faxes, mail, or email or respond to written requests.
- Fail to make customer delivery commitments.
- Delay in responding to customer service problems.

Figure 87. Do's and don'ts of working with reps and independents.

Rep Performance Rating Scale										
	Unsatisfactory						Excellent			
Focus on the right market segments	1	2	3	4	5	6	7	8	9	10
Compatible or non-competing product lines	1	2	3	4	5	6	7	8	9	10
Technical background and knowledge	1	2	3	4	5	6	7	8	9	10
Response to leads and account opportunities	1	2	3	4	5	6	7	8	9	10
Ability to sell into markets\segments	1	2	3	4	5	6	7	8	9	10
Use of telemarketing as support	1	2	3	4	5	6	7	8	9	10
Consistently asks for more leads	1	2	3	4	5	6	7	8	9	10
Knowledgeable of firm's product line(s)	1	2	3	4	5	6	7	8	9	10
Obtains pre-sale information	1	2	3	4	5	6	7	8	9	10
Uses direct mail for market probes\promotion	1	2	3	4	5	6	7	8	9	10
Responds to technical\product training	1	2	3	4	5	6	7	8	9	10
Follows up on lost orders	1	2	3	4	5	6	7	8	9	10
Ability\prepares proposals\quotations	1	2	3	4	5	6	7	8	9	10
Reports on sales and quotations	1	2	3	4	5	6	7	8	9	10
Demonstrates good territory management	1	2	3	4	5	6	7	8	9	10
Good overall communication with factory	1	2	3	4	5	6	7	8	9	10
Achieves sales coverage and forecast	1	2	3	4	5	6	7	8	9	10

Figure 88. Rep performance rating scale.

It incorporates subjects covered in the book, such as marketing, market segments, preparing quotations and lost orders analysis, territory and sales coverage, and sales forecasting.

It lists various items the company would want its reps and independents to perform. However, keep in mind that reps are independent contractors, not employees, and there are limitations on what they can or will agree to do. Nevertheless, the rating scale provides a good basis for helping a company consider what it would want a rep to do and for establishing a framework for negotiating and discussing the specifics of the relationship and desired outcomes.

When duties, responsibilities, sales targets have been agreed to, ideally in writing, the company will have a basis for objectively evaluating reps' or independents' performance at least quarterly. This is obviously a

Table 65. Use of a Recruiting System for Reps

| | Recruiting system for reps | | | | | | | | | | | |
| | Job shop | | | | Product | | | | Type | | | |
	1	2	3	Total	1	2	3	Total	1	2	3	Total
Use reps	6	7	10	23	5	27	16	48	11	34	26	71
Do not have system	1	6	7	14	1	22	11	34	2	28	18	48
Have system	0	1	1	2	0	4	4	8	0	5	5	10
Not asked, answered, don't know	5	0	2	7	4	1	1	6	9	1	3	13

generic example and should be tailored to the firm's customers, products, markets, and territories.

Incidentally, questionnaire responses show that only 10 of the 71 companies using reps have a system by which to hire or recruit them (see Table 65). It is possible that not having a clear picture of what you want the rep to do gets in the way of having a system or well-thought-out procedure for hiring a rep.

Collins' third guideline shows that performance evaluation is a two-way street: Reps and independents, too, can evaluate the company's performance. Just as SMMs should evaluate the performance of their inside/outside sales and reps/independents, the latter should also evaluate their clients' performance in supporting them.

The **Company Performance Rating Scale** (Figure 89) is designed to provide a quick assessment of factory support of reps and independents. Scores below seven indicate red flags that sales management should discuss with the rep to better understand how to help the factory better support reps.

Rooftop Industries, Inc., previously introduced, asked its 84 nonexclusive reps and dealers to provide feedback about what it could do to provide better support. Rooftop's management was surprised at the number of different areas mentioned: pricing, delivery and lead times, product development, response time to special pricing and RFQs, promotional literature, software to facilitate the pricing of features and add-ons, and lower costs. As with the Rep Performance Scale, the company version is generic and should be tailored to the company.

Company performance rating scale										
	Unsatisfactory							Excellent		
Number and quality of sales leads	1	2	3	4	5	6	7	8	9	10
Sales\engineering support	1	2	3	4	5	6	7	8	9	10
Responses to phone, fax, mail/email	1	2	3	4	5	6	7	8	9	10
Reliability of deliver promises	1	2	3	4	5	6	7	8	9	10
Introduction of new products	1	2	3	4	5	6	7	8	9	10
Sales call support in field	1	2	3	4	5	6	7	8	9	10
Customer service	1	2	3	4	5	6	7	8	9	10
Parts support	1	2	3	4	5	6	7	8	9	10
Effectiveness of product/technical training	1	2	3	4	5	6	7	8	9	10
Response to customer problems/inquiries	1	2	3	4	5	6	7	8	9	10
Accuracy and response with quotes	1	2	3	4	5	6	7	8	9	10
Overall commitment to quality	1	2	3	4	5	6	7	8	9	10
Commission payments accurate and on-time	1	2	3	4	5	6	7	8	9	10
Knowledge of target markets	1	2	3	4	5	6	7	8	9	10
Assistance in defining markets	1	2	3	4	5	6	7	8	9	10
Product and training manuals	1	2	3	4	5	6	7	8	9	10
Effectiveness of advertising	1	2	3	4	5	6	7	8	9	10
Trade show support	1	2	3	4	5	6	7	8	9	10
Accurate and useable pricing sheets/info	1	2	3	4	5	6	7	8	9	10

Figure 89. Company performance rating scale.

Summary

When growth plans don't meet expectations it's generally for three reasons. The first is inadequate analysis upfront, for example, *C-P-M*™—market opportunities and competitive situation not sufficiently researched—and questionable financial condition—financial ratios and working capital not supporting cash or credit needed to grow.

Second, most SMMs don't do a good job of configuring their sales organizations to their customers and markets and managing and evaluating sales force performance. Section Five of the questionnaire, "Market Planning, Strategies, and Sales Channel Management," contains several questions about sales organization and composition and evaluation of and satisfaction with sales force performance and sales coverage. Half of the firms in the survey reported the performance of inside and outside sales as good or satisfactory and about half using reps also reported good or satisfactory performance. Satisfaction with sales coverage also was about half. Companies can do a good job at C-P-$M^{\text{™}}$ and be financially sound, but if the sales force does not perform or doesn't do a good job of implementation, a growth plan's goals and objectives will not be achieved.

The third is failure to conduct structured periodic review meetings—specifically performance reviews using objectives and factual data for evaluation and follow-up. The adoption of an agenda that specifies attendees, their role and responsibility, the data to present for actual versus planned attainment of the goals, objectives and strategies stipulated in the growth plan, and someone to record minutes for assigned follow-up and timelines can greatly improve the chances for a successful implementation.

Many SMMs, particularly Types 1–2, do not prepare sales and marketing budgets so they really do not have a way to look at sales and marketing from an ROI standpoint as they would do other investments: They report sales and marketing expenses in SG&A together with office salaries and wages, supplies, subscriptions, lodging and travel expenses, trade shows, and advertising and promotion. Sales and marketing expenses budgets are infrequently prepared as shown in Figures 82 and 83 for ABC, Inc.

ABC, Inc.'s examples of sales forecasts (Tables 63 and 64) show that SMMs can create a blueprint for growth based on market insights and a sales organization configured to the number and location of customers and prospects and conduct structured follow-up and review meeting to evaluate not only sales performance but also the company's progress on attaining growth goals and objectives, Figure 86.

CHAPTER 11

Advertising and Promotion

There is a popular saying about advertising attributed to John Wanamaker,[1] "Half the money I spend on advertising is wasted; the trouble is I don't know which half." This apparently holds true for SMMs, according to their responses in the questionnaire. Of the 126 companies, 89 reported they advertise: About two-thirds thought their advertising was at least somewhat worth it, yet many reported not measuring its effectiveness. Table 66 shows the breakdown of their responses.

Most firms reported using more than one type of advertising, but brochures, trade shows, and trade journals were the most frequently used, though few compaines measured the results. Brochures were considered most worth it, presumably due to their relatively lower cost than trade shows and trade journal advertising. Table 67 summarizes the responses of 79 Type 2 and Type 3 companies: Type 1 companies were asked only if they advertise; not the media used.

Questionnaire results suggested that SMMs do not spend much on advertising as most reported it consumed little as a percentage of sales or did not have much of a budget. Another indication that advertising is not that important is few companies reported even measuring it; of 89 who advertise, only 21 measured the results.

Not unsurprisingly, companies selling into consumer markets reported a higher percentage of advertising than those selling into industrial markets (although the number of consumer-markets firms was low), see Table 68 and Figure 90.

Also not surprisingly, Product companies advertised more than Job Shop companies: 83% versus 55%; and larger firms advertised more than smaller ones: 81% versus 38%, Table 69.

Table 66. SMM's Advertising and Promotion

Advertise	Job shop				Product				Type			
	1	2	3	Total	1	2	3	Total	1	2	3	Total
Yes	2	16	12	30	8	33	18	59	10	49	30	89
No	9	11	4	24	3	3	3	9	12	14	7	33
Not asked	1	0	0	1	3	0	0	3	4	0	0	4
Worth it?												
Yes, worth it	1	7	4	12	0	18	9	27	1	25	13	39
Yes, measure	0	2	2	4	0	10	2	12	0	12	4	16
Don't measure	1	5	2	8	0	8	7	15	1	13	9	23
Some worth it	0	5	4	9	1	6	5	12	1	11	9	21
Yes, measure	0	2	1	3	1		1	2	1	2	2	5
Don't measure	0	3	3	6	0	6	4	10	0	9	7	16
Advertising not worth it	0	0	1	1	0	0	0	0	0	0	1	1
Don't know, not asked, not answered	1	4	3	8	7	9	4	20	8	13	7	28
Measure?												
Yes	0	4	3	7	1	10	3	14	1	14	6	21
No	1	8	5	14	0	14	11	25	1	22	16	39
Don't know, not asked, not answered, not worth it	1	4	4	9	7	9	4	20	8	13	8	29
Total	2	16	12	30	8	33	18	59	10	49	30	89

Websites and Social Media

SMMs' use of websites and social media as advertising was not mentioned in the questionnaire because they were not as common then as today— the questionnaire was administered in the late 1990s and early 2000s. Almost all companies now have a website and social media is becoming widespread. However, the jury is out on their effectiveness with respect

Table 67. Types of Advertising Used

	We use	We measure the results	Worth the cost	% Worth it	Don't know
Brochures	70	6	48	69%	5
Trade shows	62	10	33	53%	9
Trade journal advertising	61	18	27	44%	13
Direct mail	39	7	20	51%	9
Internet advertising	37	4	14	38%	11
New product releases	34	5	20	59%	6
Thomas' Register	34	7	15	44%	11
Promotional giveaways	30	2	12	40%	3
Catalogs	28	1	20	71%	2
Magazine articles	27	2	16	59%	1
Publicity releases	27	3	14	52%	4
Product sales or specification sheets	20	1	11	55%	7
Demonstrations	19	3	11	58%	1
Yellow pages	19	1	8	42%	1
Coop advertising	15	2	6	40%	2
Telemarketing	12	2	8	67%	1
Post card packs	11	6	4	36%	2
Facilities fact sheets	8	0	3	38%	1
Radio advertising	5	1	0	0%	2
Mail order	3	1	2	67%	0
Television advertising	0	0	0	0	0

to B2B industrial companies relative to the traditional types of advertising shown in Table 67. Internet searches for B2B advertising and for B2B social media will produce several sources advocating the effectiveness of websites and social media and as many others taking the opposite position.

While the debate continues, guiding principles of the advertising industry still prevail: A company should know its target audience, as suggested by these questions:

Table 68. Advertising to Consumer versus Industrial Markets

Advertise	Job shop				Product				Type			
	1	2	3	Total	1	2	3	Total	1	2	3	Total
Industrial	2	13	11	26	5	22	17	44	7	35	28	70
Consumer	0	1	0	1	2	7	1	10	2	8	1	11
Both	0	2	1	3	1	4	0	5	1	6	1	8
Total	2	16	12	30	8	33	18	59	10	49	30	89
Do not advertise												
Industrial	7	9	4	20	3	2	3	8	10	11	7	28
Consumer	0	0	0	0	0	1	0	1	0	1	0	1
Both	2	2	0	4	0	0	0	0	2	2	0	4
Total	9	11	4	24	3	3	3	9	12	14	7	33
Not asked	1	0	0	1	3	0	0	3	4	0	0	4
Total	12	27	16	55	14	36	21	71	26	63	37	126

	% Advertise		
	No. of Firms	Advertise	%
Consumer	12	11	92%
Industrial	98	70	71%
Both	12	8	67%
Not asked	4	0	0
Total	126	89	71%

Figure 90. Adverting to consumer versus industrial markets.

Table 69. Advertising by Type of Company

	Job shop				Product				Type			
	1	2	3	Total	1	2	3	Total	1	2	3	Total
No. of Firms	12	27	16	55	14	36	21	71	26	63	37	126
Not asked	1	0	0	1	3	0	0	3	4	0	0	4
Do not advertise	9	11	4	24	3	3	3	9	12	14	7	33
Advertise	2	16	12	30	8	33	18	59	10	49	30	89
%	17%	59%	75%	55%	57%	92%	86%	83%	38%	78%	81%	71%

- Who are you trying to reach through advertising?
- Who normally buys from you or is likely to buy from you?
- Who in a company usually places the orders (e.g., the plant manager, purchasing, engineering, executive committee, other)?
- What types of businesses are likely to buy from you? For example, do you normally sell to small, medium, or large companies, high-tech companies, hospitals, hospitality, and so on?

Much of the preceding material shows that many SMMs do not have the information by which to answer these questions. A SMM desiring to use advertising effectively can improve its chances of a better advertising ROI by profiling customers using SIC/NAICS codes, employment sizes, and customer profiles, which would allow advertisers to understand clearly the company's target audience and tailor advertising programs and media to those target markets and customers.

	2013	Market 1	Market 2	Market 3	Total
Sales	4,680,000				
Advertising and promotion	5,000	1,500	2,500	1,000	5,000
Trade show	2,500	2,500			2,500
Total	7,500	4,000	2,500	1,000	7,500
Budget % of Sales	0.2%				

Figure 91. ABC, Inc.'s advertising and promotion budget by market allocation.

ABC, Inc.'s 2013 sales and marketing budget (Figure 91 and adapted from Figure 83 ABC, Inc.'s Sales and Marketing Budget shown earlier) illustrates a good format for budgeting advertising and promotional expenses to target markets. It spread its $7,500 advertising and promotional expenses accounting for 0.2% of sales, across its three markets while choosing to concentrate trade show expenses on Market 1 because it is the firm's bread and butter segment. This format shows how it intends to target expenses to specific groups and will be able to measure and evaluate sales, profits, and sales activity, such as leads, quote production, sales, and sales calls from each of the markets.

Summary

SMMs do not spend a lot of money on advertising and sales, but when they do it usually involves brochures, trade shows, trade and industry magazines and journals, and direct mail, which were the most frequently mentioned of 21 different types of media. Although a majority thought advertising worth the cost, most do not track its effectiveness or ROI.

Websites and social media are becoming increasingly more prevalent as advertising and promotional strategies, and they might be good at creating awareness and generating some sales, but their effectiveness as a key generator of B2B sales—if that is the objective—is debatable. At a minimum, they can be used to create awareness, interest, and inquiries in conjunction with selling strategies based on lead-generation and customer profiling, quotes and bids and lost order analysis, and target marketing, all of which would comprise a comprehensive sales, marketing, and advertising and promotional strategy.

However, whatever a company's overall growth strategy entails, there is no substituting for having sharp, clear definitions of target markets and segments and knowing the number and location of prospective customers.

CHAPTER 12

Conclusion

U.S. manufacturing has been steadily declining since the 1980s, losing about 1% to 2% of businesses per year. It simply will not be able to overcome macro factors over which they have no control—foreign competition, U.S. trade policy, national and local politics, lack of educated new employees entering the workforce, globalization, the shift to a service economy, and to technological innovation that replaces labor with capital.

I have attempted to answer the question I posed in the Foreword, "How can SMMs cope with and overcome these macro forces that counter efforts to help manufacturers grow?"

Two Success Factors

SMMs' success depends on deciding if they are ready to grow—truly committed to invest the time and expense to fully analyze their situations and take the necessary steps to successfully develop and execute a growth plan based on:

- Knowing costs and margins
- Determining if existing or new customers and products are needed to attain desired growth
- Gaining insights into why products and services have or lack competitive advantage, and
- Better understanding markets and where opportunities exist for new customers and products.

They also must make sure good there is a sound financial base—sustainable working capital, cash flow, or credit—before pursuing growth.

This book presents several illustrations and examples by which to assess SMMs' readiness to grow and how to obtain, develop, organize, interpret, and apply strategic data to create growth strategies appropriate to their situation. Moderate, low-risk strategies involving existing products and existing customers will serve some SMMs very well. Financially stronger and resourced SMMs can accommodate more robust, aggressive strategies to penetrate new markets with new products. Owners and managers need to ensure that growth strategies they adopt are appropriate to a company's core competencies and weaknesses and that it has the ability to execute those strategies.

Still Relevant

Almost 30 years ago, professors Raymond E. Miles and Charles C. Snow, distinguished professors at Berkeley and Penn State, specializing in organizational behavior and management thinking, wrote their seminal book, <u>Organizational Strategy, Structure, and Process</u>, in which they described four types of business organizations: defenders, analyzers, reactors, and prospectors.

- *Defenders* seek stability and entrenchment.
- *Analyzers* are cautious innovators, particularly "at the margin," but also favor stability.
- *Reactors* respond to "whatever is happening in their environment," vacillate, have no strategies, and do not prosper.
- *Prospectors* seek innovation and growth, and take risks finding new products and markets.

The future will bring opportunities for SMMs to expand their business and there will be a lot of help from public and private resources, but they will need to be Analyzers and Prospectors. Adopting the *C-P-M*™ methods and solutions presented in this book will help them assess those opportunities and choose growth options commensurate with their readiness and ability to implement.

Roy Bob

In my early years as a private sector consultant, the company for whom I worked took an approach similar to *C-P-M*™ in discovering opportunities to reduce clients' costs and make them more efficient. Our recommendations, based on rigorous and thorough analyses, often called for major restructuring of plant layout and workflows, equipment modifications and upgrades, methods and procedures, quality control, and management information and reporting systems. Many clients balked at the scope of our recommendations although our findings were dead right on, substantiated, and logical. One of our senior partners, an astute and crusty old southerner, shared some of his insight in the context of explaining clients' reaction to and often skeptical adoption of our recommendations.

He said, "Companies would rather live with a problem they understand than accept a solution they don't." Unknowingly, he had described shotgun marketers who would rather defend current practices than invest in customer, market, and competitor analyses to gain insights and to find growth opportunities. His comment, after all these years, still resonates, particularly in light of the findings in the questionnaire and substantial data and research about the reasons for the failures of growth plans and new products. SMMs who are Defenders and Reactors (the shotgun marketers) will not survive the intense competition for new customers, markets, products, and services that future opportunities create.

Nevertheless, as Roy Bob advised, "You can't let a technicality stand in the way of good judgment." SMMs must confront their financial and operational constraints and lack of good strategic information in order to be able to develop growth strategies around the three basics—customers, products, and markets. They should not let the technicality of not knowing or not having strategic information get in the way of investing to obtain or generate that information.

There is no magic key to finding new customers and markets and developing new products. SMMs that are truly committed to growth must step back, take the long perspective, and invest resources to get cost and margin information about customers, products and services, markets, growth opportunities, and about their competitors.

Looking Forward

The following is adapted from an article written by Mike Collins that appeared on Dec. 27, 2012 in IndustryWeek Magazine, "Can We Grow

American Manufacturing?" (Originally published in IndustryWeek, December 27, 2012. © 2012 Penton Media" Inc. All rights reserved. Not to be reproduced without written permission.)

"American manufacturing has stabilized around 11% of GDP because all of the internal efficiency programs that kept us in the game. But I am making the argument that to grow in terms of sales revenue, GDP%, or jobs it is going to take a different approach then what has been accomplished in the last 3 decades.

It will take a mindset change from an internal to an external focus. By external approach I mean more aggressive techniques to monitor customer wants and needs, market trends, and competitor products. It is all about doing a better job of finding out what is going to happen before it happens.

Instead of waiting for things to change or waiting on the government to change policies, I would advocate that companies should go on the offense, take matters into their own hands, and develop strategies that are within their control. There are seven factors that any company who wants to grow should consider.

1. Finding out if your products and services have a competitive advantage.

2. Learning methods to find new customers and markets. Instead of leaving it up to the sales force to find new customers, it is much more efficient to provide them a plan of what kinds of customer profiles you are seeking and markets you are targeting.

3. Learning how to use internal information and inquiries to help you sell.

4. Considering a different kind of organization to allow you to prospect for new market opportunities. The pyramid or functional organization used for so long to efficiently manufacture products doesn't work very well for finding new customers and markets. I would like to suggest that American manufacturers need to adopt a new type of organization—the Prospector Organization—to be able to grow in the future.

5. Gathering enough information to make sure your new products will sell and there are enough customers to justify the investment costs.

6. Using future technologies and other methods to modify your products or invent new products.

7. Analyzing the way customers want to buy and considering different types of sales channels for different customers and markets.

Changes to the American economy marches relentlessly on. I think it is realistic to say that there are going to be many winners and losers as we try to adjust to the global economy. However many companies will "freeze in the headlights" of global change or will hunker down and continue to use the same strategies with the hope that we will somehow return to the good old days. But there are a variety of American manufacturers that are changing their strategies and taking advantage of the new market opportunities being created.[1"]

Notes

Chapter 7

1. H. Igor Ansoff (December 12, 1918—July 14, 2002) was a Russian American, applied mathematician, and business manager. He is known as the father of Strategic management. The matrix is a tool he created to plot generic strategies for growing a business via existing or new products, in existing or new markets.
2. Cooper (2011), p. 60
3. Bonner and Walker, Jr. (2004, May), pp. 155–69.

Chapter 9

1. The Rorschach inkblot test is a psychological test in which subjects' perceptions of inkblots are recorded and then analyzed using psychological interpretation, complex algorithms, or both.

Chapter 11

1. John Wanamaker (July 11, 1838—December 12, 1922) was a United States merchant, religious leader, civic and political figure, considered by some to be the father of modern advertising and a "pioneer in marketing".

Chapter 12

1. Collins M. P. (2012, December), Can we grow American Manufacturing? IndustryWeek.

References

Bonner, Joseph M. and Walker, Jr., Orville (2004, May). Selecting influential business-to-business customers in new product development: relational embeddedness and knowledge heterogeneity considerations. *Product Innovation Management*, (Vol. 21), pp. 155–169.

Cooper, Robert G. (2011). *Winning at new products: creating value through innovation* (4th ed., p. 60). New York, NY: Basic Books.

Index

OTHER TITLES IN THE MARKETING STRATEGY COLLECTION

Naresh Malhotra, Georgia Tech, Collection Editor

- *Developing Winning Brand Strategies* by Lars Finskud
- *Conscious Branding* by David Funk and Anne Marie Levis
- *Marketing Strategy in Play: Questioning to Create Difference* by Mark Hill
- *Decision Equity: The Ultimate Metric to Connect Marketing Actions to Profits* by Piyush Kumar and Kunal Gupta
- *Building a Marketing Plan: A Complete Guide* by Ho Yin Wong, Roshnee Ramsaran-Fowdar and Kylie Radel
- *Top Market Strategy: Applying the 80/20 Rule* by Elizabeth Kruger
- *Pricing Segmentation and Analytics* by Tudor Bodea and Mark Ferguson
- *Strategic Marketing Planning for the Small- to Medium-Sized Business: Writing a Marketing Plan* by David Anderson
- *Expanding Customer Service as a Profit Center: Striving for Excellence and Competitive Advantage* by Rob Reider
- *Applying Scientific Reasoning to the Field of Marketing: Make Better Decisions* by Terry Grapentine
- *Innovative Pricing Strategies to Increase Profits* by Daniel Marburger
- *Designing Service Processes to Unlock Value* by Joy Field
- *Grow by Focusing on What Matters: Competitive Strategy in 3-Circles* by Joel E. Urbany and James H. Davis

Announcing the Business Expert Press Digital Library

Concise E-books Business Students Need for Classroom and Research

This book can also be purchased in an e-book collection by your library as
- a one-time purchase,
- that is owned forever,
- allows for simultaneous readers,
- has no restrictions on printing, and
- can be downloaded as PDFs from within the library community.

Our digital library collections are a great solution to beat the rising cost of textbooks. e-books can be loaded into their course management systems or onto student's e-book readers.

The **Business Expert Press** digital libraries are very affordable, with no obligation to buy in future years. For more information, please visit **www.businessexpertpress.com/librarians**. To set up a trial in the United States, please contact **Adam Chesler** at *adam.chesler@ businessexpertpress.com* for all other regions, contact **Nicole Lee** at *nicole.lee@igroupnet.com*.

www.ingramcontent.com/pod-product-compliance
Lightning Source LLC
Chambersburg PA
CBHW061128220326
41599CB00024B/4203